GOWER OF THE HILLS

an EPIC AUTOBIOGRAPHY

by

Kingsley R.

Published in Swansea Wales by King of the Castle Publishing.

ISBN 978-0-9879493-4-9

Front Cover Artwork by Sylvia Nicholson

To contact Kingsley Hill
email at gowerofthehills@gmail.com

Printed and bound with IngramSpark

Dedications

*T*his book is dedicated to my "Great Guide", the Lord Jesus Christ, who guides me continually, and strengthens me. I rejoice in the assurance that His guidance is perpetual. The promise covers the whole range of my life and being. The Lord shall guide me continually... not merely for a day, or week, or for a year, but all my days; and wherever I go in the busy roadway of the world, and amid the quiet duties of home and family. I need never lose my way. There need be no gaps, or intervals during which I must navigate my way alone.

And to my wonderful mother, "JOY", who took me as a boy to Linden Chapel, in West Cross, Wales, where I first heard the Gospel of the Lord Jesus Christ, who became my own personal saviour!

And to my dear friend and brother in the faith, John Sampson. Thank you for speaking the Gospel to me, John. When you spoke and proclaimed the Gospel, God wrote His word in my heart, and I believed! You are a mentor to me, and I thank my God for you.

∿

To my Son Ben. Your integrity, and outstanding athletic and academic achievements, have both inspired me, and made me very proud!

∿

To my wonderful friends Sylvia and Charle. I regard myself extremely fortunate to call you both my friends. Sylvia, your wonderful painting is such an inspiration for me. And you and Charle, along with Penny and Bow, are as family to me. Thank you all for being my friends.

∿

And to my wonderful friend Linda. We go back further than the cell-memory Celts. A connection that cannot be understood, and need not be! Your love and friendship is deeper than the Emerald Sea!

"Son Of Wales Award"
For best new author and poet
2016
Gowerton School
"Excellence Of Literature award"
2016 For the outstanding achievement
of the epic autobiography "Cave Days".
"Best Adventure Autobiography"
For Great Britain and Ireland
2017
King Of The Castle Publishing.

"Best Adventure, And Romance Award"
2018
For the outstanding autobiography
"Gower Of The Hill's"
South Wales, Book And Literature Development ASSN.

"Best Adventure And Historical Award"
2018
For the outstanding autobiography
"Gower Of The Hill's"
King Of The Castle Publishing

About the Author

*K*ingsley Ross Hill, was born near the city of Swansea, in Glamorganshire, South Wales. And grew up in the village of Pennard, on the Gower Peninsula. [The word Pennard, means "village without a gate" in the Welsh language] Kingsley, describes growing up in Pennard, and on the Gower Peninsula, as "living this most wonderful adventure, with no gates."

It is interesting that the Gower Peninsula Series, which includes the books, "Cave Days," "Gower Of The Hills," and "I'll Meet You On Cefn Bryn", all give the reader, such a sense of freedom and adventure; like walking through a land without gates or fences. The authors books are full off romance and humour, and are extremely accurate in their betrayal of the history and geography of the Gower Peninsula itself.

The author is humble about his many awards, and I am pleased that he is becoming well known in his native Wales, and throughout the United Kingdom. And more recently in Canada and the United States, for his unique style of writing and poetry.

Kingsley Hill, lives with his family on Vancouver Island, British Columbia. And is also a pastor and counsellor, and works in youth outreach, and has a prison ministry, sharing his faith with others. He says, that growing up on the Gower Peninsula in Wales, is a great heritage. And one that God used to reveal to him his wonderful gifts of writing and poetry.

I look forward to you coming again to encourage the men. And congratulations on you new book, "Gower Of The Hill's", which is destined to become a classic!

Captain and Commander,
Horatio Tucker
Royal Navy.

Kingsley Ross Hill

Table of Contents

Chapter One

Coming Home to the Gower

My plane landed at Heathrow Airport at ten twenty-five in the morning, local time. I'd taken a night flight, leaving Vancouver, Canada at 11:45 p.m., and I didn't get much sleep, maybe forty winks here and there. But all said, it was a good flight with very little turbulence, and the flight crew did their best to take care of our needs.

Going through Customs looked more like the Berlin Airlift during World War II than checking in baggage. People were running around everywhere, and trying to find someone who spoke British amongst all the confusion was rather a tall order.

"No, I don't want a flight to Delhi! Just the way out, please! "Oh It's that way, is it?"

Finally, I got out of the terminal, and stepped into the cool misty air of the London morning. It had been so hot in Vancouver, and I welcomed a cooler day.

Now, where was the bus? There was a sign that read 'Oxfordshire and South Wales, Stand 3,' and a bus pulled up almost immediately.

"Excuse me, Sir?" I asked the driver. "Is this the right stop for Swansea South Wales?"

"Next one over, stand 4," he replied.

I lugged my heavy suitcase and saddle over to the sign, and read: 'Newport-Cardiff-Swansea, via Bristol and Oxfordshire'.

"Oh, I'm so happy to have arrived in England, I could kiss a sheep!" I said to a middle-aged lady wearing a fur coat. She hurried away at my word, and I was tempted to shout, "Don't worry Madam; I won't kiss you, even if you do look like a sheep!"

I was just so happy to know that there were no more plane rides and oceans between my beloved Wales and me. Once I crossed the Severn Bridge into Newport, I would be on Welsh soil again! As much as I enjoyed my life on Vancouver Island, Canada, the Gower Peninsula of South Wales would always be my home!

And there at the bus stop was a lovely girl wearing a T-shirt that read: "You may be able to take the girl out of Wales, but you will never take Wales out of the girl!"

I went over to talk to her. "I love your shirt!" I said. "I've been in Canada for over 20 years! They couldn't take the Welsh out of me either!" She laughed and obviously understood. I had made a new friend to sit with on the bus!

"I'm Kingsley!"

"I'm Gwendelyn."

We shook hands and chatted for 15 minutes before the coach arrived. The driver, with his assistant, labeled all the suitcases and loaded them onto the bus. Soon we were on our way to South Wales, and Gwendelyn fell asleep before we were out of London.

It was just as well; I soon began to feel tired, having traveled 19 hours already, including a four-hour journey from Victoria on Vancouver Island to Vancouver International Airport, via bus and ferry, and a lengthy wait at the airport.

But tired as I was, I was too excited to close my eyes! It seemed that we stopped at every town this side of the Severn Bridge! Reading, Chepstow, Cheddar (but there was no cheese)! I had only the ridiculously priced ham and cheese sandwich I'd bought at the airport.

Finally, a sign appeared that read: 'Newport, 50 miles.' We would soon be in Wales! The bus was full of sleepyheads as we traveled under grey skies, past old brick buildings and churches that were as grey and dull as the sky above.

And there was one sign on an old church wall which read: "I am the way, the truth and the life!" And for a fleeting moment, I felt Him whisper: "Kingsley! I am still with you in your life!" I dared to believe, that maybe God might still have a plan for me, even though it seemed that I had lost so much of my faith, falling so far from the man I once was.

I was coming home broken, with pain in my heart. Six years before, my wife and I had separated and then divorced. I'd been a single father ever since. I'd dated the odd time, here and there, but it never felt like the right time.

I had served God at my local church, as an Elder and as a Sunday school teacher. But as soon as I needed some help or support, I was treated with indifference and condemnation. My non-believing friends would say: "Those so-called Christians showed their true colours, didn't they? And that's why we don't go to church!"

Unfortunately, they were right! So much for coming alongside someone in their time of need and showing God's love.

But I have three wonderful children who are the joy of my life! And for that, I am so very thankful. And I hope to meet a lovely lady to share my life with.

"You're coming home, boy!" "Yes, Sir, I am! Home to the Gower, boy! Where the wind blows free! Yes, Sir, where the wind blows free!" I smiled.

We now reached the Severn Bridge. Sweet memories tugged gently at my heart, as I remembered family holidays with my mother and father and my brother Fraser.

Every summer, Dad would drive our family car to Devonshire, dropping my brother and me off for a month's holiday with Grandma and Grandpa. Once we crossed the Severn Bridge, there would be a different feeling in our souls because we were now in England, and would soon be spending our summer holidays with our wonderful Grandma and Grandpa. And our holiday would include the celebration of our birthdays! This was special, because Fraser and I were born on the same day – August 16th. Mum and Dad usually bought us a new fishing rod each. Then Grandpa would take us fishing off 'Hopes Nose' – our most favourite fishing spot in the whole world! We always had the most wonderful time! So much so, that we often did not want to go home when our mum and dad came back to pick us up!

In my soul today, it wasn't much different – only I was traveling the other way –from England to Wales. I was so excited to be going home to the Gower. Grandma and Grandpa had both gone home to heaven now, but their love and their heritage still lived in our hearts.

I was going to be staying with my brother Fraser and his wife Lynn, who had now been married for over 18 years! So there was hope for me yet, if I meet the right woman! I had not seen Fraser and Lynn, or my father, for six long years!

We passed the toll gates on the bridge, and there was the sign that read: "Welcome to Wales." The Welsh flag flew proudly in the wind, and it looked like the red Dragon was going to walk right off the flag and come with me to Wales! Maybe he would join me later? I felt such a great sense of pride being back in Wales, because I'm such a proud Welshman!

As Max Boyce once sang: 'It was the Welsh that first landed on the moon, not the Americans! Only we landed on the dark side of the moon. With a rocket that was built in the Rhondda, and powered by anthracite coal.'

The grey sky, and the grey buildings and churches, continued as the short winter's day drew to an end. But there was just enough light to see the signs as we passed by various Welsh valley towns with wonderful Welsh names like: Cwmbran, Caerphilly, Pontypridd, Bridgend, Porthcawl, and Merthyr Tydfil, to name just a few!

It was almost dark now, as I decided to read a couple more signs and then lie back in my chair to rest. And suddenly, there it was! A sign that read: Rhondda Valley – 15 miles! That sign provided a wonderful memory for me!

When my brother was young, and I was bit older than young, Dad took us both to one of the coal mines in the Rhondda Valley: to watch the big men coming home from the mine. My brother and I complained bitterly because we both didn't want to

Kingsley Ross Hill

go. (Wales was playing England in rugby, and we were going to smash them again! It wasn't a question of England losing in those days; it was just a question of how much they lost by as Wales played for the Triple Crown again! I think the English feared going to Cardiff Arms Park more than the IRA bombs going off in Northern Ireland! That may be an exaggeration, but I am a keen Welsh Rugby Union fan!)

But back to the story: Rugby game or not, my father said, my brother and I had to come with him to the mine to 'see a part of history' that would soon be gone. And it was indeed gone soon after that, as coal became a 'dirty fuel' and most of it then went to China, that didn't have environmental laws to keep its air clean. Anyway, its mainly natural gas now, and very little coal is mined.

I will never forget going to the Rhondda Valley with my father that day and seeing the big men coming home from the mine. First, we heard the loud ring of a bell. And then there was no noise for what seemed like a long time.

Then suddenly we heard wonderful singing! As good as any choir! The men were singing hymns as they walked down the road together. And it looked more like a march than a walk. They looked as tall as mountains to my brother and me. And strong! The muscles on their arms were as big as my stomach! And they marched their way to the pub.

They wore hardhats with lanterns on top that made them look even taller! And their faces were as black as night, with white rings around their eyes. "They aren't black men," my father said, in reply to my brother's question, "just hard-working miners covered in the black soot that comes out of the mine!"

They sang the most wonderful songs, and even though I was young, I wept with my father because those Welsh hymns rang in my Welsh soul! I was so proud that day to be Welsh! And so was my brother!

Then all of a sudden they stopped singing. "Why have they stopped, Dad?" I asked.

"Because they've arrived at the pub and they're going inside for a drink."

Dad said they were met inside by their wives and girlfriends, who made sure they didn't spend all their wages on beer. After about an hour, they came out of the pub, and they got in a line and started singing again as they walked down the road to their grey houses that all looked the same, apart from the brightly coloured doors!

I asked my father, "Why are the miners' doors so brightly coloured?"

And he answered, "To break the grey, boy, to break the grey!"

As the miners continued singing their way down the road, they would stop outside each others houses, and one of the miners would go inside to be with his family, and his wife would already have a hot bath waiting for her coal-dirty husband.

As my brother and I watched, at some of the houses, two men went inside – father and son or two brothers. At one house, four men went inside. And my father said that all the family must be miners except for the mother of the house and any sisters.

As we followed behind the shrinking queue of men, my father said that they would soon walk out of history, and groups of men would never walk and sing down the road again!"

My father's words tugged at my heart! I shouted, "I don't want the men to walk out of history, Dad! I want them to stay here forever!"

"Everything has a time, son! And the miners' time is coming to an end!"

"But what if I become a miner, Dad? I can help?" I cried.

"Yes, me too," My brother Fraser said! "If King and I work hard, we can save the mine! You said that we could do anything, Dad, if we work hard!"

"Oh, my boys!" my dad said, with tears in his eyes. "You have the hearts of young lions! But you are not meant to be miners! Gallant as knights you are, my sons! But saving the mine and the coal industry is not your fight! A wise lion knows when to fight and win his spoil, and when not to get involved because an era has run its course, and its time has come to ease into history!"

My brother and I looked at our dad, not totally understanding what he was saying but feeling sad.

"But when you boys are older, you will be able to keep this history alive in your hearts! Because you have seen the big men coming home from the mine! You have heard them singing. That's why I wanted you both to come today!"

"But I want to help and change history, Dad," I wept.

"So, do I," my brother added. And we walked together out in the middle of the road in front of the marching miners!

"No, come back boys!" my dad shouted!

But then the big men stopped, and a man turned toward us. "What do you boys want?" he asked.

"We want to be miners, Sir, and to save the mine!" we both answered.

The big man smiled with caring in his eyes. All the men stopped singing, and I thought we were in trouble!

"So, you want to sign up to be miners?" the big man asked.

"Yes, Sir, we do."

"Well, how old are you boys?"

"I'm nine years old," I replied, standing up as tall as I could.

"And I'm seven," my brother stated.

"And I told you not to go into the road," my father added.

The big man then said that we had to be sixteen before we could go into the mines! And we were only nine and seven, but together that made 16 years, right? My dad, who now stood behind us, said, "Yes, together they are sixteen!"

Then, two of the men gave both my brother and I a shovel to carry. And along with my father, we marched down the road in front of all the big men! And I know on that day that my brother and I became miners, and we made our dad proud! Because when I looked into his face, his eyes were smiling.

My father had said that the miners would walk out of work and into the history books. And he was right! Less than five years later, they closed the last working mine in the Rhondda Valley. And the valley became even greyer! Even though the Welsh singer Tom Jones still sings "the green, green grass of home!" the Rhondda will always remain Rhondda grey!

♪❋

RHONDDA GREY

In the Rhondda, there are 24 shades of grey, or so Gwyneth, the artist, told me in the tea shop the other day.

"And the stories of the Rhondda are told with those shades of grey; 24 different colours come and go every day, and I have tried each one of them – green, blue, orange … and I saw a purple one the other day," Gwyneth said.

"But what I find most interesting, as I mix my paints each day, is that no matter what picture I paint, it always ends up grey. It is the greyest when it rains and the green hills are covered in their blankets of mist, and the men are sad because the mining jobs have gone bad, and families are left to dream of what they might have had – especially my dad! Look! There's that Maggie Thatcher, still wearing her tartan clad. It's a wonder that woman comes out of her house when the miners are so mad. Mrs. Jones runs the hair salon down the road with the bright red door. And she can be heard singing, because in her heart she knows that she is not very poor. And she cuts Mr. Davis's hair for free, as she has heard his wife crying from behind the purple door.

The post office opens at 9 o'clock and it is also the general store. And it seems the whole village is mailing letters these days, and asking for a bit more, while Mrs. Lewis stands proudly at her door. And between customers she peers out as it rains, and the grey wind blows her nose some more.

Young Gwynn arrives at the general store, wearing his father's boots and expecting a birthday parcel from a grandmother who doesn't live here anymore. "You like wearing your father's boots, don't you, Gwynn?" calls out another Mrs. Jones, from in front of her orange door. "Your parcel hasn't come yet, Gwynn. But it will! I've never known a day for your grandmother to be ill. Maybe the weather is bad in Myther Tydvill? Because she walks almost every day over that big hill."

As Gwynn walks away in his big boots, Mrs. Jones stands outside and lights a cigarette, and she wonders why Gwynn's father is still his hero. His mother came in with bruises again yesterday, and the ones around her eyes never seem to go away. And I paint this picture with the darkest shade of grey, even though her eyes are sky blue; because behind there is the dark, dark grey! "Oh, Hello Mrs. Jarvis, have a lovely day, between the raindrops and 24 shades of grey."

"Hello back to you, Mrs. Jones, God must be crying up there today, with all the rain. Maybe He heard of more mine closures coming this way. I wonder what His favourite colour is? It must be grey."

"Oh yes," they said together, "it's Rhondda grey!"

In the spring, the birds sing, so joyful and loud, and the crowns of the bryns can be seen green and proud, as the wind puffs away at winter's last cloud. The bryns songs are silent, yet the music plays so loud, and old Mrs. Evans takes off her dark shroud. Her husband is gone, but Spring is in full song, and the robin sings the Summer won't be long.

It has not rained in three days, and Mrs. Hughes' naughty boys climb the biggest hills to play. There are kites to fly, and balls to throw, and sling shots aimed at the crows, and it's time to frighten their little sister with big brown spiders, you know.

The clouds roll in and roll away, their fast shadows moving across the grey rocks, and the sheep dog barks. "Why is he barking, Mr. Thomas?" young Gwynn asks.

"He will be bark at anything, boy! Even the clouds when they are low enough." And in the town, it's another blue-grey day, and it's hurray, hurray! For the merry, merry, month of May, as the sitting cows chew their cud and dream of fresh hay.

The green fields of the blue bell waving Rhondda, waved back at the shower-throwing April, while May shines her sunshine upon the newborn lambs, who suckle, skip and play, and Winter's shades of grey are becoming forgotten, amidst the kissing saplings and the hay that will become golden on yesterday's hill and then dance with June's hottest day – hurray, hurray! I am happy in the Rhondda today

"Tell me again, Mum, what is Rhondda grey?"

"It's in your soul, Son; it's in your soul every day!"

"I know what you mean Mum. Can I go out to play?"

"Heaven's yes! You must make the most of Farmer Brown's hay, because in the Rhondda, the summer can last only an hour and a day."

The singing brook whispers his happiest song along the way, and with my brush, I mix all the colours in my tray, because I am going to paint August today! 'Tis my favourite month in Rhondda grey! And look, here comes Heather Lewis, out to start her day. With one hand, she holds her feathered hat while the wind tries to blow it away. Her dress blows high and spins like Dava, the butterfly. And the boys on the bench at the bus stop all dream of going for a walk with Heather one day.

She walks past and the boys try not to stare, but this time the wind blows her hat high into the August singing air, and she runs after it, faster than Jack the wild cat! "What are you staring at?" she asks all four boys glued to the bench. "Did you have a good look at my knickers then? I hope you took a good look, 'cuz that's all you're going to see!"

One boy snickered, and the others laughed, and she said, "I suggest you all go and look at your mother's knickers hanging on the clothesline." And instantly the laughing stopped and there was silence on the bench.

"Look!" one of them said, "it's the bus!"

Oh yes," the others said, relieved. And they all hurried on while Heather walked along to meet September on her way. I think I have had enough painting for today. Good night, my Rhondda Grey!

© *Kingsley Ross Hill*

Then the bus arrived in Newport, waking me from my day dream and Gwendelyn from her sleep. "I must have nodded off," she said.
 "Aye! A long nod off. Almost four hours!" I replied.
 "I'm glad I didn't miss my stop," she said. "I'm getting off at Bridgend, which is the next stop."
 "I thought maybe I should have woken you a long way back because I wasn't sure where you were getting off. But here we are, and you didn't miss your stop. You timed that right, didn't you!"
 "Yes," she replied. "Do you have somewhere to go? Because you can get off at my stop if you like!"

"Oh, I'm alright, thank you! I'm going on to Swansea. My brother will pick me up from the bus station. But thanks for asking!"

I must have looked lonely, because after all, I was forty, and she was all of twenty-five! I don't think her mother would have appreciated her bringing me home with her! And, even less her father! I laughed at the thought of it.

"Well, this is your stop. Bye, Gwendelyn!"

With the promise of romance now gone from her eyes, she moved to collect her belongings, but before walking away from the bus, she looked back and said wistfully: "Bye Kingsley!" The doors closed with a bump and the wheels began their slow grind on towards Swansea.

As I watched her go, I saw the most beautiful red sunset in the western sky, now only 30 miles from Swansea! I wanted to sing that old Gene Pitney song: 'I'm only 24 miles from Tulsa.' But that was in America. So instead, I sang with my welsh accent, which seemed to have come back stronger since we crossed the Severn Bridge; "if I could see the Rhondda One More Time".

⤳

The next stop was Swansea! With the orange and red of the sunset now fading behind the night clouds, my memories of sunsets and colours were waking like a new morning in my soul. And I remembered a girl named Gay! And a boy named Kingsley! They made colours of their own. One was orange, and the other indigo! They are the colours of our love, you know! Yes, my love, you are orange, and I am indigo!

Then galloping through the pages of my mind came the Thunder Child! Who became Great Thunder! And the rest of the horse family arrived. "Hello, Thunder Spring and Little Thunder, it's so wonderful to see you again!"

"It's time to get off the bus," shouted a voice. We have arrived in Swansea."

"But you were on another journey, my boy, said the driver to me.

"Yes Sir, I was."

The man unloaded my luggage, and I stood alone on the platform, except for a lone pigeon to whom I said hello.

I reminded myself how long it had been! Six long years! Which seemed to me like six lifetimes. And I'd come back to the Gower Peninsula to find another lifetime! Or even a past one! I'd be happy either way; I needed to find what my soul was in search of!

"What is it that you are looking for, boy? The past? Or the future? Or both?"

"I don't know Sir! I'm a broken man!" I answered.

"That's alright! You've come to the right place – where the wind blows free. The Gower, she has many secrets, boy!"

"Yes, she does, and that's why I'm here to find one."

Just then an old familiar car came around the corner. It was my brother Fraser!

"Kings, it's great to see you! Here, let me get your suitcase!" he exclaimed.

After throwing my case in the back seat, we were on our way to my brother's house. Fraser lived not far from the city in a small town called Gorseinon. And we would soon be there. It was a quick hello and then a good night, to my brother's wife, Lynn, and I was off to bed.

"Good night, Kings!

"Good night, Fraser. See you in the morning."

Chapter Two

Good Morning Swansea

I woke to the distant cackle of a magpie. Looking at the clock on the wall, I saw that it was 11 a.m. Fraser and Lynn had left for work, and they wouldn't be home until five this evening, so I would have the day to myself.

Lynn had put a bowl and a box of cornflakes on the table. A little note was jutting out from under my teacup. "Dear Kings, Fraser and I have left for work. Help yourself to anything. Hope you have a good day and get over your jetlag. See you tonight. Love, Lynn and Fraser."

I thought: how pleasant! Those nice words meant so much to me this morning. After a hot shower and a bowl of cornflakes, I decided to walk into Swansea. I've always felt that cities and towns, even little villages too, are very much like people, with their different personalities and moods. And old Swansea town, which I hope I will always call it, has a personality and mood that are so compatible with mine! First, I would go into the Swansea market!

As I stood outside one of its four entrances, inhaling the strong smell of the fishmonger's shop, I thought: "Oh, how that wonderful, awful, sinus-burning smell has instantly melted the years away!" As I walked into the market, I stood for several minutes, reminiscing about times and people; it was "yesterday once more."

Next to the Fishmonger was the vegetable stand, unchanged in over 30 years! After one stands there for a few minutes, the smell of fish and vegetables seem to mingle into one. And then it is time to go and find another smell – and it is my favourite smell of all!

Kingsley Ross Hill

The wonderful smell of Welsh Cakes! Here they bake them on old stoves that are almost as old as the recipes themselves. Mother to daughter, and daughter to granddaughter, this wonderful heritage is passed down.

Today, an elderly lady takes pride as the next batch is ready to come off the stove top. And passersby, like me, stop their morning to smell and recall their memories of Welsh Cakes and of wonderful mornings in the warm embrace of the old Swansea Market.

In the crowd I see faces; some I think I recognize. And if I went over and talked to them, I'm sure they would recognize me. But for now, I'm just happy. Happy to watch and let them be. For there is so much to feel, to see, to think about, after having been away for these six long years!

The sweet smell of Welsh cakes now dances with my taste buds, as I stand in line to get some hot off the grill. Only so many are made each day and then put on a rack to cool.

"How many, love?" I hear the old lady's voice, full of enthusiasm and the joy of the morning.

"I'll have twelve!" I say, as my own voice matches her enthusiasm. "I'll have six to eat hot! And six to take home!"

"And six to take home. Right you are!" she says, with a gleam in her eye. "And here's an extra one for luck!" And she watches with pride as her granddaughter, who is maybe eight, sprinkles the sugar over the cakes. "That's enough," she says. "The nice gentleman is sweet enough as he is."

As I walk around the market eating my Welsh cakes, I say to myself, "Oh, what a rich heritage I have!" With every bite, a wonderful memory takes me back to a time and place when I walked the market with my mother and brother.

And if my brother and I didn't fight, we could have a toy knight or a box of soldiers from the toy shop that sold everything a boy or girl could ever want! Certainly what boys could ever want! Girls were more mysterious and wanted other things, not tanks or robots or potato guns to shoot at people.

Girls are still mysterious to me at 40! But then that's part of what makes them so wonderful, isn't it? And painted toes, too! I like that! And when I went over to the toy shop, the same man who had sold me a goldfish when I was ten, said he didn't have any girls for sale, at least not today – but to come back on Saturday and see what had come in.

I was tempted to say, "I don't think you understand, Sir! I want a real girl, with blue toe nails and her hair like a horse's tail, like my friend Gay used to have!

Next to the toy shop, I could smell another wonderful smell! The smell of 'cockles'! And there serving the cockles were the Penclawdd cockle women. Famous throughout all of Gower land! I first heard about the Penclawdd cockle women when I was an innocent nine, in primary school.

"Those women will beat the shit out of you, if you argue with them," my friend, John Majors, said. He and his family used to live in Penclawdd, until they moved to my home village of Pennard. "They just look like anyone else," I thought, as I bought a large basket.

"Vinegar and pepper, love?"

"Yes, please," I said, biting into the soft, juicy and slightly chewy little shellfish. "Oh, what a wonderful taste thrilled my taste buds, like so many times before when my mother had taken me to the market and we'd enjoyed cockles together."

In Swansea market, one can buy almost anything you need, from Italian leather jackets and jewelry to all kinds of men's or women's clothes. There's even an old- fashioned wedding planner if the lovely lady you met in the market was more beautiful than you could resist! If she wanted a ring, like they commonly do, two stalls down was Dye, the jeweller, who made a comfortable living in the magic of the market.

But, back to the Penclawdd cockle women for a few more minutes. It wasn't an easy task to gather the cockles from the beach, to bring them to the market for people to enjoy. In the old days, the cockle women's day started, as it still does today, on the sand flats of Penclawdd sands, where they followed the tide as it continued its journey to low water. In those early days, they marched down the sands with their donkey-pulled carts until they reached the cockle beds, where they raked the cockles by hand and put them into buckets, which, in turn, they lifted into the donkey carts, and then headed up the beach under donkey power, to the waiting trucks. Then the cockles would be cooked and washed before they were taken to the Swansea market and other markets in South Wales.

The donkeys are long gone now, and only their memories come in and out on the storytelling tides. But the cockle beds are still there! They are carefully managed and harvested by several hard-working families that go back almost as far as the cockle beds themselves.

I have only one memory of the donkeys on the sands. I was about eight years old when my father took me down to the cockle beds, with a wooden rake that we had made just for this occasion. As my father began to rake up the cockles, he handed them to me to put into my red and white pail. Soon, we were surrounded by large, fat, armed cockle women, who threatened my father but smiled at me with missing teeth!

"Why were they so angry with you, Dad?" I asked, when we reached the safety of the car.

"Well, they each think they own a piece of the beach, old son. And I'm not going to argue with them, are you?" he replied.

"No dad, I'm not!" And, we both laughed. "And why are their arms so big?" I continued.

"That's from lifting and carrying the heavy buckets of cockles. And, of course, from beating up their husbands when they spend all the cockle money on beer at the pub." And I laughed some more.

In middle school, I had a girlfriend. Not a real one, who gave me hugs and kisses under Park Mill Bridge. But one who protected me from a gang of "bad boys" that terrorized shy boys like me. I watched Hazel Thompson punch out three bullies all at the same time! And I felt safe. Hazel's mother was one of the Penclawdd cockle women. And all Hazel wanted in return for her protective service was to stick her tongue in my mouth and squeeze my John Thomas with her hand. A small price to pay, I think, when I considered the painful alternative of the bullies. And do you know, I began to enjoy the kissing and the squeezing, but I never told my father. Only Hazel's mother's donkey! The donkey said, "Heehaw, what are you telling me for? I don't give a squeeze! Just give me another carrot, will you?"

Back to the present day at the market. After finishing my cockles and saying thank you to the cockle women, I walked around the rest of the market shaking hands with memories and making new ones with my fellow countrymen.

There was only one more thing to do now before heading home to Fraser and Lynn's. And that was to go and have a cup of coffee with steamed milk and sit among the working people of this town that I'd left behind all those lifetimes ago.

As I stood in line, the smell of coffee and the sound of chit chat filled the vibrant market air! Then, I saw a face that I knew from my boyhood. "What would you like this morning, Sir?" he asked.

"I'll have a steamed coffee with an ice bun, Mr. Griffith, Sir!" I replied.

He was surprised that I knew his name. Clearly he didn't recognize me, and he was too busy to ask! Mr. Griffith had been one of my Sunday school teachers at Linden Chapel when I was a boy. He now owned and operated the Swansea Market coffee shop. I would have to introduce myself one of these mornings. Meanwhile, I sat at a table and sipped my coffee, and I watched and listened to the wonderful world around me, where it seemed that most people knew each other's names. And if they didn't, they were genuinely interested in meeting you! Sitting here this morning and listening to my fellow countrymen, it brought such comfort and soothing to my life that had recently gone so wrong! Surely there is no place like home to return to and heal your wounds!

　　　　　　　　　　　　　　　　Kingsley Ross Hill

Tis the Gower, boy! Here you are never alone!
Welcome home, boy!
Thank you, Sir! It's so good to be home!

Morning turned into afternoon, and I decided to walk around
Swansea town. There were, of course, some things that had changed.
But to me, Swansea city would always remain Swansea town! When
I was a boy, they made a big fuss about Swansea being given the
status of becoming a "city" rather than a town. I told my father
that I was quite happy for Swansea to remain a town.

My father answered me by saying: "If you want Swansea to
remain 'good old Swansea Town,' it's up to you, boy! Swansea will
always be as you hold her in your heart! And this is true of so many
things in life! And be wary of people who say, 'they say that, or
they say this'! Ask yourself, old son, who are 'they'? And do they
agree with your conscience and heart? Do they care for the things
and beliefs that you do?"

I have asked myself these questions ever since! Who are they?
And do they care about my heart?

As I walked along the familiar streets, so much was the same
– unchanged since I was a boy! The shops and sights greeted me
like old friends. And there, right in the middle of the Kings Way, I
stopped, and looked up to the old castle on the hill.

The hills shouted down their songs to me, and I shouted back
to them, remembering that in old Swansea Town, the past and
present walk together, hand-in-hand like lovers down the lane. And
time only sweetens these songs, and this kind of love never grows
old. Oh, my beloved Swansea, one of your sons has come home!

Just then a double-decker bus came down the street, and I
jumped on.

"Where are you going?" the driver asked.

"I don't know. Where are you going?"

"I'm going to Mumbles," he said.

"Then, I will come too!"

"Been away, have you, boy?" he asked.

"Yes, Sir, I have."

"Well, welcome home!"

I got off the bus outside the Mermaid Pub, and went in to find a mermaid who would serve me lunch. She was a mermaid alright! With jet black hair and eyes that made me excited! They were as green as the emerald sea.

"What can I get you, love?" she asked with a smile!

And I answered, "You!" But, I didn't say it. I didn't have to! It was in my voice and written on my face; and soon we were both nervous.

"Where are you from then?" she asked, her eyes running away from mine and then coming back again.

"Oh, Vancouver Island." I said. "And, I was just thinking how lovely it is to be called 'love' again! It's a far cry from downtown Vancouver, where people pass like ships in the night, even where it's crowded."

"Will we pass like ships in the night?" she asked.

"No, we have already met," I said, looking into her eyes that retreated shyly away again.

"Come back?" I said. "I just want to talk to you."

She looked at me with her emerald eyes again, and said "Tell me more about Vancouver?"

"Well, as I said, it can be pretty cold and unfriendly in a city like Vancouver. People stand on the Sky Train like robots and rarely say hello. But I'm not complaining. I do love my adopted land, the 'west coast,' and the vibrant, cosmopolitan City of Vancouver. You just have to have a nice group of friends; that is the key.

"Anyway, may I have the Ploughman's lunch with a pint of beer, please?" And the mermaid walked off, on legs, to give my order to the chef. And I said to myself: "I guess her legs become a fish tail when she finishes work and heads back out to the bay! Mermaid by night, and pub maid by day! That must be quite a life!"

She sat with me and we talked while I ate my ploughman's lunch. Before I left, she squeezed my hand and gave me her phone number, with a promise that we would go out for coffee and a Joe's ice cream sometime soon.

> *Bye Meredith! Bye Kingsley!*
> *Hope to hear from you soon.*

Well, it was late afternoon now, and my jet lag was catching up with me. Plus, I was eight hours ahead of Vancouver time, so I caught the bus back to Fraser and Lynn's.

We spent the evening catching up on all the news, over tea and biscuits. Lynn had made a lovely Shepherd's Pie for supper; a nice meal for a traveler, I thought. As the evening wore on, I was so tired I could hardly keep my eyes open. But I hung on until 10:30 p.m., as Fraser recommended: "Try to adapt to local time right away. That's the quickest way to adapt to the time change!"

> *Good night everyone!*
> *Yeah, good night, Kings!*
> *See you in the morning.*
> *Tomorrow is Friday, and then we will have the whole*
> *weekend to spend together.*
> *Yeah, I'm looking forward to spending*
> *time with you both.*

Chapter Three
My Father's Words

*I*woke up at my usual time this morning, 7:30am. And I was just in time to see Fraser and Lynn out the door to work. "Bye," I said. "I'll see you both tonight."

In some way, I was glad to have another day to myself before the weekend. Just to reminisce and think about what I needed to do for me, instead of taking care of everyone else! And the weekend would be family time, spending time with Dad and visiting friends with Lynn and Fraser.

So, what would I do today? I thought, as I poured myself another cup of tea. Yorkshire tea too! By Jove! Gold and strong it was! I'll have a nice walk along the marina into Swansea, and then catch the bus out to Pennard Cliffs on the Gower. Or should I get off the bus at Pennard Village first, and walk to the castle? I'll decide when I'm on the bus.

I finished my breakfast of bacon and eggs, with marmite on my toast, then looked at the date on the fridge. It was February 26, and on Monday it would be March 1, Saint David's Day! Saint David was the patron saint of Wales. I felt excited about celebrating Saint David's again in Wales, after all these years. I had always celebrated in Canada too, and I had celebrated it with my children, as part of their heritage. . But it wasn't the same as celebrating it in Wales, with the music, food and culture that went along with it.

The morning was crisp and clear as I walked along the marina path towards Swansea town. As I stood on the new "sail bridge," I looked down at the always dirty looking brown water of the River Tawe. The River Tawe flows down between the two hills of Town

Kingsley Ross Hill

Hill and Kilvey Hill. My father's house was almost at the foot of Kilvey Hill. When I was a boy, and my father was particularly pleased with me, he would say: "Kings, I'm very pleased with you, old son! I think I'm going to rename Kilvey Hill, the 'Kingsley Hill', after my eldest son." At my father's words, I would feel larger inside than the Town Hill and Kilvey Hill put together!

And my mother would then say to my father: "What did you say to him to make him so happy?"

My father knows how to bestow a blessing upon his two sons! My father's words are a "mountain" to me, where no man can climb up and put out my fire! A father's words can bless you or curse you. Blessed is the son or daughter whose father lifts them up and blesses them through his words. Cowardice lives in the man who remains silent and doesn't engage with or build up his children. It is interesting that my father's house is at the foot of Kilvey Hill, renamed "Kingsley Hill," and I only have to look up at that hill to be reminded of my father and remember his love for my brother and me.

Unlike rural Kilvey Hill, Town Hill is built over, and the inhabitants of the big municipal housing estate have the finest view in Swansea, which includes not only the sweep of the bay towards Gower, but also the great view Northwards over the ever-rising series of hills, through which the River Tawe (pronounce the 'e' by the way) cuts its way to the sea. In the background, 25 miles away, is the long, impressive line of summits, rising to over 2,500 feet, which form the range of the Carmarthenshire Vans. The northward view from Town Hill includes the coalfield of West Glamorgan. And, it was coal that changed Swansea's destiny! But that's another book! But I will tell you that my father also changed the name of Town Hill, to 'Fraser Hill,' my brother's name!

Fathers and mothers, if you want to ensure that your son's and daughter's destinies are great, then teach them to revere God, who is the greatest mountain! And name your children after the towering hills!

⌒

Now back to my walk to Swansea. As I arrived, Swansea Town was waking up.

And I'd almost caught him in his pyjamas! Not quite though! The Swansea Market would soon be opening! And I waited outside the fish-smelling, chewing-gum-stepping, seagull-shitting entrance, where a few noisy trucks broke the otherwise quiet misty morning.

The mist rolling in from Swansea Bay added an aura of mystery as the waking town said good morning to the new day. Fresh fish lay still in ice trays, as they dreamed of their sea-swimming days. And in their staring eyes they spoke not sadly of their end, for they would be eaten by fine ladies and gentlemen, and boys and girls who would dip them into tomato ketchup and tartar sauce. 'Better than dying in the sea!' one happy sole said to me.

Now the fat man arrived – with loaves stacked high on trays as high as the Eiffel Tower, still warm and smelling in the pigeon-flapping air. Oh, and then came the baker's van from Eynon's Bakery. A strong youth, with a Welsh Dragon tattoo on his arm, carried in a tray of one of my favourites: 'ice buns' with their yellow bread and white icing! I watched and almost drooled at the sight and smell that sent me and a nearby pigeon into a dither.

Next, he carried in a tray of 'custard slices' with dollops of custard and crumbly pastry, crowned with sweet warm icing – almost too much for my taste buds to bear! 'I will have to have one of those forthwith!' I vowed to the pigeon, who seemed convinced that I had something for him in my pocket, as he walked back and forth in unison with the movements of his head. Maybe he was excited about breakfast, and the crumbs he would find today? And we both waited and watched in anticipation, as the shy day grew to a shouting morning, but still misty and full of song.

Next arrived the 'Welsh cake ladies'!

"Couldn't wait, could you love?" one lady said.

Kingsley Ross Hill

"No, sorry, I couldn't," I replied. "I can't wait for a dozen hot ones fresh off the stove."

All of a sudden, the large market doors were wound open by two men pulling on chains. 'It's 8:30 a.m. on the dot,' said my pigeon, who now wandered off, and I wondered into the market to buy my lunch for the day.

Two French baguettes, with Welsh ham and cheddar and tomatoes, were the order of my day. And I also bought a large basket of cockles from the cockle women, who smiled at me with full sets of teeth. Guess they hadn't been fighting lately!

Well it was time to head to the bus station, where I'd only just arrived from London less than 48 hours ago. It seemed I had been here so much longer now that I was home. One of the first things I'd noticed was how much slower the rhythm of life was here in Swansea, compared to the fast-forward Vancouver. I felt myself already slowing to Swansea's rhythm!

I waited in the bus garage for the Pennard 14 to arrive. In my growing up years, the Pennard bus had been the number 64. And after being away in Canada for a few years, and coming home, it changed to the number 14. Oh well, most other things were the same, I thought, as I looked around. A queue had begun now at the bus stand, and I got in line. I wanted to get a seat upstairs so I could get a good view as we traveled along the country lanes. One good thing about catching the Pennard 64 in the past, and the 14 in the present, was that the Pennard bus was always a double-decker! Because a single-decker was too long to get around the Murton corner. I remember the day they tried it, and they took down half the wall of the Plough and Harrow Pub! Needless to say, they never tried a single-decker again. And it was free Guinness for all when that wall came down, I can tell you that!

Riding on a road-level decker bus was not half as fun as the double-decker! On a double-decker, I could see the world from the top deck – the world that was so dear to me!

The bus arrived, and I hurried upstairs like an excited school boy! An angry looking old lady behind me almost smiled. I sat in the very front seat. As there were no children on the bus, I wouldn't have to give up my seat to excited boys and girls who, like me, wanted to look out over the fascinating world below.

As the bus pulled away from the depot, I was a boy again! But the old lady's look reminded me that I was still a 40-year-old boy before I even got on the bus!

The Pennard boys were the worst behaved boys in all of the Gowerton School. The bus conductor, Mr. Merrill, told my mother this. Even worse than the Penclawdd Cockle Women's sons. And that is saying something, he said. At least we weren't bullies, frightening and beating up the new boys as they tried to find seats on the bus. We only had to sneak upstairs, where the girls sat, segregated away from us bad boys! As we snuck up the stairs to kiss the girls, Mr. Merrill would pull off our hoods and discover that we were boys. We were given one warning per trip to and from school, and if we did it again, we were put off the bus to walk the long miles home. But it was worth it to see your pretty girl's face, beaming at you from the back window of the bus. You were a hero to the boys and a romantic prince to the girls. A 'win-win situation,' even if you did get the strap from your father, or the wooden spoon from your mother, when you got home. And on Monday morning, you were more popular at school than you had been the week before.

The bus takes a good fifteen to twenty minutes to get along the Mumbles Road, before turning inland towards Clyne Common and more of rural Gower. Once the bus has climbed the hill to get onto the Common, there is a feeling of open space. And today, the view back over Swansea Bay, and the wilder Gower before me, gave me a feeling of excitement and anticipation as I entered my beloved land! From my seat, I could see a herd of wild horses roaming on Clyne Common. And they provoked such wonderful memories and emotions – I was instantaneously taken back in time!

My very first job was working on the golf course at Clyne Common. Each day I got to visit with the horses. And also, during my school days at Dumbarton House School, Mr. Gibson, who drove the school's minibus, stopped at the top of Clyne Common and picked up my beloved Gay! Oh, I felt her so strongly this morning! After all these years! Was I just having an emotional reaction to my memories of her? Or was I actually feeling her in my heart again, as I once did, as true as the wind blows.

Twenty years had come and gone since Gay and I lived and loved in the most beautiful love story that my soul has ever known! And often through the different times and seasons of my life, my heart has gone out to her across the expanse of time and distance. I remember a time about ten years ago, when I realized I'd made a big mistake and married the wrong woman! It wasn't just the understanding that my wife and I weren't compatible. There was always an 'awareness' and a 'knowing' that I'd met the love of my life in Gay! We had lived a lifetime in two seasons – spring and summer! In our hearts, we had planned a lifetime together. *I love you Kingsley! I love you too, Gay!*

And I wondered, today, why we had met. If she indeed was the love of my life, then why did she have to go away? And I remembered some words that my great friend Maggie Davies had said to me all those years ago when Gay and her family moved away to England, and my love went with her!

"I can't leave, Kingsley, my love, if your love doesn't come with me!" my Gay said. And it seems that all my life, "my love" had gone with her and never come back.

My friend Maggie said that "real love lasts forever, and never dies!" And she promised me, on the day that Gay left, that God had a bigger plan for my life! I can testify that He surely did! He took me to Canada, and I was able to live out my boyhood dreams of hunting and fishing, while exploring the wild west coast of British Columbia! And He also gave me three wonderful children, who have brought such love, meaning and purpose to my life! I am exceedingly blessed to be a father! And I wouldn't give up this blessing for anything in this world.

But sitting here today on the Pennard 14 bus, I could feel my heart going out in longing for a love that I once knew so long ago. And in a strange and wonderful way, all the time and experiences that I had lived between saying good bye to Gay and today, had evaporated away. It was like this was the next day! And I was off to meet Gay! And in my heart I began to sing and rejoice, because somewhere in this world was my Gay! And my love was still with her! And I felt her love with me, in my heart. How could I be back in yesterday?

We were approaching Pennard village now. I decided to get off and walk to Pennard Castle. I would walk the same way as Gay and I used to walk. I got off the bus at Brown's post office and went into the store to buy myself a Cornish pasty and a pop. Mrs. Brown still ran the Post Office. I recognized her immediately but she didn't recognize me. Not that it mattered, and I didn't feel like talking anyway. My heart was still full of thoughts of Gay. But seeing Mrs. Brown in her shop made me think of Maggie in Penmain Post Office and Heather at the stables. I'd lost contact with Maggie and Heather soon after leaving my home in Devonshire, with my Grandma and Grandpa, and moving to Canada. It wasn't that I'd wanted to lose contact with them, it was just, as they say, that life gets in the way! And besides, I'd spent the last six years healing from a divorce.

I wolfed down my Cornish pasty and guzzled my pop as I walked across the golf course towards the castle. And I smiled as I thought of Gay and I holding hands and stopping every few minutes to look into each other's eyes and kiss. And as I walked, I heard the sweet song of a skylark. A few rays of sunshine briefly broke through the grey, and in the late winter's air, I felt the promise that Spring was on her way!

Arriving at the castle, I stood amidst its storytelling walls and listened. And the gentle winds of memory stirred!

♪❄

MR. PENNARD CASTLE

Hello, Mr. Pennard Castle. It's so nice to see you again.
Six long years have come and gone since
I last held your hand,
while running and playing on your golden slopes of sand.
Today I have come home!
And again, amidst your ancient walls I stand.
I hope you can still look into my heart,
and see, and understand, of course, you can.
Oh, Mr. Pennard Castle, please take my hand,
And tell me another story, and make it very grand!

© *Kingsley Ross Hill*

I decided to sit on the hill beside the castle wall, where Gay and I used to look down over the valley, and see the Killy Willy River winding its way to the sea. And now the wind blew crisp and fresh upon me, as my soul remembered those warm, tawny afternoons and evenings when Gay and I sat here enjoying each other's embrace.

And I felt this deep desire to try and find her. In my heart, it was as if I could feel her presence on the gentle wind, as if she were near and searching!

After sitting for a while, watching the still valley below, it seemed that Winter and Spring were walking and talking together. The wild flowers and the skylarks sang of the arriving Spring, while Winter continued to ride on the chilly wind, blowing the grey clouds to the beat of his own song. The yellow flowers of the gorse bushes were in bloom, but only on their south-facing sides as they serenaded the sun. And the sun popped in and out between the clouds as if taunting old man Winter, who in turn would blow again, covering the sun with his wardrobe of fashionable greys!

And with his next gust, it was time for me to get going. I ran down one of Pennard Castle's golden paths of sand, until I stood at Killy Willy's edge, his waters still flowing quickly after the winter rains. And there was no sign of any horses in the valley today. They were probably sheltering inland, or maybe in the secluded opening in Park Mill Woods, away from the sea wind's cold reach. I walked along the river's edge and communed with my memories of Gay and our horse family that time and tide would never wash away!

I reached the stepping stones at the bottom of Penmaen Burrows, which are just before where the Killy Willy River turns and points almost straight out to sea. Then I climbed the dunes to the Burrows and walked towards Penmaen village. Once across the Burrows, I turned left on the narrow road underneath Cefn Bryn. And it all seemed to be the way I'd left it, all those lives ago! There were sheep on each side of the road, and there on the slopes of Cefn Bryn was a herd of horses. There looked to be four mares and a young stallion, who was not more than a year old. Some of the mares were probably pregnant and would give birth in the late Spring. But the herd was too far away for me to make any real predictions as to who would be having their foals first!

Suddenly, I arrived at a piece of road that could never be ordinary to me! It was the place where, Helen, Gay's mum, would drop off Gay, and then pick her up again after she had come and spent the day with me. How my heart would fill with joy as I saw the car coming to drop off my Gay! And then my heart would tug, and even the summer wind felt cold, when she took my Gay away. And for a few minutes today, I stood and hoped and wished for a time machine! Come on, man! Pull yourself together, Kings! Yes, okay, just a minute! I want a few moments with my memories. I stood and thought about our picnics, up on Cefn Bryn. Gay would make us the most wonderful picnics and we'd climb up to King Arthur's Stone, or 'Kingsley's Stone,' as we renamed it!

I continued my walk to the village, and my heart began to beat faster as I reached Maggie's Post Office and General Store. It had been over twenty years since I'd last seen Maggie in the store, or in her cottage that was ten minutes up the road. Twenty long years! Would she even still be alive? If she was, she'd be an old lady in her nineties! I opened the door and went inside.

A middle-aged woman said, "Can I help you, sir?"

"Yes, I hope so," I replied. "I'm looking for Maggie Davies, who used to run the Post-Office here. I'm an old friend of hers!"

"Oh, I'm afraid I've got some disappointing news for you! Maggie passed away almost two years ago now!"

I just stood still for a few minutes, and then asked if she had been well over the years I had been away?

"Oh, yes!" the lady said with a smile. She walked almost every day, and even climbed up onto Cefn Bryn, right up until she was 95! And she lived to be 98. And then she died suddenly in her sleep. The best way to go if you ask me! What is your name?" the lady asked.

"I'm Kingsley Hill," I said.

∽

"I'm Mary Parsons. Pleased to meet you!" And we shook hands.

"I've owned the store for ten years," Mary continued. "Maggie's sister from Bristol bought the old cottage. She only lives there during the summer months; it's empty during the rest of the year.

"Where is Maggie buried?" I asked.

"In Port Eynon church, next to her husband, and her mother and father. They are a real Gower family, the Davies!"

"Yes, they are," I echoed. "I can remember Maggie telling me that her mother and father ran the Port Eynon farm!"

"That's right, Kingsley, they did! Maggie grew up on the farm. Just a moment, Kingsley. Did you say that your last name is Hill? Yes, that's right! Well, Maggie left some things here for you! And she made me promise that I would give them to you in person if you ever came back."

Mary disappeared into the back room bringing three letters that were addressed to me! She handed me the letters and said, "They must be years old now. Maggie had them for at least ten years before I took over the Post Office. And I have been here for almost ten years."

I was surprised to get the letters, but I didn't say anything except "Thank you".

Oh, there is one more question I wanted to ask." Whats that, Kingsley? Do you know if Heather Griffiths, still lives at the stables? Why, yes she does! I know Heather, very well! In fact, I was just about to phone her to see if she needed any groceries from the store. Would you mind if I spoke to her, I asked? No, not at all! Heres the phone, why don't you give her a ring. I'm sure she would love to hear from you. I picked up the phone and dialled. As the phone rang, for a few moments I felt hesitant, wondering if she would still remember me, it had been so long! Of course she will! I told myself. Heather answered the phone, and I recognized her voice immediately . Hi , Heather, its Kingsley! Kingsley! Did you say, Kingsley? Yes Heather, its Kingsley! She was so excited to hear from me, and after talking for about five minutes on the phone, she invited me over to her cottage at the stables, for tea on Wednesday night. I was so excited! Thank you, Mary, for letting me use your phone.

༄

Oh, Mary, before I leave, "Do you have any fresh flowers?" "And do you know when the next bus is going to Port Eynon?"

"There is a bus in 10 minutes," she said. "If you hurry you will catch it up on the corner!"

"Thanks, and I'll take these lovely flowers too. How much?"

"There's no charge if you're taking them to Maggie"

"Thank you so much, Mary!" And I hurried out of the door to catch the bus!

"Catch me a fish some time, Kingsley! Maggie told me all about you catching her a bass and riding wild horses!

"I will catch you a fish sometime, Mary," I shouted back.

I just made it to the bus. "Port Eynon, please."

Chapter Four
Love and Letters

As I rode the bus to Port Eynon, I began to grieve Maggie's loss. Not that it had come as a surprise to me. But how could there ever be a good time to lose someone so special in my life?! Knowing that Maggie had lived a long and fruitful life, and had enjoyed good health until she died, was something to celebrate. But to know that I was separated from her by death, was a huge loss! Even though I had been away from her for all these years, I'd always thought of her as being there! I wished I had come and visited her, after I'd moved away to Canada. But in Maggie's words, that I had heard her so often say: "Life gets in the way!" And I knew she would not think any less of me for not having visited.

As I walked around the gravestones, I thought about the time Great Thunder and I had been chased around the church yard at Ilston Church! A silly looking man wearing a brown cloak had taken offence to a horse being on the grounds. As Great Thunder and I escaped from the capped pursuer, we separated a woman and her dog out on the road. I began to roar with laughter at the happy memory. And I'm sure Maggie was laughing too!

Just then I came upon Maggie's head stone.

"Here rests the shell of beloved, Maggie Davies,
her soul now re-united with her husband, John Davies,
and her Saviour, Jesus Christ.
Born June 9th, 1915, and went to be with her Lord
on March 19th, 2014."

Next to Maggie's stone were her beloved parents, Celwyn and Gwenneth Llawellyn. Maggie always spoke so fondly of her husband, John Davies, and her mum and dad, who had pioneered Port-Eynon farm, long before I was even a twinkle in my father's eye! And as I looked upon their headstones, they were not divided in death, but rather, "united," and all together with the giver of life! The Lord Jesus Christ.

Maggie once told me, when I had shared with her that I was scared of dying, that I need not fear! She said that when a person has a personal relationship with God, He sends His Holy Spirit to live within their heart. She said that the Holy Spirit testifies to our own soul, that we belong to Him! And when we die, God will take us home to be with Himself! The grave then becomes a place of hope – a doorway to Heaven! Maggie was such a woman of faith and inspiration to me! God did use her mightily in my life, in building my own faith in Him!

Some daffodils, now old and dry, had been placed on Maggie's grave. I replaced them with my flowers. They were irises, one of Maggie's favourite flowers! After placing the flowers, I began talking to Maggie. I told her about my life and what was going on in my heart!

"Maggie, I'm glad that you have gone home to be with the love of your life! As for me, I lost the love of my life! When Gay left the Gower, and went to live in England with her parents, all those years ago. And I still miss her, Maggie! She still lives in my heart. And I don't think I've ever stopped loving her! Oh, Maggie! Do you remember how upset I was, the day I had to say good bye to her? And you comforted me and told me that God had a greater plan for me, and that one day he would bring the right person into my life! Well, Maggie, I still think Gay is that person!"

Suddenly, a gentle wind blew around me. And I heard Maggie's voice! "Kingsley, the cottage is sold now, as is the shop. But go to your cave and pray to God! And share your heart with Him! And, if you haven't already opened your letters, go and open them on top of the Tor, where you used to greet each new day. I love you, Kingsley!"

I wept at her words. Her voice was silent, yet strong. And, oh so real within my heart! And with shivers running up my spine and excitement in my heart, I headed off to the Great Tor to open my letters.

I sat again on top of the Tor. But this time as a "broken man" of Leathers Hole! And I looked out over the green sea of the Bristol Channel. I had once sat up here as a King, wearing my rabbit fur robe and with my beautiful princess in my arms! Where had the years gone?

It was time to open my letters. I examined the postmarks on the envelopes, and I planned to open the earliest one first. On one of the envelopes, I could only make out the day and the month, and on one of the others, just the year, which read 1995. That was 20 years ago! As I held the letters in my hand, I had this feeling that I should have come home many years before. The third letter had both the year and the month – October 4, 1993. That was 22 years ago!

For a few moments, I wondered if the letters were from Gay? Or were they from Samantha, who I had met after Gay had moved to England? How would my life change if I opened these letters, I wondered. For I could not go back in time! "Open the letter, Kingsley," I heard Maggie's voice say again. So I opened it.

Dear Kingsley,

Eight years have come and gone since we said good bye and I moved away to England to start university. There is so much to tell you! Yet I don't know where you are! I came back to the Gower in October, hoping that I could find you. Like a young girl in love for the first time, I came back and looked for you on the beaches and in the valley. I looked for you in all our special places.

As I write to you, I am wearing the Celtic cross that you gave me with my birthstone in it. Evening emerald, do you remember? I want you to know that I never take it off! And one day, I pray that it will lead me back to you! Oh, Kingsley, my Prince! I wish you were here. I need you so much! Where are you? (At her words, I cried, and then read on.)

I don't know where to start? So, I guess I will start at the beginning. I finished university five years ago and I became a vet! Yes, that's right, Kingsley, a vet! And I can picture your smile as I'm writing. My dad wanted me to be in business management and administration. But as you know, I had always wanted to be a vet, ever since I was a little girl. And do you know that my experience with you and our horse family really affirmed my dreams! Not everyone gets to go to the university of "Pobbles Beach," like you did! But I had the privilege of going there for a whole Spring and Summer, didn't I? And when I told my classmates of our adventures, I was the most envied girl in the school!

Now my tears turned to smiles! And I continued to read.

My first year of university, I did what my father wanted. I started into a business major. But my heart wasn't in it! And I soon realized that I was living out my father's dream, not mine! I tried to talk to him, but he just wouldn't listen. He missed my heart by not realizing how much becoming a vet really meant to me! It was all about him, his dreams for me! Once in the middle of an exam in class, I shouted out, "What about me?" I pictured you riding Thunder Child across the university gardens and rescuing me. As we escaped on horseback, we made it back to the Gower! See, I am as wild as you, my Prince! (Now I was laughing and crying at the same time. And if Great Thunder was here, he'd be neighing too.)

Wiping the tears from my eyes, I continued to read.

After a year, I switched my university and began my studies to become a vet. Mum was supportive and understood me. But Dad became like a different person! When I came home on weekends and holidays, he hardly spoke to me! And when he did, it was only to lecture me about how I had ruined all his plans for me and for the family business.

What family business? That was his dream, not mine! I ended up going to a school counselor. She helped me to understand things and encouraged me to live out my dreams. Do you remember when you told me that God had brought Maggie into your life to help and guide you? Well, I feel that is what my school counselor did for me. When I was here, I went to talk to Maggie at her cottage. She gave me your news of how you saved Thunder Child's life! And brought him back to health by walking him in the sea. You did ride him Kingsley! I knew you would! And I'm so proud of you. I hope you still have my saddle that I gave you; I so wanted you to ride him with it.

Maggie also told me about how you moved to Devonshire and went to live with your grandparents. I tried contacting them, but they no longer lived at the address that you had left with Maggie. Maggie had been trying to contact you too. One day she received a letter from you in Canada, saying that you had immigrated to Vancouver Island in British Columbia! She tried to find the letter for me, which had your address on it, but somehow she had lost it.

Your dad and Fraser were away during the time that I was in the Gower, and I had to return to Oxfordshire to my job. I managed to get a job as a vet's assistant. It's mainly cats and dogs, but sadly no horses! It's my dream to work with horses again.

Well, Kingsley, I don't know if you will ever get this letter. In my heart, I pray that you will. I am leaving this letter with Maggie, in case you come back. Deep in my heart, I know that one day you will! Just like your stallion, you will return to the Gower. And by the way, Maggie told me why you changed his name to

Great Thunder!

Kingsley, please know that your love came with me! And it has never left my heart! I have never stopped loving you! And I can still feel your love washing over me. You are with me every day. The first few months I moved away, I thought I was going to die without you! But somehow, I was able to carry on. It was your love that came with me, that helped me to carry on! I love you, Orange. Please come back to Indigo!

After reading Gay's first letter, I couldn't open another! Not yet! Not until I had dealt with these feelings and emotions that rolled over my soul and threatened to drown me. I cried out to God like I hadn't done in years!

"O God! Great waves are crashing over me as in a wild and angry sea. And I need your strength to stay afloat! Please help me! My heart is troubled and my soul is overwhelmed by the rushing waters as I try to understand. Gay came back looking for me! And I had moved away to Canada. You did send her my love as I prayed you would! To watch over her and give her strength. For that I am thankful! Oh God, my love has always gone out to her, even though Gay and I have been living separate lives on two different continents, with oceans between us. Mum once told me that real love transcends time and distance!

O God, you are love! Please send Gay my love. And please help us to find each other again! Amen."

⟡

"You alright, Boy? You're praying on top of the Tor!"
"Yes, Sir, I am. I'm okay, Sir.
"Well done, boy. You tell God all about it and He will help you."
"Yes, Sir, I will."

Kingsley Ross Hill

After finishing my prayers, I had peace in my heart again. It had been a long time since I had prayed and poured my heart out to God. Especially after how the church leadership had treated me. They had judged me and condemned me, as I went through the pain and loss of a divorce. The so-called Pastor of the sheep even phoned me at work and threatened me with death. No wonder people are put off by Christians, Mr. Donald, Sir. I received more mercy, love and encouragement from the pagans – and judgment and a critical indifferent spirit from the so-called 'followers' of Jesus. How sad! But God is bigger than the pretenders and the hypocrites – those who do not love.

I know today that God didn't judge or condemn me. As my Grandmother said: "God left the room when the church showed no love! God is righteous and holy, but He dearly loves and understands His creatures, and most of all, the sons of men. He wants to help and heal our hearts and our broken lives."

After my prayer on top of the Tor, I headed back to Fraser and Lynn's. It was Friday night, and Dad and his significant other, Mary, had invited us over for tea (or 'dinner' as my fine friends on Vancouver Island call it).

I arrived back just as Fraser and Lynn were getting home from work. And after a shower and change, I was excited to see Dad and Mary. They had been away in England for the first few days I'd been back. It was going to be fun catching up with all the news. Dad was a great collector, and a restorer of antiques and old furniture. And I had collected and restored some great pieces on Vancouver Island. In fact, I don't think I have any furniture newer than the 1950's. The rubbish they sell today never lasts. And yet, people buy this made-in-China junk! Oh well, each to their own, leaving more quality stuff for people like me.

We had a great meal with Dad and Mary. Mary had cooked a nice organic chicken with lots of veggies and homemade gravy. They all laughed at me when I told them that I ate a lot of organic food. I reminded them how fortunate they are to live in a place where the ancient farming and growing techniques are practiced and protected, as part of the heritage of the Gower Peninsula. You have to work hard to determine what is truly organic food in Vancouver, with all the pesticides and imported produce from places like China and the United States.

Well that was enough talk and we got into the food. "Very nice meal, Mary!" my brother and I echoed across the table, and we ate until we hurt. After tea, Dad took Fraser and I down to his workshop in the back shed. Dad had purchased an old table from a farmhouse in Carmarthenshire. He had stripped off the paint – three layers of old lead paint, that had been used over a hundred years ago. Then when he turned the table over to varnish the underside, he found a secret drawer.. It was stuck with age when he first tried to open it, but he tapped it lightly with a rubber mallet and it finally opened. Inside, he found several pieces of jewelry: Two necklaces, a gold watch, and several gold lockets with pictures in them. The most treasured item was a pear-shaped ruby in a gold ring, and when he polished the gold, he found a date inscribed on the back: 1761.

"Wow, Dad, that's amazing!"

"It's worth a fortune, boys! I had it appraised – 20,000 pounds! And I only paid 20 pounds for the table."

"We felt that we'd robbed a bank and gotten away with it," Mary said.

Dad then showed us a few other pieces of furniture that he'd been working on. I had such a great time with Dad. I shared with him about my finds in Vancouver, and in the Cowichan Valley on Vancouver Island. Classic wooden boats and antiques had always helped to keep my father and I connected. Even with me living so far away in British Columbia, if I found a good piece of furniture or needed some advice on restoration or repair, I just called Dad, and he was an encyclopedia of knowledge.

Spending time with my father this night was both healing and stimulating for me, as the sting of my divorce became gradually less acute.

"It's good to see you are doing alright, Kings," said my Dad. "Mary and I were a bit concerned that the wicked witch of the north was getting you down."

At his words, I roared with laughter. And soon Dad, Mary and Fraser were laughing too. Oh yes, laughter is the best medicine.

Lynn said it was ten o'clock and we best be going. Dad wanted us all to go to Carmarthenshire the next day to do some antique hunting.

"Let's get an early start," he said, "how about we meet here at the house at 9:30 a.m.?"

When I arrived back at Fraser's, it was off to bed for me. I was tired from all my walking around Penmaen. As I lay quietly on my bed, I thought about Gay and her letter, and I read it through again. And I wanted to open another letter; I couldn't wait until tomorrow as I had planned to do. I had chosen not to mention Gay or the letters to Dad and Fraser. Reading Gay's letter, and thinking about my experience at Maggie's grave site, had brought the memory of Gay too close to me again. I didn't want to share her with anyone; only God. But I might share things with Heather, on Wednesday, when I go over for tea.

I would open the second letter, dated 1995. It was the only one that had a year on it. So, if this letter was from Gay, it had been written two years after the one I had just read, which was dated October 1993. I examined the handwriting on the envelope with my brother's magnifying glass that he used for his stamp collection. The writing looked the same alright! But it was also very much like the writing on the third letter. One of them could also be from my friend Samantha, I thought. She had already written to me once all those years ago. Well here goes! I opened the letter and as I hoped, it was from Gay!

Dear Kingsley,

It's been over two years since I came back to the Gower and left you my first letter with Maggie. And it looks like I will be leaving this one with her too. I have been here in Swansea for two weeks now and must leave to go back to Oxfordshire tomorrow.

I paused in my reading. Good! I hadn't missed another letter in between and I could try to piece together any gaps. I continued to read.

Oh, Kingsley, where are you? I wish I could find your address in Canada. Your dad and brother have moved away from your old house on Browns Drive and gone to Swansea to live, according to your neighbor, Mr. Heath. But, he doesn't have your dad's new address and it's not listed in the phone book!

Kingsley, I feel I am going crazy trying to find you. It's like you dropped off the face of the earth. And yet I feel you close in my heart. I can feel your soul, Kingsley, like there is something wrong! I need to connect with you.

O Kingsley, I hope you don't mind me telling you that I love you and that I need you so much. Of course I don't know for sure if you are married or have a family. You don't have any reason to contact me again, but deep in my heart, it's like there is a knowing that you love me and you are searching for me too?

I feel you so strongly, and your love is always with me. It gives me strength, along with my faith in God, and it keeps my hopes and dreams alive. O Kingsley, so much has happened since we last met.

My dad and I have completely drifted apart. In fact, since I last wrote, our family has split up. I mentioned before that Dad and I hardly talked because of my decision to choose a career that he didn't approve of, but I still came home sometimes to see my mum and my sister. But recently I noticed that my mum was depressed, and whenever my dad would come into the room, she would tense up like she was afraid of him.

When I came home for Christmas last year, Mum had a black eye and bruises! My sister Pearl was acting really strange too. So I knew something was really wrong! I could feel it in my spirit. I asked my Mum how she got her injuries, and she cried and told me she had fallen down the stairs. Then I saw a strange look cross my sister's face.

And then I knew! My sister's face said it all! Thankfully, Dad was out, and I pulled my sister aside and demanded to know what was going on.

"Dad's beating Mum!" she cried, "and I don't know what to do. When he gets angry, he hits her."

I thought back to when I was there over Christmas. "How could I have missed this?" I asked myself.

After the holidays, I called in at the University where I had received my degree. My old counselor from college, Debbie, now worked there and she provided a name so my mum could get some help.

Mum and Pearl finally fled one night to a Transition House for battered women. In the end, my mum had to put a restraining order on Dad because every time he got mad, he would be violent with her. It was really hard on me and on Pearl, because Mum would forgive him, to give him another chance – he vowed to change – but then when he lost his temper, he would hit her again.

Oh Kingsley, I'm so sad. My life is in such a mess.
A year after leaving my father, my mum went back to work. She and Pearl now have a house of their own in Cardiff – a long way from my dad, who still lives in Oxfordshire.

I have some other news to tell you. I pray you won't judge me, as so many people have. Thankfully, Mum and Pearl stood by me. Last year, Mum ended up having a nervous breakdown, and she and Pearl leaned on me for emotional support but I was really struggling myself. I reached out to one of my college friends in Oxford who said he'd be there for me. Well, as soon as he found out I was pregnant, he took off.

I have a little girl, Kingsley, and I've named her Melody, after my sisters middle name, to thank her for her support during my pregnancy. My sister has been amazing and she watches her little niece like she's her own child when I'm away at work.

Well, I must stop writing now. I will love you always, Kingsley! One day I pray we will be together again. I will leave my letter with Maggie. Love, Gay

I stopped weeping and put down the letter. I could feel Gay's pain as if it was happening to me. She had such a wonderful family, or so I thought! It was hard to think about her mum being subjected to abuse. But at least they were safe in Cardiff.

I ended my day by praying for Gay and her family.

Chapter Five

Gower of the Hills

*I*woke up excited, but mentally drained after the events of the day before. I reminded myself again that I'd come home to the Gower for a holiday – to relax and to do some healing myself. I was not here to try to solve the world's problems, even Gay's. Back on Vancouver Island, I was a busy Pastor and Counselor and I needed a break.

After a wonderful breakfast of bacon and eggs and toast and marmite, Fraser, Lynn and I headed over to Dad's house to meet him and Mary for our day trip to Carmarthenshire. It was a lovely spring day as we left urban Swansea behind us and headed up the narrow winding roads through the woodlands and fields, with their hedgerows and wooden gates where farmers crossed the road with their cows and sheep – forcing an otherwise busy world to slow down. And if one is stared at by an inquisitive cow, then the wait is longer.

On our trip this morning, there were four sheep (or was there five?) that were more stupid than the other one hundred and forty-one, the farmer said, as my father beeped the horn as gently as a horn could sound. And with the last sheep kicked by the farmer's boot into the field, the farmer said to my father: "The dog is sick! So I have to round them up myself with a whistle and a staff."

And suddenly, the world started to move again – until we reached the next corner, where a herd of cows was now crossing the road. My father swore, Mary laughed, my brother farted, his wife complained, and I opened the window and told a cow: "Hey, for a moment I was happy to be going somewhere!" The cow moo-ed, the farmer closed the gate, and we were once more on our way to the 'Gower of The Hills' and the Carmarthenshire Vans – they stand like proud soldiers on the horizon guarding Wales from the always invading English.

Dad asked if we would like to stop at Carreg Cennen Castle. "It's not much off the beaten track," he said. My father was much like me, in that if there was something worth seeing, it was always 'on the way'! We had explored many wonderful places by getting lost. And we had been chased by a bull and by "a jealous lesbian sheep," as Mary had described it. On one occasion, we were chased by a sheep with horns! Of course it was a ram, and as my father described it: "Ram us, he did." He rammed his rack into my father's backside, as we tried to climb the farmer's gate. Once we were over the gate, Dad suggested that *I* might like to open it the next time! Then as I walked quietly behind my father back to the car, his buttocks stared back at me through the holes the ram had made in his trousers – but I didn't get into any trouble, because I was only eight. And as the ram looked at us through the gate, he reminded me of Jeffrey Morgan, the bully at my school who was ten.

We arrived at Carreg Cennen Castle, and Lynn, with her bramble-beating walking stick, raced us all to the toilet that stood up on the hill like a lonesome Catholic priest waiting for confessions.

"There is only one confession he's going to get from me," I thought, as I waited cross-legged for Lynn to come out.

Dad said loudly as we all waited: "She must be knitting a quilt!" I always loved Dad's sense of humour.

Carreg Cennen Castle dates from the 13th Century. It's perched 300 feet above a precipice and is the most theatrically-situated ruin in Great Britain. And this Arthurian castle of one's dreams is complete with a subterranean passage. Its ground-plan forms a square, and its walls are exactly aligned to the cardinal points.

After climbing the steep hill to the castle, Lynn pulled out a picnic of egg-and-tomato sandwiches, along with a flask of tea and chocolate-covered biscuits. And as my stomach shouted "full," my father announced we'd have a fine pub lunch when we reached Carmarthen. As we explored the castle, I was drawn to the south-east wall, where one can stand looking from the heights across the rolling hills to the sheep meadows below, where Red Kites and Sparrow Hawks dance with the north wind. The sheep on the distant hills are like white dots on a sea of green. And along with a raven and several crows, and a magpie that had just landed, my soul sang a song to the hills that were singing with the spring, and to the waving heather that made the sun smile and the clouds dance in their thirty colours of grey. Wow, Day, what a thrill!

"Look Kings, there's a magpie," Dad said. "Do you remember Jerry the Magpie?"

"Yes, Dad, always!"

After we finished our snack, Dad took some pictures, and then we headed slowly down the long hill to the car park. Soon we were on our way to Carmarthen, travelling through narrow lanes with hedgerows 10 feet high! We then picked up the main road, passing by Welsh-named villages and farms. And I felt such a wonderful sense of belonging! My beloved land of South Wales once again caressed my soul. I whispered to a mountain: "I'll never leave you for this long again!"

By the time we reached Carmarthen, the old clock tower read 1:30. Dad said, "Let's go into the antique stores first and all meet back here about 3:30?"

Fraser and Lynn decided to walk around the town by themselves, allowing Dad, Mary and I to spend some time together. And the years felt as if they slowly melted away as we walked and talked amidst what seemed like an endless line-up of antique shops full of wonderful treasures. I helped Dad pick out several pieces of china that completed sets he had been collecting since the last time we walked the antique stores together. I felt much like a 'complete set of china' now that I was with my father again.

Well, I was almost complete; there was only one piece missing, and that was Gay!

We found a picture of a mysterious Celtic woman standing in the shallows of a misty green lake. "She looks like the mermaid that I met in the pub in Mumbles the other day, Dad!"

And he said, with a twinkle in his eye: "You better have this picture then, hadn't you?" And he gave me the picture to take back to Vancouver. "She can remind you of your home," he said.

"Thanks, Dad, I'll treasure her!" The picture was titled 'The Celtic Enchantress of the Green Pool.' And I thought that when I got back to Swansea, I would contact the black-haired women I'd met in the mermaid pub and see if we could have a mermaid adventure together.

It was now just before 3:30, and Dad, Mary and I headed off to meet Fraser and Lynn at the clock tower. The lunch rush was finished at the pub, and we sat at the main window and looked out on the town square. Mary ordered fish and chips and we all followed suit. I had smoked haddock with my chips instead of the cod, and, of course, tartar sauce and a mountain of good old H.P. sauce to dip the chips in.

"Another pint of cider, Kings?" Fraser asked. He'd already had two.

"Aye," I said, "I'll have another pint."

Dad and Mary had a custard slice for dessert, and I couldn't resist an ice bun. "Better make it two, love; my diet doesn't start till tomorrow!" I said to the waitress, and she laughed.

Mary said, "You're not on a diet, are you, Kings?"

"No," I said, "I'm only joking."

It was time to head back to Swansea, and I felt excited because Liverpool was playing Manchester Smelly United, and Fraser had taped the game. A cup of tea in my antique tea cup that Mary had bought me, along with chocolate biscuits, would be the order of the evening. And several cans of Canadian beer that I had managed to smuggle in my suitcase.

"And the Hill brothers watching the footy together! What more could I ask for? I said out loud.

"Maybe a mermaid?" Dad said.

"Mermaid, my arse!" Mary said.

And Dad replied: "I'm not talking about your arse! I'm talking about a mermaid with a tail!" Fraser and I roared with laughter.

And Lynn said: "You boys behave!"

I sat in the front with my father on the way home, while Mary squeezed into the back. It was a great sitting next to my father and feeling close to him again. It's just not the same talking to him on the phone from Canada.

Being away from Dad for such a long time had made me appreciate him even more. Distance sure does make the heart grow fonder. And it is so easy to take our loved ones for granted when we see them often.

As we drove along, Dad made it clear how much he was enjoying my company. I felt such a strong love for him! This man who had been, and continued to be, such a wonderful Dad. Mary was a wonderful step-mother too. I loved her sense of humour, and I loved the fact that she didn't take any guff from anyone and at the same time she had a heart of gold.

Before we got out of the car, she leaned over the seat and put something in my hand. It was a British fifty-pound note. "Use it towards your holiday," she said.

"Mary, you didn't have to do that!" I responded.

"Now shut up and take the money, boy," she ordered.

Fraser, Lynn and I enjoyed a wonderful evening watching the footy, and Liverpool beat the Red Devils, 3 to 1.

To top off a great day, Meredith the Mermaid called and asked me if I would like to meet for coffee and a walk on Sunday evening. And I eagerly agreed. Then after the football and a movie, I headed to my room to retire for the night.

But before I went to sleep, I decided to open the last of the letters from Gay. Only this one was not from Gay as I had thought. It was from Maggie.

My dearest Kingsley,

The months and years have gone by since I got a letter from you in Canada. I am concerned for you, Kingsley, and can only conclude that you are going through some deep waters of trial in your life! I love you and I'm here for you if you should ever need me. Remember, if you need a place to stay, the cottage is always your home. I pray for you every day and ask the Lord to keep you safe and close to His heart. I know He does, Kingsley, and I want you to know that whatever the trouble is, everything is going to be alright. Don't forget who you are! You are a true child of God! And He still has a wonderful plan for your life. Sometimes our hopes and dreams don't work out the way we want them to. But remember this, Kingsley, God's love and faithfulness never changes, He is the same yesterday, today, and forever!

"For I know the plans I have for you," declares the Lord, "plans to prosper you and not to harm you, plans to give you hope and a future". Jeremiah 29 verse 11:

And if you are hurting, remember that God is preparing you for something 'great'! He will give you hope in your heart and dreams to dream! And He will help you to live your dreams.

I wept with joy after reading Maggie's words. She had died and gone to heaven and still her words reached out and held my heart in her hands. Her letter continued, and she talked about Gay.

I want to tell you also, Kingsley, that Gay has come back to the Gower at least twice to try to find you. She is not doing well at all. Her Mum and sister have moved away to Cardiff to start a new life away from the father, who has been abusing their mother.

Gay has gotten pregnant and she now has a little girl. That's the big news, Kingsley; she is quite heartbroken about her life. I don't want to say too much more, not by letter anyway. But after pray-ing over this letter as to what I would say to you, I feel I need to tell you that Gay is still very much in love with you. And I don't think she has ever loved anyone else. I will leave that with you, Kingsley, and trust God to use these words as He sees fit.

Remember, dear, I love you always.

Love, Maggie

Chapter Six

Sunday, Sunday

*S*unday was another beautiful spring day. I spent the morning relaxing with Fraser and Lynn. In the afternoon, Fraser and I went for a walk along Swansea Bay. It was so good to be spending time with my brother, my only brother, and as we walked almost the full length of the beach, I felt like we were getting to know each other again. When you grow up together as brothers, there are always childhood memories of people, time, and places. And of course, our family heritage! But, six years away from any relationship is a long time. So, our walk was rich in the revelation of our development and who we were becoming as people.

When the conversation came around to how I was doing, in what I referred to as my 'relatively new life as a divorcé and single dad,' it was nice to be able to share almost everything. We had both grown bigger and stronger, and we had grown beyond the walls of independence and pride that used to guard each of us from getting to know one another. We had both become secure with who we were, and we were learning to appreciate our differences. All I needed now was to find the woman with I could do the same.

When we arrived back at the house, Lynn had made a lovely dinner – a lovely leg of lamb with mint sauce, gravy, roast potatoes and vegetables; and Dad and Mary had been invited too.

Fraser and I looked at each other across the table and said: "Sunday, Sunday! It's the best meal of the week!"

Roast lamb had always been our Sunday dinner when Fraser and I were growing up. And now he and Lynn were carrying on the family tradition! And for 'afters,' as we call it in Wales, Lynn continued our grandmother's tradition of serving Bird's custard on a treacle pudding.

And the silence around the table shouted loudly: it said "fan-flipping-tastic!"

Fraser and I ate until we hurt, as usual, and then retired to the living room to watch another game of footy. It was West Ham United versus Chelsea, and it would be a good game! Fraser and I both had supported Chelsea when we were very young. We talked about how Mum had bought us both a full Chelsea football kit, including soccer boots, for our birthdays (which of course were on the same day!). And our grandparents had bought each of us a leather football – made in England, mind you! Those were the days! None of this Chinese rubbish they sell today. Anyway, we played football all day long when we could. On my 11th and Fraser's 9th birthday, we saw the light and we became Liverpool fans! I was Ian Rush, and Fraser was Kevin Keegan. But today, I was happy to be Kingsley Hill, and my brother was Fraser Hill. The Hill brothers were together again!

"Quick! Alert the media and call the police! It's Sunday, bloody Sunday... and the Hill brothers are together again!"

I lifted a glass to him and he lifted a glass to me: "Cheers, Bro!"

In the late afternoon, the phone rang. It was Meredith, the Mermaid from Mumbles.

"I was just about to call you," I said. We arranged to meet in a coffee shop on the Mumbles Road.

"I know where that is, Kings," my brother said. "I'll drop you off if you like."

"Thanks Fraser. That would be great!"

It was nice to be in the company of a lovely lady. I felt wonderfully uncomfortable as I shrank away from her big, beautiful eyes each time we stopped talking. The eyes are truly the window of the soul and Meredith allowed me to see her lovely self.

After a while, our shyness left us and we were able to focus on having some good conversation, rather than just reacting to the powerful attraction between us. A large part of my initial perception of Meredith had been wrong! I had perceived her as perhaps a shallow, materialistic type of person, but I had been wonderfully wrong! I found her to be sensitive and engaging, and we enjoyed our conversation. We talked about our mutual interest in art and Celtic music, and, of course, exploring the wonderful Gower Peninsula. We had both been away from the Gower for extended periods of time in our lives and we both appreciated being home again.

Back on Vancouver Island, I had recently taught a class on discovering individual love languages in dating relationships – or courting, as we call it here in Wales. As I talked to Meredith, I became aware that meaningful conversation is one of my love languages. Conversation is very much the doorway to intimacy for me, as is touch. I can't imagine not touching or caressing a special someone's hand, or not having my arms around them and kissing them passionately. As I sat across the table from Meredith, I learned that conversation was one of her languages too!

No, dear reader, I didn't kiss her in the cafe or dance with her in the doorway. That may have been a little bit forward. Or not? Not if the feeling is there. You will have to read on, won't you!

Meredith and I laughed a lot about life and children, especially children. As I talked about my fab three, who I missed terribly, I began to weep! Minutes later, I was sharing about my daughter Samantha, about some of the crazy things we had done together, and I roared with laughter so loudly that I thought we were going to get kicked out of the cafe. Meredith agreed; she joked that if we were in the Mermaid Pub, she would have had to kick me out!

Oh, this laughter and conversation was doing me so much good! I felt that I hadn't had this much fun since forever and a day! And Meredith was also clearly enjoying our time together, which made me feel very good.

"How about a Joe's ice cream?" she asked, referring to Joe's Ice Cream Parlor just a few doors down from the cafe.

"Joe's!" I exclaimed. "I'd love a Joe's ice cream! It is one of the things I miss living in Canada – not being able to enjoy a Joe's ice cream."

To my delight, Meredith said: "No, I could not live without my Joe's ice cream either."

And we both ordered the largest tub this side of a family bucket. Gosh, it was fan-flippin-tastic! I didn't come up for air or conversation until I had finished half the tub. Meredith had ordered a "ninety-nine" chocolate bar with hers, which stuck out of her ice cream like the Blackpool tower.

"I love a ninety-nine bar of chocolate in my ice-cream!" she exclaimed. "And I love eating the crumbly flaky chocolate first and then the ice cream."

My taste buds had no words to say to such a wonderful description of pure pleasure. So I dived back into the orgasmic experience of my ice cream until I was finished, and then I lay in an exhausted heap on the floor! No, I didn't; I merely slouched over in my chair, breathing heavily!

As the lights on the lamp posts flickered on one-by-one, Meredith and I walked along the promenade. We passed the Yacht Club and walked on to the Mumbles Pier. We paid the toll of 10 pence each to get onto the pier and Meredith took my hand.

Yes, touch is definitely a language that I speak. As the warmth and gentle touch of her hand caressed mine, we walked further out to where we could see the winding sweep of Swansea Bay and the inviting lights of the city beckoning. There in the distance was the beloved Kilvey Hill, which stood like a guardian over the orange glow of the city. It wasn't much of a sunset tonight as the clouds were thick and heavy over the bay. But it was sure romantic being out on the Mumbles Pier in the evening with a lovely lady.

When we reached the end of the pier, our eyes met and danced. I touched the side of her face and gently kissed her in the breath of the breeze. Meredith sighed. As we walked back, we caressed each other's hands.

"I must agree with Forest Gump's mother, Kingsley: 'Life is like a box of chocolates and you don't know what you are going to get!'" said Meredith with a smile. And Meredith was dark chocolate and marzipan, and tasted so good!

After our lovely evening in Mumbles, Meredith walked me to the bus stop where she waited until the bus arrived. She said she was off work the next day, and after she dropped her daughter off at school, she would pick me up from Fraser and Lynn's place and we could spend some time on the Gower together.

"I'm looking forward to it!" I said, jumping onto the bus.

"Bye, Kingsley!"

"Bye, Meredith. See you tomorrow!"

As the double-decker bus went along Mumbles Road towards Swansea, I sat on the top and looked out across the bay where the cargo ships were now lit up, ready to come into the Swansea docks on tomorrow's tide. A few small boats were starting back to the marina, like people's lives trying to find a safe harbour.

And, on this night, I, Kingsley Hill, felt like I was finding my way. I didn't know where I was going, and I didn't need to. I knew that I was home! The Gower would show me the way!

When I arrived home, Lynn made a pot of tea and we all watched Coronation Street, with chocolate biscuits, before drawing the curtains of the day.

"Good night, Kings!"

"Good night, Fraser and Lynn! See you tomorrow when you get home from work."

Chapter Seven

Meredith the Mermaid

*M*onday morning arrived and I was excited to be spending time on the Gower and enjoying the company of Meredith again, after spending such a special evening with her the day before. After breakfast, I sat in the living room and waited for the mermaid to arrive. Suddenly, like a gentle wind, my thoughts blew back to Gay. And I began to experience the same feelings and emotions that I'd had when reading her letters!

Why was I still so emotionally connected to her? Was she close by somewhere? It's been 20 years, I reminded myself! Pull yourself together, man! You have to move on!

The doorbell rang, so I stuffed my thoughts and my feelings about Gay into a secret drawer within my heart, to bring out again another time.

I opened the door and said: "Hello Meredith the Mermaid, how are you?"

Meredith laughed and replied: "Can we head right to the Gower? Because I've packed us a picnic."

"That's great!" I said excitedly, and we were soon on our way.

"Where would you like to go?" she asked. "My daughter is going over to her friend's place after school, so I have all day!"

"How about we go to Bishopston Valley?" I said. "We can walk down through the valley to Pwll Du Bay."

"Wonderful!" Meredith replied. "I've never been down to Bishopston Valley or Pwll Du Bay."

As we drove along Fair Wood Common towards Bishopston, it was becoming a beautiful spring day. At least half the sky was blue now, out across the bay, and we would soon reach the village where we could walk down to the valley. I pointed out one of the local pubs in Bishopston called 'The Valley.'

"We can always have a drink on the way back," she suggested.

We reached Pennard Parish Church, where we parked the car, and then we walked along the narrow lane toward the cliff tops. I carried the picnic basket, and when the narrow path opened wide enough for the two of us to walk side by side, we held hands, only to have to let go again when we had to walk single file. Again, I thought how nice it was to have the company of a lovely lady! Her light perfume drifted my way in the gentle breeze, and as the birds sang, Spring's joyful song was all around us.

Suddenly, the narrow path opened out to a wide meadow, and Meredith took my hand again as we walked toward the cliff top. Then we came to a point that looked down on the tooth-shaped rocks known as 'The Seven Slades.'

"Come and look!" I said, as I stood on the edge of the cliff top. Meredith didn't like heights and I had to coax her to stand on the edge with me. Then I put my arms around her and she said she felt safe.

"Wow, you can see for miles!" she exclaimed.

"We are standing on Pwll Du Head," I said. "It's the highest headland on the Gower! It stands over 300 feet, or 97 meters, high!"

We climbed down the steep path from the eastern side of the head to Pwll Du Bay.

"Look at all those beautiful pebbles!" Meredith said excitedly.

"I'm glad you're enjoying it," I replied, as Meredith took my hand again and gave it a gentle squeeze. "Pwll du Beach has the finest pebble beach in all of Gower Land." And the pebbles chattered as we walked and tripped across them.

"How do you know so much about the Gower, Kingsley? I've lived here all my life, and you've lived away in Canada for years!"

"Well, I come back when I can, and before I left to go to Devonshire and then Canada, I lived out on the cliffs and beaches!" I said.

"Like in the wild?" Meredith said, with a slightly puzzled look on her face.

"Aye," I replied. "Out here in the wild was my home for almost two years! Would you like to know more about Pwll Du?"

"Yes, Kingsley, I would love to."

"Well, the name Pwll Du means 'The Black Pool' in Welsh!"

"The black pool?" Meredith echoed. "Is there a black pool?"

"Come and see," I said, as we continued to trip our way across the shifting pebbles. "Look! The huge mound of shining stones stretches right across the bay."

"And here's the black pool!" I shouted in excitement, not having seen it myself in so many years.

"Oh, it looks so mysterious!" Meredith exclaimed. "And look how deep it is!"

"It's deep alright! And cold! My dad and I swam in it once. The waters are from the Bishopston stream that runs through the valley."

"The pool is dammed up by the pebbles," I explained. "And the stream seeps out onto the sands through the pebbles. Can you see the line of wet sand on the beach?"

"Yes, this is lovely, Kingsley! I never knew about this. Thank you for sharing this with me! How about some lunch – are you hungry yet?"

"Yeah, I'm getting hungry. Shall we have it by the pool?"

Meredith had packed us a lovely lunch. Salmon and tomato sandwiches, with ice-buns for dessert! And she even pulled out a tub of cockles!

"Cockles!" I shouted in excitement. "And...ice-buns! How did you know they are two of my favourite things?"

"You told me when we first met in the Mermaid pub, remember?" she replied.

"Yes, I remember now. Come here!" I cried, and I gave her a gentle kiss.

"Mmm," she said. "So it's true that a way to a man's heart is through his stomach!"

"It's one of the ways," I said, smiling.

"Hmm, just one of the ways," she echoed. "You will have to tell me about the others!"

"Are you flirting with me, you naughty mermaid? And do you know what we do with naughty mermaids?"

"No, but please tell me," she said, giggling.

"It's kind of hard to explain. I'll have to show you," I said, smiling.

"Show me," she murmured back, now blushing brightly. And I pulled her towards me and kissed her tenderly, until our tongues darted and danced, and the pebbles shouted a song of romance under our feet.

"Thank you for being such a beautiful woman!" I exclaimed, "And for helping me to feel so glad to be a man again!"

"And thank you for making me feel so glad to be a woman, Kingsley!"

We finished our ice-buns and kissed some more. And then it was time to climb back up to the cliff path, up on to Pwll Du Head, and down the other side to Hunts Bay. As we climbed down towards the bay, my mind and heart became full of wonderful memories that swept through my soul like a crashing wave! There before me was "Hunt's Bay"! Where I had found my message in a bottle! And there on the side of the cliffs, to the west, was the haunting entrance of Bacon Hole! That had once been my home!

"Are you alright, Kingsley?" my mermaid asked. "You look like you are miles away. Like you are back in another time and place!"

"Oh, I'm definitely alright," I replied. "I was just remembering. Would you like to come and see Bacon Hole? It's where I lived for a while when I lived on the cliffs."

"I'd love to see it, Kingsley, as long as you keep me safe. I get claustrophobic when I go into caves and small spaces. When I was in my teens, my dad took me caving with him, and I had to come running out of this long cave that was really scary!"

"Oh, it will be nothing like that," I assured her. "My cave has a very wide entrance, and if you are not comfortable going in, you can stay near the entrance. I just want to go inside for a few minutes and check things out."

We climbed up the rocks and along the cliff path until we were right above the entrance. I found the old path, through the gorse, that I had so often used to climb up and down to my cave, all those years ago. As I took Meredith's hand and led her down, the path was quite overgrown. Clearly it had rarely been used, and we got pricked here and there by the sharp thorns of the gorse.

"It's a wild gorse chase!" I said, laughing. Meredith was a good sport and she didn't complain; we arrived at the entrance with a feeling of accomplishment. Some of the gorse had begun to flower just outside the entrance, and its dainty yellow petals and sweet coconut smell welcomed us!

"I'll stay here if you don't mind," Meredith said, as we stood and gazed into the still entrance. It called out loudly to me to come inside!

"This place gives me the creeps," she shouted to me as I disappeared inside!

"Fear!" I said in a loud whisper. "Are you here?"

"Of course, I'm here! Where do you think I'd be, in Las Vegas? I've been waiting for you to come back."

"What's the matter, fear? Short on friends, are you? No one to haunt – is that what you mean?"

"Yes, that's what I mean," replied Fear. "Say, why are you whispering, wild boy? Cat got your tongue?"

"No, I just don't want my lady friend to hear me talking to spooks like you! Bad for the image, you know."

"Now, is that the way to talk to an old friend?"

"Old friend, my arse! I don't remember you and I being friends!"

"Then why have you come back, wild boy?"

"I'm a wild man now, Fear, not a wild boy, in case you haven't noticed! I learned a lot of things through you, most importantly to overcome you! And, I came back to remember the victory that God gave me over you!"

"God! You're not still hanging out with him, are you? Oh, I get it! He's told you that you're now a man, has he? What a joke! I know why you have come back! You came back like a little boy missing his Gay! She's gone, hasn't she? And, like a little boy with dreams too big for his boots, you have come back searching for her. Well, I've got news for you, Kingsley! She's gone for good! And just think, you have to live with the fact that she came back looking for you, and even wrote you letters. But you went to Canada, and you missed your chance!"

"Oh Fear, I thought you might have changed! But you're still the same negative father of lies you always were! You are no longer a part of my life. Because God has shown me who you are!"

Oh, shut up about God, wild boy!"

"Jealous Fear! Jealous because you don't control my life anymore! Well, like I told you years ago, keep your chin up, old man, I'm sure that in another ten thousand years, someone else will come and live in Bacon Hole, and you can haunt them!"

"Kingsley, who are you talking to in there?" Meredith called out from the entrance.

"Out in a minute," I shouted back. "I'm just muttering to myself."

Before I headed back out of the cave, I dug around in the clay to find that most of my stones were still in place, forming the circle of my old fireplace! There were several pieces of half burnt wood where someone had started a fire and then put it out. I guess Fear had frightened them away.

"It's a dark abode in there!" I said to Meredith, as I came out into the daylight again. "It's hard to believe that I lived in there once. It was so dark and spooky that I tried to keep a fire going all night to chase away the fear and darkness."

"You are pretty brave to have lived in there, Kingsley! You wouldn't catch me in there anytime, let alone at night!"

"Let's go," I said. "Shall we walk back to Pwll Du Beach and then walk back up through Bishopston Valley? Then, we can stop in at the Valley Pub on the way home."

"Great plan, Kingsley! I was going to suggest that we have tea in the pub. I'm having such a lovely day with you, Kingsley, I don't want it to end!"

I hugged Meredith and kissed her again.

After climbing over the headland and down the other side to Pwll Du, we walked across the pebbles to the black pool again.

And Meredith asked again: "Why does it look so mysterious? Maybe it's the dark deep water?"

"I wrote a poem about it when I lived in Bacon Hole," I replied. "Would you like to hear it? It's a poem that I memorized."

"Yes, Kingsley, I'd love to hear it."

♪✽

THE BLACK POOL

There lies at the bottom of the Bishopston Valley
a dark and mysterious pool.
Cradled within the pebbles its secrets are kept.
Its magic waters call out to the brave and pure of heart
Who may come and bath in its essence,
and be given a special wisdom and strength.
As for those who are cowards,
whose hearts are still ruled by fear,
They may not enter the black pool within the singing stones,
Lest they be pulled down to its deep dark depths.

And they are held by their own transgressions,
so the Friar of Bishopston has said!
But the joys that await the righteous flow down
from the Bishopston Pill,
As through meadow and woodland,
and underground chambers, she travels
Collecting the secret wisdom of life's seasons to impart
within her sacred waters
To those whom she allows to swim therein!
"'Tis true, boy!" the voice said.
"Yes, sir, I know!"
Because when I was a boy,
I held on to my Father's shoulders as he swam around the pool.
"It's black, Dad, I can't reach the bottom!"
"Hold on to me tight, Dad," I said,
starting to slip off his shoulders.
Suddenly I slipped off!
And I thought I would surely sink!
But my Father spoke powerful words to me:
"Cast that fear out of your heart, boy."
And his strong hands held me fast!
And he said, "Kick your legs, Son,
and push your arms out gently, and you will not sink!"
And my Father let go of my waist,
and I was swimming all on my own!
And I shouted, "Look Dad, I'm swimming
in the black pool, and I'm not afraid!"
And he said with his eyes smiling,
"Well done, my son, you are now one of the brave!"

© *Kingsley Ross Hill*

Meredith clapped her hands, and I bowed, and we carried on our way.

As we walked once again, I thought about the sounds and smells of the Spring that filled the air, reminding me how unique and sacred the Bishopston Valley is!

"It is so beautiful here," Meredith echoed back to the singing hills on each side.

And the stream sang to us a chorus, as the valley twisted and turned inland, between densely-wooded slopes and rocks all dressed in fine moss. Meredith held my hand as I led her up the twisting path, stepping and jumping over fallen boughs of sycamore and birch that could no longer stand up to the strong winds and rain. But they lay not as soldiers killed in battle, but as bridges to climb and cross, becoming a part of the song of nature.

And how special it was to lead this lovely lady through this sacred wood.

Suddenly, we came out of the woods into an open meadow, and the clear waters of a trout stream flowed beside us. I reached for Meredith's hand again.

"This is so romantic, Kingsley! Like it's our own world! Just the two of us."

"It is," I replied. And I pointed out several trout in the stream and vowed to come and catch them another day.

The meadow was full of bluebells, my favourite of the wild spring flowers. I picked a bunch for Meredith who invited me with her eyes to kiss her soft lips again.

"You smell like the wild flowers," I said, as I enjoyed her woman's fragrance in the fresh meadow air.

We reached the original little hamlet of Bishopston, which is wedged in at the bottom of the valley. There's an ancient church here that is dedicated to St. Teilo. The Welsh name of the village is Llandeilo Ferwallt. St. Teilo was a contemporary of St. Illtud in the sixth century, when Wales was being Christianized by the travels of the Celtic Saints. St. Teilo may well have founded a church in this then remote place.

To my delight, Meredith had a keen interest in history, and especially ancient churches! This was very stimulating for me and we walked hand in hand to explore the church.

Bishopston Church has a great charm, with its small nave and chancel with a typically castellated tower. In the early days of the Conquest, they built the tower more for defense than for the bells. And as Meredith and I stood in the shadow of the tower, I vowed to protect her, by sword or fist! against any marauder who would try and conquer us!

The Bishopston stream springs surprises, and, as one can expect in 'limestone country,' it rises on Fairwood Common in the Millstone Grit belt but sinks underground in dry weather at Barland Quarry, where it hits the limestone. For a mile beyond Bishopston Church, it remains hidden, although you can detect its presence in strange sink holes. As we walked along in search of the stream, Meredith was fascinated by the sink holes. And I tried to remember a place that I had found with my father long ago, where one can hear the stream running far out of sight below!

"There it is!" I said excitedly. "It's called 'Guthole'! Put your ear to the ground and listen!"

"I can hear it, Kingsley! I can hear it singing and bubbling underground like you said."

"And I can hear it making a different sound," I said, "as it travels further and further away in its secret chamber underground."

"What's it saying, Kingsley?"

"It's singing, 'let's go, let's go, let's go!'"

"Oh, I can hear it singing now! It's singing: 'let's go to the pub for lunch!'"

And I agreed that we should go to the Valley Pub. We parked in the car park and went inside. Its age and heritage caressed my soul.

And I said aloud, to all the patrons already seated: "It's so good to be home!"

"Was this your local pub when you lived in the Gower?" Meredith asked.

"No, but I'm remembering the age of everything here! The old oak tables and chairs. Look at the old beams on the ceiling! Solid elm! There is nothing like this in Canada! There are some nice pubs in Vancouver, but compared to ours here in Britain, most of them are relatively new buildings that are fixed up inside to try and look old. I'm not much of a pub-goer, but my local pub here in Wales was the Plough and Harrow, in Murton. The new part of the pub is over 400 years old!

"'Put that in your pint and drink it!' I tell them in Vancouver, when I hear someone boasting about how old their local pub is. When I come home to the Gower, my heritage is something I appreciate and celebrate so much more since I've been living in Canada. The beer in Canada is great, though! Better than that piss they drink in the United States – Bud Light. What a joke – it tastes like bull piss!"

"I've never been to Canada or America," Meredith said. "So, I haven't seen anything to compare our pubs with. Apart from Europe, that is. There are lots of old pubs in France and Spain."

"Right you are, my mermaid, right you are!" I replied.

"Stop calling me a mermaid, Kings, or I will drag you out to sea and do all sorts of things to you!"

"Promises, promises! Come on then, mermaid, drag me out to sea!"

Meredith slapped me on the back, laughing, and we sat down.

As we enjoyed our food, we talked about our day with its many adventures. We both agreed that we must go on another Gower adventure soon!

"I will be away for the next week, Kingsley. I'm taking my daughter to my mum and dad's in Somerset. I'm going to spend some time with a girlfriend and have a spring break too. How about you, Kings? What's next in your plans?"

"Well, I'm looking forward to spending time with my Dad and brother. And on Wednesday, I'm going to visit an old friend at the riding stables in Penmaen."

"Can I call you when I get back from Somerset, Kingsley? I've had such a wonderful time with you today and I would like to see you when I get back."

"Yes, I would like that too," I said.

But I also thought that I didn't want to get involved in any serious relationship until I'd dealt with what seemed like such an unfinished journey with Gay! Everything happens for a reason! And I believed that there was a reason I had received these letters from Gay and Maggie all these lifetimes later. And it was clear to me that Gay still lived in my heart, and I believed that she still carried my love within hers!

Now I felt the need to tell someone about Gay and the letters. But who? I didn't want to tell Dad or Fraser. As for Mary, she was great to talk to, but a lot of what I'd shared with her in the past had found its way back to Dad. And I was sure that Meredith didn't want to hear about the love of my life! Oh, how I wished Maggie was still here! And I knew that in some ways she still was. She had spoken to me in the wind at the churchyard. And in her letter, I could hear her voice! Tomorrow, I would go for a walk to Pennard Castle and collect my thoughts.

Meredith kissed me good-bye as she dropped me off at Fraser and Lynn's.

"Bye, Kingsley! Thanks for making me feel so special!"

"Thank *you*, Meredith! See you when you get back from Somerset."

And I thought to myself that no matter what the future might hold, it was so nice to have a mermaid in my life! And what Dad had said was true ... there is such a thing as mermaids!

After an evening of watching Coronation Street and Inspector Frost with Fraser and Lynn, I toddled off to bed.

"Good night, Fraser and Lynn, see you tomorrow."

"Yeah, Kings, good night and see you in the morning."

Chapter Eight
Pennard Castle and Mr. Bryn

On Tuesday morning, I was up early enough to have breakfast with Fraser and Lynn, and we talked about our plans for the following weekend. We were looking forward to spending some quality time together. As they headed off to work, I decided to go to Pennard for the day and visit my old haunts. It would be great to visit the castle and go down to the Three Cliffs Valley! Then the next evening, I had been invited to go and have tea with Heather. I was so looking forward to seeing her and getting caught up with more of the news from around the Gower. But in my heart, there was a deeper reason! I hoped that, in some way, my time with Heather would give me more connection with Gay! Reading Gay's letters had brought me close to her again. But I needed more – to give me the faith to believe that I would see her again.

After walking into Swansea, I stopped in at the market to buy my lunch and connect with my fellow countrymen. The Welsh Cake and Cockle ladies were getting quite used to seeing me in the market most days as I walked around basking in the friendship and fellowship that was offered to me so freely!

"Why, this is Wales, and of course we are friendly," a lady said to me, as she listened to my conversation with someone else standing in line at the cockle stand. "We are always friendly here," she continued, with passion in her voice!

"Yes, you are," I echoed. "And it's so wonderful to be home – having been away for so long has made me appreciate being here so much!"

Pennard Castle and Mr. Bryn

It was time to catch the #14 bus to Pennard. And I stood in the bus depot even more excited than the pigeons – who walked around with their heads moving back and forth, charming people into giving them a share of their breakfast.

There was one that was almost white, with a ginger-red head and tips on his wings. "Here you are, handsome fellow," I said, breaking off a piece of Welsh cake for him.

Just then I heard a familiar voice call out: "Are you talking to yourself, Kings?" It was my friend Martin's mother, Beryl.

"No." I smiled. "I was talking to the pigeon. I haven't quite got to the stage of talking to myself yet, not in public anyway! And how are you, Beryl? It's so great to see you!"

"You too, Kings! I haven't seen you in years. How long has it been?"

"Six years," I said.

"Six years, Kings! I can hardly believe it. It only seems like yesterday that you and Martin were always doing something together. You boys were always in trouble, weren't you, Kings! And our Martin was just talking about you the other day. He said that it's pretty boring in Pennard without you. He was telling us stories about you and your Stallion. And how you left home and went to live in a cave for two years. You were a wild one, Kings! But we love you all the same, don't we! So how are things in Canada?"

It was so nice to meet up with Beryl. And we sat together all the way to Pennard. It turned out that my friend Martin had had his troubles too. He'd met a woman, married, and then divorced, all while I was away in Canada.

"He dropped out of university when he got married," Beryl said with a sigh.

"And how is he doing now?" I asked.

"Oh, much better," she replied, smiling. "He's met someone who he really gets along with. He's living in Gorseinon now, just outside of Swansea.

"Well, my stop is coming up, Beryl. It's been great talking to you. Please give my regards to Martin."

"I will, Kings! And you take care of yourself."

I got off the bus in Southgate Village and walked across the golf course to Pennard Castle.

The word Pennard, means 'a village without a gate' in the Welsh language. And I can remember my mum telling me that the word 'Pennard' was very appropriate for my personality!

"Ever since you could walk, Kings, you didn't like gates or fences. You would climb over them just because they were there! I remember when you were about four years old, a neighbour opened the gate for you to come out of her garden, and you climbed over her fence instead! And if I told you to 'stay somewhere' and there wasn't a fence, you would most likely stay there. But, if there was a fence or gate, forget it! You were gone!"

When I think of what my mother said, I do believe that growing up in Pennard had a special significance for me. It's interesting that names and places have specific meanings for different people, if only they are 'aware and open' to receiving their messages and meanings!

For me, 'a village without a gate' represents freedom! And fences and gates represent captivity! Unless they are to keep your enemies out, of course, like the walls of Pennard Castle.

As a boy, I would climb the walls of the castle with my brother Fraser. Mother would shout to us to come down before we hurt ourselves. I remember the feeling I had standing high upon the castle walls. The walls were ruins and had already been conquered! – so it wasn't a feeling of *wanting to conquer* that I felt inside, but rather a feeling of *wanting to be a part of protecting the walls*. As I approached the haunting walls in the distance today, the feeling in my soul was much the same! I felt a feeling of ownership and protection, of wanting to rebuild the walls!

I arrived at the castle, and stood amidst its ancient ruins. And as they had always done, the years melted away, and I stood again with yesterday.

My Friend Pennard Castle

I stand amidst the ruins of my great friend, Pennard Castle. And I am here alone. I can still feel within my soul that I am the first! The first to find it! And explore its ancient of days, even as it reaches out and explores my soul, as it tells me its forbidden secrets. Only as shared with a best friend, you know. We feel each other's nakedness and caress that which time cannot cover or disguise with dress. You are ancient and you are young, and everything they think they know has been said or done. But not for us! We are new and fresh, and more alive than when your first stone was laid . You shout loud and tell my stories like you always did! Now that I am a man, and when I was a kid. You still whisper your secrets to me in the wandering winds, where I tell mine to you. And no other soul has heard the silent shouting sound of you and me dancing to our songs of the coming spring, or our sadness when autumn falls and kisses us both. And I love our favourite song that we sing when summer dresses fade, and the children stop digging with their spades, and lovers' dreams fly on skylark wings and reach the golden sunsets on the distant hills. My soul thrills to your songs and secrets that echo through the years, and that meet me today. It's so good to see you, My Friend Pennard Castle.

As I was finishing my lunch at the castle, I suddenly remembered something that I had long forgotten! Before I left the Gower to go and live with my grandparents in Devonshire, I buried a poem that Gay had written for me under the castle wall. And I vowed that one day I would return for it; and today would be that day!

I remembered that I had walked to the end of the southwest facing wall and buried the poem in a little leather pouch underneath the archway where Gay and I had looked out across the Three Cliffs Valley below.

Could it still be there? My heart raced as I walked along the wall. I stopped and stood under the archway.

"This is the spot," I said aloud. And I started to dig in the clay and stones. It was too hard to dig with my hands. I had used a trowel to bury the pouch, if I remember rightly. The ground had become hard over the years with the wind, rain and sun. I looked around for a stick I could use to break the hard surface. Finally, at the end of the castle wall, I found one. Once I broke through the clay, the sand was soft, and I began to dig with my hands. At first there was nothing – only hard pieces of clay and small stones. I was down about a foot now, and I wondered if I was in the right place?

"It had to be here!" I said, speaking out-loud again. "I'm right under the arch at the southwest facing wall!"

Suddenly my fingers gripped something long and soft! Excitedly, I lifted it up to inspect it, and it was my leather pouch alright! Its once grey leather was now stained a deep red by the clay. Brushing off the sand, I took it to the castle room to open it. The 'castle room' was a sacred place of mine. I had played there as a young boy and hidden my secret treasures in the deep sandy floor. It was where I had buried my love letters and poems that I'd written for girls, when I was too shy to give them what I had written. But, I wasn't shy anymore. I was searching for my Princess!

The 'castle room' was also Gay's and my special place where we hugged and kissed on those warm summer afternoons. And even when It was cold, the high walls sheltered our kisses from the strong sea winds that blew up the valley from the Bristol Channel. During the long summer nights, we would watch the sunsets, and then the night sky, from our sacred room. So today, after twenty years of sunsets, I would read again her poem in our room!

I opened the pouch and found the poem. I wept as I read through the poem and remembered the most precious love of my life!

♪✳

THE SONGBIRDS SONG

A POEM FOR MY PRINCE

The songbird sings a song,
so sweet that God in his heaven smiles!
Only one song he sings.
And many searching hearts hear it!
But for only two, the song sings the same!
Listen my heart to the chorus, he sings our song!
The song of our own hearts!
We sing and dance as our souls take flight,
having been woken from our winters sleep,
by the songbirds song of love!
As we sit here together,
your are in me and surround me at the same time!
Your voice sweet and gentle,
blows as the sea breeze over the fragrant hill.
I breath you in, and my soul rejoices!
As I touch and taste the purity of your heart,
In this song I've never sung before, yet my soul knows every word!
A love song, as innocent as children,
who discover they speak the same tongue,
and somehow know they are one!
Touch me again my love!
That I may tremble, and fall into your green
and mysterious eyes, where I see you, and you see me,
our souls melting together, deep, deep, I fall into your eyes,
and travel to the depths of your soul, my Prince!
The place no one else has ever been before!
Only the God, who made you for me, my love!
Suddenly, I see myself!
My own reflection within your soul!

And we are dancing.
I am breathing with your breath, and beating with your heart!
Oh, breath for me, my love, and beat for me my heart!
For I have fallen so deep, because I followed my heart.
I am here inside you my love!
And you are here with me!
I sing to you, Kingsley, my love!
With the songbirds song.
One song! It is our song of love.

© Kingsley Ross Hill

♪✳

PRINCE OF SUMMER

A POEM FOR MY PRINCESS

Years and distance,
and even people in different lives
have not been able to quench the love that
still lives and breathes and shouts
within my heart!
Like the spring that sleeps within the
bulbs of the wild
flowers that lie under their winter blankets
dreaming of the prince of summer,
who will come and kiss them with the sun.
So my soul wakes, and leaps to the kiss of your
poem, my love! And cries out:
Where are you, my Gay!
Where are you, my love?
Surely you can feel my love that travels through
distance and time to find you and kiss you,
as the Prince of Summer!
You came looking for your Prince, my love,
and could not find me!

But you have found me now!
My heart has heard the longings of your heart.
My soul hungers and pants for you, my love!
Your poem has woken me from
my winter's sleep,
and I must search for you and find you!
My forever love!

© *Kingsley Ross Hill*

With my poem in my pocket, and my Gay within my heart, I ran down the golden slopes of the castle to the valley. As I ran, I remembered a game that my brother Fraser and I used to play as boys. We would both run down the sand slope, which was just big enough for the two of us to run side by side. We would try to trip and pull each other down on the way, and whoever was still standing when we reached the bottom, won! Sometimes we would come crashing down on top of each other. And if that was the case, it was a draw!

And today at 40, I only fell once on my way down.

The sparrow hawk above shouted: "There's that Kingsley Hill again, still running down the slope at 40!" And he shook his head from side to side as I picked myself up from the sand.

As I reached the bottom, I shouted back to him, "I haven't had so much fun in a long time, have you?"

"No, I haven't!" he said, and glided off.

The valley was full of Spring's song this morning, and I lifted my spirit to sing with its golden chorus. The song we sang then was called 'Promise.'

As I walked the valley, I followed the Killy Willy stream as it twisted and turned its way to the sea. Apart from a few people walking their dogs, I had the whole valley to myself. As always when I walked here, almost alone, I had this wonderful feeling of ownership! As if this wonderful paradise was all mine! Not that I wouldn't share, it, mind you; I would! But only with a select few! I wonder if God felt the same way as me, when He walked in His garden? And as I looked around, I thought He must be a better sharer than me.

I came now to a bend in the river where I had once speared some big skate. But the river was running too fast and deep after the winter rains for me to see any fish on the bottom. Its waters become more shallow as it flows to the sea; and when I walked further, I could hear the song of the water as it raced over the pebbles. Then I crossed over the large stepping stones as the river turned, and I was facing the sea.

Oh, what wonderful memories caressed my soul, as I remembered long summer days, and having picnics with Gay up on the hills, and swimming in the sea.

Once I had passed Three Cliffs' Woods, I looked up to Cefn Bryn. Gay and I would climb the dunes and walk across the cliff tops to Penmaen Burrows, and then on to the path that leads to the top of the Bryn. Today, Cefn Bryn was wearing his spring wardrobe. At his feet, the wildflowers shouted, especially the yellow daffodils and bluebells. The gorse flower shone brightly around his middle, contrasting with the green ferns that he wore like a belt. And the sun shone down on his summit, illuminating the grey rocks like an Irish tweed hat.

"Good morning Mr. Bryn," I called.

"Good morning, Boy," he called down. Cefn Bryn always called me Boy! It was an affectionate term, he had told me, even though he knew that I was a man! And a prince at that!

"You have forgotten who you are, Boy! Because you had your heart broken in Canada. But don't worry; you are on the Gower now, Boy, and it will all come back!"

"Thank you, Mr. Bryn, Sir, thank you!"

"You have a good day now, Boy!"

"Yes sir, I will."

Chapter Nine
Ruby Tuesday

I sat on the river bank on the other side of the stepping stones and faced the sea. It looked about half tide as I looked out across the wet sand to where the Killy Willy shook hands with the waves.

There had been no signs of any horses in the valley, and I wondered where they were? Often from early spring time to late summer, the Three Cliffs' herd established itself in the valley, laying claim to its grazing areas and drinking from the river, until well after the foals were born. Then, in late summer or early autumn, the herd moved inland to shelter from the driving rains and sea winds that blow up the valley from the Bristol Channel.

"Maybe they have gone on to the beach and around Three Cliffs Point to Pobbles?" I suggested to myself. "Sometimes they like to walk up the path through the dunes and on to the Pennard Golf Course. I will go and investigate!"

I crossed back over the stepping stones and onto Three Cliffs' Beach. Sure enough, there on the wet sand were a number of hoof prints. I walked along, trying to figure out how many horses there were in the herd. The Three Cliffs' herd used to average between five to eight mares, of which at least half were pregnant. And there were at least two or three yearlings, either stallions or mares. And then, of course, the dominant stallion! Like my "Great Thunder"! The leader and protector of the herd!

As I inspected the hoof prints further, there looked to be eight or nine horses in all. Pregnant mares are generally heavier and their hoof prints go deeper into the sand. It's far easier to track humans with two legs than horses with four, but I concluded that there were about eight or nine horses. Eight or nine mares is a manageable size for one stallion! In my experience over the years, when there has been more than ten or twelve horses in a herd, a younger stallion, or even a mature stallion from another herd, will challenge the current dominant stallion.

Regarding my stallion, Great Thunder, he was a younger stallion who was not accepted by the Three Cliffs' herd until he fought the dominant stallion and won the possession of the herd! And what a great and terrible battle it was! But that's another story!

I continued along the sand toward Pobbles. And there, in front of one of the caves, stood a stallion! Instantly, I was back in yesteryear, when my stallion, Great Thunder, had stood outside guarding what became our 'family cave.' My heart raced and the memories flashed in my mind and in my heart. And I thought: Could this be one of Great Thunder's descendants? If he was, I could expect to be chased into the sea at any moment! And, I had no spear or bowie knife to protect me.

My heart raced faster and faster as I got closer to him. But I decided not to change my course. I took the risk of walking right past him! I talked to him as I passed within yards of the cave he was guarding, and it was my cave alright! The cave where a mare named "Thunder Spring" had saved my life by keeping me warm all night on her belly when I had hypothermia. I would surely have died without her warmth!

Wow! I could hardly believe it! It was twenty years since my stallion had stood on guard at this cave – which then became 'our cave' when his mare, Thunder Spring, saved my life! And then she had given birth to a baby stallion, whom Gay and I named "Little Thunder." And it was yesterday once more. Seeing this new stallion standing outside our family cave brought back so many memories of Gay and I, and the wonderful times we spent roaming the beaches and the hills.

I now walked in front of the stallion, who just stood on guard and allowed me to pass without baring his teeth or chasing me into the sea like Great Thunder had done.

"Hello, Boy," I said. "That's my cave that you are guarding, but if it's yours too, I'm not going to argue. And, I believe you must be a relative of my horse, Great Thunder! Have you heard of him? He won the greatest battle the Three Cliffs herd has ever seen!"

The stallion neighed, lifting his head up and down as if he was answering me! Shivers ran down my spine as I thought that the stallion was probably one of Great Thunder's great-grandsons. Standing outside my cave like this, he just had to be!

I would have to ask Heather about the wild horses when I visited with her tomorrow. I remembered her saying, before I left the Gower to go and live in Devon, that when she brought her riding school down to the sands to practice, she would also let Great Thunder free to roam and visit with his family. Plus, he got Thunder Spring pregnant again before I left for Devon!

"Yes," I said to the stallion, "you must be one of Great Thunder and Thunder Spring's descendants!" And believing this, I went right up to him to pat his neck and say hello.

"Old Boy! I'm Kingsley, and I knew your great, great grandfather, Great Thunder." He neighed and lifted his head again, as if understanding what I was saying.

As his eyes connected with mine, there was a 'knowing' I didn't fully understand. I didn't need to! It was just there! A wonderful connection and understanding between us had been born today! I noticed too, that on his forehead, this stallion who was all black apart from two white front feet, had a deep red mark on his face in the shape of a ring! It wasn't a complete circle, but almost! So I could call him Ruby Red! Then I thought that today being a Tuesday, I would call him something 'Tuesday'? Red Tuesday? No, that didn't sound right.

"How about 'Ruby Tuesday'? I asked him. And he neighed and nodded his head up and down in approval. "Then that's what we will call you, old boy – Ruby Tuesday! And we chose it together, didn't we!" And he neighed and nodded again! Wow, what a connection I had with this stallion already!

Excited now, I spent the next couple of hours with Ruby, and I had dreams of putting my saddle on his back and thundering across the sand like I had done with Great Thunder! Only Ruby wasn't wounded like Thunder had been, so he might be harder to train. But Ruby wasn't as wild either! That would surely make a difference. I was glad now that I'd gone through all that interegative nonsense at the airport, to bring my saddle back into the country. They wanted to take it from me, but I held onto it like a second skin. I remembered what Gay had said to me when she gave me the saddle.

"Kingsley! This is my most precious possession that I can give you! And I want you to ride Thunder Child with it. I know that one day you will ride him! And this is the saddle to ride him with. And I want you to think of me every time you use it. I want it to remind you of my love for you, Kingsley. I will always love you!"

Oh my Gay, where are you? I still love you and I send you my love wherever you are. Tomorrow I'm going to visit Heather, and maybe I will find out where you are. Or where I can find you. I don't know whether you know, but Maggie has died and gone to heaven now. I sure miss her. And I could hear her speaking to me through her letter, and at the churchyard the other day. She knows how much we love each other! And I know in my heart that she prayed for us, prayed that we would find each other again one day!

Well, it was time for me to head back to Fraser and Lynn's for supper and enjoy the evening with them.

"Well, Ruby, old boy, thank you for your friendship and for not chasing me into the sea. I didn't fancy swimming to Ireland today. You have a good rest of the day now, and I will come and see you tomorrow on my way to visit Heather in Penmaen." And I sang the song 'Good Bye Ruby Tuesday' as I walked away.

It was a long walk up through the dunes to the golf course. The deep sandy path made my legs tired. Once on the golf course,

I was rewarded by finding the Three Cliffs' herd! And my estimate of how many horses there were had been correct! Nine horses in all. Four of them were mature mares, pregnant with foals; three were young stallions, born last spring, by the size of them; and two were young mares. In my view, that was a good balance for the herd. There's nothing like a few young mares to keep the young stallions on their hooves, just like in the human species – there's nothing like a few young ladies to keep us men on our toes. But then we also fought like wild stallions over the women when I was growing up!

I would like to have spent more time with the herd, especially watching the young stallions. Ruby was the only mature stallion – their dominant leader! I would have to spend more time amongst the herd another day.

The walk back to the village to catch the bus was a long one. And I felt tired as I sat at the bus stop. The schedule said a bus would be along in fifteen minutes. Good, I had timed it right! I would soon be on my way.

I arrived home at Fraser and Lynn's just in time for supper. It was leftover lamb, roast potatoes and vegetables, and Fraser had picked up a few cans of beer. Over supper I told them about my adventures. They always seemed amazed at how much adventure I could get into in just one day!

"I take life as it comes," I would say. Heather had once said that I was as wild and free as my stallion. At forty years old, I had to agree with her – and I wouldn't have it any other way!

Fraser, Lynn and I enjoyed a nice evening in. After the excellent supper, we watched a movie and finished the beer. Then off to bed again for me, falling asleep as soon as my head hit the pillow.

Chapter Ten
Remembering Great Thunder

*A*fter breakfast, I walked into Swansea to start my day. And as usual I went into the market to buy my lunch. I'd almost had my fill of welsh cakes by now, having had some almost every day since I'd arrived. But I still had a craving for cockles, and I ordered a large basket of them for lunch. I also bought a backpack so I could carry some apples and carrots for Ruby. I was still excited about the fact that I had discovered him standing outside my cave! Surely he was one of Great Thunders' descendants, I said to myself again. He had to be!

I headed off to the bus depot to catch the #14. As the bus drove along Clyne Common towards Pennard, I thought about my upcoming visit with Heather in the evening. I tried to tell myself that I couldn't expect too much! It would be unlikely that she would know where Gay was living. But who knows? I might get some clues!

I got off the bus at Southgate Village and walked along the path to Pobbles Beach. When I arrived at the area where I had seen the herd yesterday, there was no sign of them anywhere, except for some horse manure, which led down through the dunes. They had probably gone back down to the valley to graze. I followed the dune path, hoping I would catch up with them in the valley, but they weren't in the valley either. I walked towards the beach, following footprints that were fresh in the soft mud beside the river. But when I arrived at the sands, the footprints had disappeared.

The tide was about half way out and still receding. This meant I could walk around Three Cliffs Point to go back to Pobbles.

I walked to my old cave, hoping Ruby might be there, but he wasn't. And I decided to go into the old family cave to check things out.

There was no pregnant mare in there today, like there had been when Great Thunder used to stand on guard protecting Thunder Spring, all those years ago. But as I stood in our family home once again, my mind and heart were flooded with precious memories of Great Thunder and our family!

"There will never be another horse like him!" I said aloud.

But there was also another hero in my life, who I didn't talk about so much. Without her, I wouldn't be here today! As I stood over the place in the cave, where I'd fallen unconscious that day upon Thunder Spring's belly, I was once again grateful that her warmth had kept me alive during the night! Suddenly, I was back in yesteryear and I remembered so much more!

This was also the place where she gave birth to 'Little Thunder,' and after his birth, we walked out of the cave together! And I was accepted as one of the family; it was the day I got to be part of Great Thunder's family! And I would never forget it, as long as I lived!

I thought about how Gay and I had brought Thunder Spring apples and carrots, and collected water from the river each day so she could drink and renew her strength. I'll never forget the look in her beautiful brown eyes as she looked at me while I fed her apples and carrots. She looked at me like a wise mother and I guess in many ways she was! Thunder Spring had saved the life of this man-child. Maybe always a half-horse-child! And Great Thunder grew from being my enemy to being a protective father, whom I trusted with my life! As I had once saved his.

With God's help, he gave my life back to me! Or should I say, helped me to experience 'life' in a way that I never could have if I hadn't met him and my horse family! I was there at the birth of his son, like a best man! And oh, how I loved him! And still love him! He will always be part of my life! I have told my children about him, and even written a book!

"See what you have given me, old boy!" I shouted out loud.

♪✲

REMEMBERING GREAT THUNDER

A POEM

You ran as wild and free as the wind.
I was just a boy when I first heard your thunder.
You thundered across the sand and surf,
and chased me into the sea.
And the four winds could not catch you.
From the very first time I saw you,
I wanted to be just like you!
Running wild and free,
with the wind chasing behind me,
and the rising sun before me.
Little did I know on that first day,
when I ran into the waves in fear of your fury,
that through your bravery and friendship,
God would set me free,
and I would discover myself,
as He had made me to be.
You taught me so many things,
my great friend,
so that my life would be changed forever!
And as I grew from a boy to a young man,
somewhere between the golden sunrise and
the sunset stories in the western sky,
I realized you were much like me.
You never fitted in with the other horses,
and I was not accepted by the crowd.
But along with our family,
Thunder Spring and Little Thunder,
we discovered that we had so much more.
We could hold the wind and ride the sea,

climb the mountains and be truly free.
Thank you, Great Thunder,
for helping me to see,
that this is the way it was meant to be,
for you and for me.

© Kingsley Ross Hill

When I came out of the cave and looked across the sands towards Oxwich Beach, I saw in the distance a black spot on the beach. After studying its shape for a few minutes, it looked like it was coming this way! And I remembered how Great Thunder had chased me into the sea when I'd tried to walk the beach at the same time that he was on his run.

"My gosh, déjà-vu! Double déjà-vu! I can't believe that this is happening!

As I walked along at the edge of the sea, I could see now that it was a dark horse with no rider, thundering across the sands. I kept thinking to myself: Ruby isn't as wild as Great Thunder. We have already met and introduced ourselves outside the cave!

Suddenly the horse spotted me and changed his course – galloping towards me!

"Oh no, here we go again!" I thought. I braced myself to be chased into the waves! But he didn't charge me like Great Thunder had done. Rather he swerved away, giving me plenty of room between himself and the sea. I let out a big breath of relief.

Surely, he must be from the lineage of Great Thunder! The fact that he's running the sands to Oxwich from Pobbles and back! And the cave! And why would he stop and then stand outside the same cave where Great Thunder had stood! But there was no pregnant mare in there to guard! Why stand and guard an empty cave? So many questions filled my mind and heart. And also a great excitement! Maybe Heather would be able to tell me more about the horses this evening.

I would observe Ruby, just like I had done with Thunder. One thing was clear though. Ruby was not as aggressive as Thunder had been. I watched him finish his gallop at Pobbles, slow to a canter, and then a trot, stopping at the cave opening. I stood like a soul in time, back in an adventure that had started 20 years before! I did a jig of excitement as wonder filled my soul.

Before heading up to Three Cliffs Valley to see if the main herd was there, I decided to double back across the sands to the cave and visit Ruby. I wanted to connect with him more and get him used to me. I hoped that we would become friends!

I approached him slowly and calmly as I had done yesterday. And I spoke to him: "Hello Ruby! You're a very fast horse galloping across the beach like that! And I do appreciate you not chasing me into the sea. It's rather cold this time of year, old boy! I didn't fancy a swim!"

Ruby stood tall and proud as I continued to talk to him. I slowly lowered my backpack to the sand and pulled out two apples. Ruby, to my surprise, ignored the apples in my hand and lowered his head to my backpack. He then proceeded to munch the apples in my bag! I was delighted at his friendliness and comfort around me.

And I said to him: "'Come on old boy, you can't eat all the apples, I'm saving some for the mares!"

And I slowly reached down and zipped up the bag. Ruby lifted up his head, still munching and dripping apple juice, and he pushed his wet nose to my face!

"My gosh, that's a nice kiss!" I said, now smelling of horse perfume and apples! "So much for my shower, old boy! Now I smell like a horse, a fruity horse!" He neighed and showed his teeth as if laughing.

"You find that funny, old boy! Well, how am I supposed to go out on a date smelling like 'horse'? Then he started to nibble my hair like Thunder used to do.

And I said, "I love you, Ruby!" I felt such a thrill of excitement and I started to dance on the sand. Ruby looked at me with his big brown eyes and neighed. I'm sure he said, in his horse language, that I was as crazy as he was!

It was time for me to continue my search for the herd.

"Well, Ruby old boy, thanks for the great visit, and I will see you again soon. I'm heading off to the valley now, to see if I can find your family."

The sun shone brightly as I made my way across the sand, and I realized how good I was feeling! I felt like I was doing some deep emotional healing. And Ruby and the other horses were a big part of me feeling so good about my life again.

When I reached the Three Cliffs, rather than crossing the Killy Willy River and then turning up the valley, I decided to walk through the archway of the cliffs. Once through the archway, I stood beside the river and walked along its banks. I soon came to one of its turns, and I remembered that this was the place where I had speared my two large skate. The river was still running too fast today for me to see any fish on the bottom. But I noticed clouds of muddy water coming down with the fresh water! This told me that the horses were further up river, either crossing or having a drink.

And there they were! And it was Ruby's herd alright! There were the same nine horses that I'd seen yesterday. I pulled out some apples from my backpack, and I was soon surrounded by the whole herd, apart from one young stallion who seemed determined to drink the river dry. The four pregnant mares were quite assertive and they wanted to eat all the apples. As the two young stallions approached for their share, the mares chased them off.

And I said, "Listen-up, girls, the old man was right. A pregnant mare can be as feisty as a women's lib gathering! Now stop pushing me, or there's no more apples for you. I know you're eating for two, but let's have some manners, shall we?" After they scoffed the apples, they went back to grazing the lush new shoots at the river's edge.

"That's not very nice," I said. "You only came to see me for the apples?"

But one of the mares more than made up for the others' rudeness. She lay down on her tummy in the grass and allowed me to sit against her and bask in the sun. She seemed so comfortable with me resting against her, and I looked deep into her gentle brown eyes.

"Thank you, girl. It's a real privilege for me to sit with you like this! How come you are so gentle, girl? Most mares are aggressive when they're carrying a foal and they chase people away from the herd. I'm glad that you trust me!"

Suddenly a little hoof kicked me from the mare's tummy. And instantly I was back in time! I remembered waking up on Thunder Spring's belly in the cave and feeling Little Thunder's hoof move across my own tummy from within his mother's womb!

I had always had such a connection with the horses! As a boy, they had been my playmates and friends! And as a youth, they had become my family, even saving my life! And now I was with them again! And they were helping me heal my broken heart!

It was a great feeling to have the mare put such trust in me! And it reaffirmed what I had learned as a boy. Horses can reflect our feelings and our emotional needs!

"You are giving me such comfort and healing from being here with you, old girl!" And as I was speaking, her foal kicked me again!

I rubbed her belly and said: "You are a lovely mare, aren't you! But you need a name!" She was white with grey blotches that looked like clouds.

"Hmm, something cloud? How about 'Sun Cloud'?" I said. "Your grey blotches are like clouds, and you are warm like the summer sun. And it's late spring now, so Sun Cloud has a lot of meaning to it. What do you think, old girl? Do you like that name?"

She gently neighed. I rubbed her tummy again until she made a quiet snoring sound.

I stayed and visited with the herd for about three hours as the spring sunshine warmed the valley. I got to know each of the mares a little, but none were as gentle and kind as Sun Cloud. And

I wondered if she was Ruby's mare? If I was Ruby, I would choose her! Or maybe Ruby had two mares? I should have such luck! But if one was as beautiful as Sun Cloud, then she would be my all-in-all! And if Gay ever comes back, I will have to give up my Meredith Mermaid!

Suddenly, like a gentle wind, Gay blew into my heart again! Visiting with the horses reminded me of how we used to name the whole herd! And we would take such pleasure in seeing the new foals being born!

"Oh Gay, I wish you were here with me, my sweet love! The mares will soon be giving birth. And it won't be the same without you! I love you Gay! I pray that you can hear me! I'm here in the valley with our horse family!"

Then it was time for me to climb the dunes and cross the burrows to Heather's home. I prayed as I walked, asking God to help me find some information about Gay.

As I rambled across the burrows, the sun was still high in the sky. And I felt so restored and refreshed in my soul after spending time with the horses! My time with Sun Cloud had been so healing! And again, I marveled at how she could sense my feelings and my mood! And then reflect what I needed back to me! She knew how much I needed her touch and she gave me her warmth and her love. I had a deep sense that she was carrying Ruby's foal, and I would even go so far as to say that she had a 'knowing' that I was family! I couldn't wait to spend more time with her and Ruby!

I arrived at the old farm house, and I remembered how Heather would often look out of her window at me when I was practicing riding on Gay's horse, Blaze. It seemed like only yesterday that I was riding Blaze across the field.

I knocked on the heavy wooden door, my knuckles making a 'thud' sound against the old wood. It always felt so welcoming.

"Just a minute," I heard a voice call back. "I'm coming!"

The door scraped open, and there was Heather!

"I was just putting a log on the fire," she said. "Even though it's spring time, this old stone house gets cold. It's so great to see you, Kingsley!" And she gave me a tight hug.

"It's great to see you too, Heather!" I said, and it was so great to hug her again.

"I've just put a pot of tea on before supper," she continued. "Now come, sit down and tell me what has brought you back to the good old Gower?"

"Well, I've lived a few lifetimes since I saw you last, Heather!"

"Just a few?" she asked, and we both laughed.

"As you know, I lived in Devonshire for about five and a half years with my grandparents, and then I emigrated to Canada."

"Come, tell me more," she said. "What else?"

"Well, I was married for twelve years and then I divorced. The wonderful news is that I'm the proud Dad of three wonderful children! They are the joy of my life!"

"I'm sorry to hear your marriage didn't work out. But I can tell how much you love your children! Your face lights up when you speak of them."

"Yeah, being a dad is the most wonderful experience in the world! And I wouldn't have missed it for anything!"

We then talked about Maggie and how much we missed her.

"I loved her like a real sister," Heather shared.

"She was like a Mum to me," I said.

"I know she was! And do you know, Kingsley, how connected she was to you? About 10 years after you left for Canada, she would come over to the farmhouse and tell me how worried she was about you."

"'Something is wrong,' she would say, 'I can feel Kingsley's heart and he is in pain.' Maggie must have been picking up on your pain as you were going through your divorce. I've never known two people to be more connected than you and Maggie!"

Yes, I could always feel her prayers watching over my heart!"

"How about you, Heather?" I asked. "You told me over the phone that you've retired from the stables!"

"Yes, I have, and my niece, Pauline, runs it now! I'm still very much involved in the riding school, though. I do a lot of the student bookings and plan the riding curriculum."

"That's great, Heather! The horses and the riding school are your passion!"

Over supper, I asked Heather about Great Thunder. She shared that for the first five or six years after I left the Gower, Great Thunder continued to run from his cave at Pobbles to Oxwich Bay and back every day. And his son, Little Thunder, would run with him!

"Yes, I remember Little Thunder," I said. "I changed his name to Clashing Thunder after he won his first fight against another stallion!"

"There was another thing Maggie started doing after you had been away for some time, Kingsley. She started naming all the horses! She wouldn't admit it, but it was her way of holding on to you! She loved you so deeply!"

At Heathers' words, I could feel a wave of Maggie's love flowing through my heart! I tried hard not to cry, but I couldn't hold it and I began to weep!

"I miss her so much, Heather!"

Heather began crying too.

And I said: "What a right pair we are! I'm sure Maggie is looking down from Heaven laughing at the two of us!"

"Yes, I'm sure she is!" Heather said. "I'm half expecting her to knock on the door with one of her famous custard pies!" Now we were both laughing.

"Another thing she did, Kingsley, was change the name of her custard pies to 'Kingsley's Pie'! After she did that, I realized just how much she loved you!"

Yes, like a son! I knew then that Maggie loved me like the son she had never had!

"Kingsley, I will tell you what I *do* have," Heather said, "I still have a few bottles of Maggie's homemade pear cider from the last Christmas I shared with her! Let's open one with our dessert. I don't know how many toasts we drank for you and your stallion!"

I smiled at the thought of Maggie having a toast for Great Thunder and me.

"This bottle is about two years old," Heather continued.

"And it tastes great!" I said, downing my glass.

Heather continued to answer my questions about Great Thunder.

"When he became too old to gallop on the sands, Clashing Thunder continued to gallop the same route on his own," explained Maggie, "keeping the family tradition alive. And the stallion that now runs the same route is Clashing Thunder's offspring! It a black stallion, Kingsley, with a red circle on his forehead."

"I know, Heather! I've already seen him down on the beach – and he even let me touch him! And I'm so glad that I brought my saddle with me!"

"Oh no! Kingsley, you're not, are you? Are you? And why am I not surprised? I once told you that you would sooner hold back the sea than tame that wild stallion! And you proved me wrong, Kingsley! And now I've started a new saying in the village! And the saying is this: 'You may as well try and hold back the sea, than try to tame Kingsley Hill.'" We both roared with laughter.

"That is certainly true, Heather. You should have seen me coming across security at the airport with my saddle!"

"That I'd like to have seen," she said, pouring us another glass of Maggie's cider.

"I am flattered, Heather, that you would have started such a saying about me in the village!"

"It's true! You wild man, you!"

"Heather, there is something I need to ask you!"

"Yes, what is it?"

"How did Great Thunder end his days?"

"Well, first of all, he became the brightest light in the stables! And I could never understand how a horse that wild could also be so gentle! It's like you and your stallion have the same heart, Kingsley! That's what Maggie always said.

"Great Thunder was so gentle with the younger children," "and I had him work with a group of eight handicapped kids. He loved those children! I didn't even have to train him to be patient; he just knew. It was as if he could perceive and understand the feelings and emotions of the children and then give them back whatever they needed, just through his behaviour. They were all different and they had different challenges, and he would work with each of them individually. He would give them kisses with his wet nose, and nibble on their hair, making them laugh when he knew they were sad! Those kids loved him! He changed their lives!"

"I remember those kisses, and him nibbling on my curls," I said, holding back my tears. "He used to nudge me gently if I was walking in front of him too slowly. And when I looked back at him, he would show me his teeth as if he was laughing!"

Heather smiled. "There was one occasion," she said, "that is more vivid in my memory than all my other memories of Great Thunder. One of the special needs' children in the group couldn't walk or stand for prolonged periods of time because he wore heavy braces on his legs. One morning, without me having to say anything, Great Thunder lowered himself to the ground while the little boy climbed on his back! In my 50 years of working with horses, I've never seen a horse do that! And he did it on his own accord. And that is why I changed the name of Penmaen's Stables to 'Healing Horse Stables!'"

I was so happy to hear all this news about my beloved stallion.

Heather continued. "And Maggie and I made sure to allow him to run free with his family in the Three Cliffs Valley quite often. So he was able to see his family grow up, and give Clashing Thunder the heritage of galloping across the sands with his father.

"And there is something else you should know, Kingsley – that cave of yours where Great Thunder stood on guard? Well, Clashing Thunder and Thunder Spring's foal (the one that was born after you left to go and live in Devonshire) both stood on guard there all their lives. They were both stallions but they never fought each other! They both stood on guard, one on each side of the cave. Now as you have already seen, a black stallion, Clashing Thunder's son, stands there too!"

"There is certainly something very spiritual and mysterious about your cave, Kingsley! Maggie and I would take walks there while Great Thunder was spending time with his family in the valley. And Maggie would say that the spirits of Kingsley and Great Thunder would always reside in this cave, and that the generations of horses understand this. When Great Thunder grew old, Maggie said it would be your wish that he be set free to end his days on the beach. And, that's what he did! He grew too old to gallop, so he walked to Oxwich and back to his cave every day. And then he would stand at the entrance to his cave, like he always did, and he stood between his two sons, one on each side of him. It was the most haunting sight to see these three stallions all standing together.

"As his sons galloped together across the sands, Great Thunder would spend hours just staring out to sea! Maggie said that he was waiting for you!'"

I wept at Heathers' words. "Where did he die, Heather? I have to ask."

"He died standing outside his cave!" she said, "and by the time they came to take his body away, the high tide had carried him away first. Apparently, they had a tractor and trailer on the beach and they were concerned about getting to the cave before the tide got too high. But as they were approaching, a big 'rogue wave' swept in and took Thunder away, right there in front of them, and he was never seen again!"

Now I was laughing and crying at the same time. "What a way for Thunder to go! He was as wild and mysterious in death as he was in life! Long live the King of the Gower!"

It was so wonderful hearing about the life of the stallions, and realizing that Heather and Maggie had loved and appreciated these magnificent creatures over the years when I had been away.

I then asked Heather about Gay.

"I'm afraid that I can't tell you any more about Gay, Kingsley! Other than what Maggie has already told you in her letter."

"But there is something I must give you before you go!" stated Heather. "Before Maggie died, she brought over this box of your treasures for me to give you when you came back. She didn't even trust her own family to give it to you, only me! Here you are, Kingsley; I hope something in here may help to answer some of your questions about Gay. One thing I do know, Kingsley, and that is that you still love her very much, don't you?"

"Yes, I do!"

Before I left Heathers' house, I phoned Fraser and Lynn to let them know that I wouldn't be home until late or maybe not until tomorrow. I wanted to take my box of treasures out to the Tor and open them there at Leather's Hole.

"You can stay here for the night if you want to," Heather said, "but I know you better than trying to coax you into doing something you don't want to do! I'd sooner try and hold back the sea!" And we both laughed.

"Thanks Heather," I said, "I really need to be alone opening this box."

"Well, you better take this," she said, handing me the last bottle of Maggie's homemade cider. I loaded kindling and a few larger pieces of wood, together with Maggie's cider, into my backpack, and then I was on my way to Leathers Hole!

"Bye Heather, I will drop by and see you soon!"

"You'd better, or I will shoot you with your bow and arrow!"

I laughed and closed the heavy door.

Chapter Eleven
Treasure Box and Promises

*J*arrived at the entrance to Leathers Hole and put down my treasure box and backpack. It was a beautiful evening alright! And I still had a few hours of light. First, I would open my treasure box! And then make a fire and look out across the Bristol Channel.

Oh, how the years melted away as I sat again outside my cave. And the view from here was even more wonderful than I remembered! Was it because I had been away for so long? That was part of it, for sure, but it was far more than an absence that made my heart grow fonder. My soul needed to be home! And to breathe in the healing winds of the 'land of my ancestors'! I felt so happy to be back as 'the Caveman of Leathers Hole'!

I shouted to a passing seagull: "Look I'm back! I'm the Caveman of Leathers Hole!"

And the gull called back, quite unperturbed, and said, "Of course you are! We all knew that you'd return one day!"

With my back against my cave, I began to open my treasure box! There, on top, was my rabbit pelt robe! – tucked carefully over everything else in the box as if guarding my treasures! And it was Maggie's hands that had touched my robe last, and wrapped my treasures with love! Oh, what memories filled my heart as I picked up my robe and draped it over my shoulders. And in the breeze, I smelt the strong smell of rabbit fur. I would need to wear it for a while and let the freshness of spring air it out. And it would keep me warm as the sun went down tonight. Next in my treasure box were my throwing knives and arrows that my Dad had bought me for Christmas all those years ago! And there was my 'Bowie Knife' with its carved bone handle!

"It's Christmas in April!" I shouted out to the gull. And he squawked out some words again. (I think he said that he had to wait until December before he opened his presents!)

Near the bottom of the box was one of my old sweaters that I had left at Maggie's cottage. And there wrapped inside it was my message in a bottle. The barnacles were still stuck to one side of the bottle! And there, folded inside and wrapped with a fresh ribbon, were my Scripture verses that had spoken so powerfully to my heart! Bringing me encouragement, strength and light! And so, as I read them again on this night, my faith became renewed! And I believed again that I wasn't alone! God was still with me and watching over me! He hadn't abandoned me like those 'Holier than thou Christians' had at the church I once attended.

And I did a dance for my God in the golden light of His setting sun. I am loved and I am free! And He has brought me home to the Gower to heal!"

[Romans 10 vs 17, Faith comes by hearing, and hearing through the word of God.]

At the very bottom of my treasure box was an envelope from Maggie! It was too dark now for me to read it, so I gathered up some gorse that grew close to the entrance of the cave and made a small fire, fed with a little wood from my backpack. I took a long breath and sat back and read the letter:

Dear Kingsley,

I knew that one day you would return home to the Gower. I trust that you have already got your letters from Gay, and my letter that I left for you at the store.

After you had been in Canada for some time. I began to sense you were in trouble, my dear boy! Forgive me, for calling you 'boy'! I suspect you are quite the man by now, and probably a father too! But you will always be as a son to me, Kingsley. I love you very much! Sometimes you come to me in my dreams, and I wake up in the night, and pray for you and your family.

Last night, I woke up with a start! You and Great Thunder were thundering across the sands with another vicious stallion chasing you! I know that Great Thunder runs from no one! So, I knew you were in trouble! But, I trust you to God, who I know always watches over you!

There is something that I feel God wants me to give to you in this letter. I believe it will speak to you regarding your situation. That is my prayer anyway! In my prayers and meditations before God, I believe that He has revealed to me, that you have gone through "a great Loss" in your life! Maybe the breakup of a marriage? Or the loss of someone very dear? I sense you might have come home to the Gower brokenhearted, needing healing and the faith to believe again. Believe me, dear boy, that God still has a wonderful plan for your life. Let me remind you that He does; there is no doubt!

I have some scripture verses especially for you! And a meditation that I want you to think upon! Now, God has likely already taken me home by the time you get this message, but please read the Bible verses and what I have written. God's Word, as you already know, is never out of date! It meets us right where we are in our lives, and at the very time we need to hear it!

I knew the experience she spoke of – how God revealed His truth through His scripture and it would speak to my heart. "You always knew my heart, Maggie, didn't you?" I cried.

[Joshua 1 vs 5, No one will be able to stand against you as long as you live. For as I was with Moses, so shall I be with you! I will never leave you nor forsake you!}

(As I read this scripture, I felt God reaching out to me, and encouraging me with His assurance that He would not abandon me nor fail me! After having gone through my divorce, I'd felt devalued, and my self-esteem had become so low! And, more than anything else, I felt disappointed that I'd let God down! But in reading His word this evening, it helped me to feel valued again! God is still for me and not against me!)

(And His love for me has not changed because of my failure or mistakes! Not like people who are quick to judge and turn their backs, without knowing me or what I am going through!)

[Joshua 1 vs 9, This is my command – be strong and courageous! Do not be afraid or discouraged. For the Lord, your God is with you wherever you go!]

(When I read this verse, I felt the Holy Spirit reminding me, and testifying to my heart, that my strength and courage is in 'trusting God' and 'claiming and believing His promises to me'! God is with me wherever I go! I do not have to be afraid or discouraged by my situation.)

[Joshua 21 vs 45, Not a word failed of any good thing which the Lord had spoken!]

(Through this verse, God said to me: "Kingsley! Not one of my words or promises will fail you. Just believe them and trust me to carry them out! And I will!")

And then I read Maggie's words and meditated on them.

Kingsley! Life can be a wonderful journey. It is a trip through a strange land where you have never been before, and you never know how much time you have ahead or where you will be going next. Strange scenes, strange dilemmas, new tangles, new experiences, and some old ones with new faces, so that we do not recognize them.

Even with all its challenges, life is full of pleasure and enjoyment, if only we will make some provision for the drudgery and hard things that seem to crowd in so thick and fast sometimes and make us forget the gladness of life!

Kingsley, life is like a big play at the theatre! The actors and actresses play their parts, but most often don't understand why they have been given a particular part to play in this grand performance! We look around at the other actors who seem to have a more attractive part to play! But let me tell you a wonderful secret! Though not really a secret, it is free for all to know and should be shouted from the rooftops! God is the Director of the play! And He sees 'the big picture'! We often think and wonder how our roles in the play can ever make sense and be a part of something wonderful.

Kingsley, your dreams may have been crushed and your heart broken, but God hasn't given up on your dreams, he still carries them in his heart! He is right now planning a wonderful future for you! The parts that you have been chosen to play may not make sense now. But they will!

I have found a wonderful truth in my life, Kingsley! And it is this! I can allow myself to feel lost in this journey called life, because I know that I have this amazing guide. And Kingsley, there is a Director who will make everything in your life work out, and your life will turn into the most wonderful masterpiece. Just trust Him to do so, and He will!

May God richly bless you, Kingsley
I love you!
Maggie

After meditating on what Maggie shared, I prayed to God and asked Him to work everything out in my life, and to give me the faith to believe He would. "And please God, help me to find my Gay."

I continued to sit outside the entrance of Leathers Hole, looking out across the Bristol Channel. I would sleep under the stars tonight, like old times, and use my rabbit pelt robe as a blanket. It had been quite a day spending time with the horses, and then going to Heather's house. But with all my experiences and adventures, I was still no closer to finding Gay! I would have to trust that 'Director God' would work out the big picture of my life!

[Romans 8 vs 29, All things work together for good for those who love God, and are called to his purpose.]

I lay there and watched the sunset, which now covered the sky with oranges, reds and purples that danced over a silver singing sea. And for the first time in such a long time, I felt happy and free!

I watched the flames of my fire dance, until I fell asleep in the flickering shadows.

Morning came and I felt that I had experienced a deep and nourishing sleep. I climbed up to the top of the Tor, draped in my robe. And I gave my weather report! The sea was a deep emerald today – my favourite colour! The wet sand and dark rocks shouted a falling tide. And far out to sea, white horses rode upon the wind and the sky smiled blue. A truly beautiful day was upon me!

Well, I was as hungry as a hunter, and packing my treasures in my backpack, I headed off to catch the bus to Swansea. As I climbed down the dunes to the beach, I noticed Ruby on his run back from Oxwich to Pobbles. And he stopped where I thought he would. Right outside our cave! And I decided to go and pay him a visit. He seemed happy to see me, and he lifted his head up and down while I patted his neck and said: "Good morning, old boy! I'm glad that you are not as wild as Great Thunder! Or you would have probably chased me into the sea already!"

As I stood in front of the cave with Ruby, I remembered what Heather had said about Great Thunder dying outside our cave. And then a big rogue wave came and took him away!

And looking out to sea, I recited a poem that I'd once written for 'The King of the Gower'!

♪✻

KING OF THE GOWER

The King of the Gower,
guarded our home like Camelot!
A Kingdom, wild, beautiful, and free!
For that's what it was – and is – and always will be – for him and me.
Our sacred cave in the Cliff's by the singing sea.
Pobbles and Three Cliff's Bay,
and our golden ring of sand, where we galloped to Oxwich,
across our beautiful land, as far as the eye can see.
Look at us run! Catch us if you can!
We thundered past the Killy Willy,
winding his way to the evening emerald sea,
as the Bell Rock rings of our arrival at the Great Tor.
Look everyone, I'm riding the King of the Gower!
Always my hero, in my life's hour.
Look, Cefn Bryn and Mr. Pennard Castle,
I'm riding the King of the Gower! Yes, we see!
Even the wind cannot catch you,
as you thunder across the sand and surf,
with your lives entwined together in body and spirit,
roaming wild and free.
Kings of the Gower.

© *Kingsley Ross Hill*

And I shouted out on the wind: "I hope you heard the poem, Great Thunder! It's my tribute to you, old boy!"

And then I recited another poem I had written about me, and I think Ruby enjoyed it.

♪❋

POBBLES BEACH

It was here on this beach where I learned to run.
I never walked, mother said, I just ran,
and I was always running to the sea.
Beach was my first word, and then it was bus.
I ran across these golden sands until I reached the sea,
and there I stood in the waves, and I jumped,
and I danced, and I shouted: This is me!
When I was a boy, I could always find God here
on this beach,
for the Angel of the Lord camped all around me.
He was everywhere.
I could feel Him!
When I danced and played in the waves,
He jumped and laughed with me,
And then I would run up on the beach trying to get warm,
And He would shine His sunshine upon me,
And blow the wind around me, making me warm
and dry again.
As I ran, I saw the seagulls flying overhead.
They reminded me that God was always watching over me.
When I reached the top of the beach,
I climbed to the high rocks, and He was always there too.
He would look out with me over all He had made.
But what I liked most of all was when
He told me that
He had made it just for me.
Even the shimmering shining sea,
He had made it for me!

© Kingsley Ross Hill

Kingsley Ross Hill

After I finished reciting my poem, Ruby said that he thought Great Thunder and I were alike!

"I must agree with you there, old boy! Maggie said that we shared the same heart!"

It was late in the afternoon by the time I arrived back at Fraser's place. After wolfing down some eggs, and beans on toast, I waited for them to come home from work.

"Hi, Kings!" Fraser said, coming through the door. "Wow! You're wearing your old rabbit pelt robe! Where did you find it after all these years?"

"It was at my friend Heather's house in Penmaen."

"I remember Heather, Kings. She used to run the stables, right?"

"Yes, that's right, and Maggie used to run the Post Office and general store."

"How is Maggie?" Fraser asked. "She must be really old by now."

"Yeah, she was really old! I found out that she died about two years ago."

"Oh, I'm sorry to hear that, Kings! I know you two were really close!"

"We still are," I replied. For I knew that Maggie would always live in my heart!

After an evening watching the footy, I headed off to bed. I was tired from all my walking.

Chapter Twelve

In my Heart there Rings a Melody

Over the next few weeks, Spring grew into Summer, and Meredith returned from her trip visiting her family in England. On weekends, Fraser, Lynn, and I went exploring the towns and villages of our beloved Wales. Life was good! Fraser and I went swimming in the sea most nights, when he got home from work. We also went fishing off the rocks, catching mackerel and bass, just as we did as kids. And we even went rock climbing on the cliffs, and climbed the face of the highest peak of the Three Cliffs! It was great to get to know my brother again and feel close to him. We had spent too many years apart, and I vowed in my heart to change that.

In the evenings, I went dancing and for long walks with Meredith, who was becoming such a wonderful friend! She got on well with Lynn and Fraser too, and we often did things together.

During the week days that followed, when Fraser, Lynn and Meredith were working, I spent time re-exploring the different beaches around the Gower Peninsula. My favourites, of course, being Pobbles and Three Cliff's Bay. I also spent time in the Valley, where the horses were now rearing their foals. Ruby, just like Great Thunder had done, moved from his cave on Pobbles, and went to watch over his family in the valley. I spent long hours with the horses, and I watched Ruby guard the herd as other horses tried to come up the valley to find fresh grazing or to join the herd!'

As I observed Ruby, he would stand on top of Great Thunders hill. There he would think and dream! And charge down the hill to protect his mare and foal. It turned out that "Sun Cloud,' the mare that I had developed a bond with in the early spring, was indeed Ruby's mare! And Ruby was a very affectionate stallion. He was often nibbling on Sun Clouds ears and lying with her in the long warm grasses that grew beside the river.

One of my highlights with the horses was sitting against Sun Clouds tummy when she 'was close to giving birth. I would sit and read, and I could feel her unborn foal moving around in her tummy! A few times the little hoof would kick me in the back.

And I would then say to Sun Cloud: "I wonder if it's going to be a stallion or a mare?"

She would reply with a gentle neigh or grunt, as if to say: "I think this one is a mare!"

Ruby seemed very accepting of me sitting with his mare while he kept watch on top of the hill. It was a family thing, you know! And we took turns! When he went on his run at about three in the afternoon, he would always come to sit with Sun Cloud when he had finished guarding the sands. Then I would go and sit up on the hill. After about an hour or so, Ruby would climb back up the hill and have a visit with me. It was then that we thought and dreamed together! And I shared with him my love for Gay!

"I must find her, old boy! What do you think?"

"Never give up!" he neighed. "The God of heaven's armies has surely heard your prayers!"

"Thanks, old boy! I know he has! I just need to keep believing!"

It was now the middle of June. Almost mid-summer's day! And as I approached the valley, I noticed Sun Cloud was lying flat on her side! I ran to investigate! And sure enough, she was close to giving birth! I looked up to Great Thunder's hill and shouted: "Come on, Rube, you don't want to miss this!"

And down he came like a prince on the way to his castle! Ruby stood on one side of her. She started grunting and lifting her head up and down, and I started to rub her tummy.

"That's it, girl" I said in a gentle voice, trying to comfort her.

Ruby neighed and said, "I'm glad it's the women that have the babies!" I nodded in agreement.

Sun Cloud looked up as if to say: "You got that right! You guys don't know what pain is till you have pushed one of these out!"

Ruby and I looked at each other and thought we'd best keep quiet. Then suddenly a head appeared! And then a pair of shoulders! And with one big push and a grunt, Sun Clouds foal was born! I glowed with excitement and joy at this wonderful miracle of birth!

The little foal sat on the ground for several minutes as its proud mother licked its face, and Ruby ran around in a circle as if creating a hedge of protection around us! Soon the little foal tried to stagger to his feet. He wobbled for a few minutes, and then stood.

What a privilege for me to have seen the birth! The years melted away as I remembered how my friend, Debbie Jones, and I would travel around looking for the pregnant mares, so that we could watch the births and name the foals! And by the end of the spring, we had named about ten foals!

Ruby spent the next few hours close by, as did I, just glowing in the joy of seeing this new life come into the world! Sun Cloud was soon on her feet, and her little one began nursing on her sweet milk. I could see now that her new foal was a mare!

And I said: "Congratulations, old girl, you have a baby girl there!"

Ruby neighed with excitement and continued to prance around us in a wide circle.

"Congratulations, Ruby old boy!" I said. "You have a brand-new daughter!"

And I began to think of a name for this new miracle. I couldn't seem to think of one and I thought some more and said I liked the word 'miracle.' And we were in the month of June! So how about "Miss Junacle! She could become a *princess* with a name like that! And both Sun Cloud and Ruby neighed in approval! So that became her name!

My days became rich, and full of the joys and glories of "the good old summer time!" But in my soul, I was aware of the part of me that was missing! I still yearned and ached for the love of my life! Sometimes when I walked along the seafront with Meredith, I would see a woman who looked like Gay! I would look and wonder if it could be her? And there was no hiding what I felt in my heart! One day while walking with Meredith, she said to me, "You still love her, don't you? Sometimes when I am with you, I feel your heart is looking for her!"

And I could only answer "Yes, it is!"

Meredith was very understanding and even supportive. Of course I had to tell her about Gay – it was only right.

"It was such a long time ago, Kingsley! And I envy the love you must have shared together! For it is so strong! And it clearly still lives in your heart! I am willing to try and understand how you feel, Kingsley! Because of what I feel for you, I hope in my heart that she doesn't come back into your life! Yet I know what she means to you, so another part of me hopes that you will find each other again!"

And I said to Meredith: "I really appreciate your honesty, and I understand if this is too hard for you. But as it is now, I can only offer you my friendship."

(Oh, dear Reader! Life can be complex at times! But I am learning that the more honest we are with our own heart and the hearts of others, the more uncomplicated life is!)

༄

Fraser, Lynn and I had just got back from a weekend spent in Devonshire, England. It was a Sunday night and Lynn called out from the kitchen window: "It's Midsummer's Day tomorrow!"

And as her words rang through the evening air, I realized that I had been in Wales for over two months now! And I was missing my children in Canada so much! We talked to each other on the phone at least three times a week, and I wrote them letters and cards. But it wasn't the same as being together! I had almost eight more weeks to go before I would see them again!

As I spent time alone on the beach, I prayed each day that Gay and I would find each other again. I wondered if God had other plans and was keeping us apart! Oh, well! What could I do! Just carry on with life, I suppose, and keep believing!

Morning came and it was Midsummer's Day! Lynn suggested that we all go out for a pub meal in the evening. And she asked if I'd like to ask Meredith to come and join us. Which I did. Fraser and Lynn headed off to work, and I decided to spend the day swimming in the sea at Pobbles, and buy my usual lunch in Swansea Market on the way.

It was another beautiful day as I arrived at Pobbles. The tide was fully in, and the breakers were crashing into the cove. This was the best time for body surfing and diving from the rocks! Excited, I changed into my swimming shorts and waded into the waves. There were several teens already taking advantage of the high tide rollers, as the waves swept them up the beach! It was my turn now as I waded out beyond the smaller breakers that crashed over my waist.

"Here's my wave," I thought, as I lined myself up about twenty feet in front of the larger swells further out. As I waited in anticipation, the swells continued to build and build! And suddenly there it was! A big one about to break! I quickly swam to catch up with its crest and dived over its front to catch it! And I did! Then I felt that magical moment when my whole body was like a part of the wave! And then I came crashing into the shore!

No sooner had I got to my feet when I jumped back over the waves to catch another one! I did it over and over again, until my legs felt like a jelly fish. There is nothing like the singing surf to wash the cobwebs out of your soul!

The teenagers looked at me as one of them now, and they complimented my efforts.

"I grew up here," I replied. I almost said, 'I hope I can do this until I'm an old, old man, and then a big wave can come and take me away like Great Thunder!' But I kept those thoughts to myself. They didn't know the King of the Gower!

All around the bay were the sounds and smells of 'glorious summer'! As the kissing sun rose higher and higher in the smiling sky, beautiful girls lay basking and painting their nails in the gossiping dunes. Their bright bikinis sparkled like summer flowers on a yellow sea of whispering sand. The lovely scent of their body oils did a dance for me on the sea breeze and excited my soaring soul!

As my eyes scanned the sands for my Gay, I was consumed by my meditative daydream, and I asked two questions of the wind! Was I looking for Gay and I as teenagers again? Or was I looking for her as the mature woman she would be today?

"Which one is it, you dreamer?" a seagull came to say.

"I think both!" I answered him, and he shook his head and flew away.

Suddenly I was back in time, as I remembered the first time I met Gay as a young woman!

I stood behind her in Penmaen Post Office, and her hair was as long and beautiful as a horse's tail and her sweet scent thrilled my soul! And today as I stood and played in the waves, my desire to find her burned within my heart again.

The sound of music and laughter filled the air as families and teens sat in groups, divided only by coloured towels. And territorial dogs barked and wagged tails at anything that tickled their fancy, and that included a posh poodle named Nancy! Cross old ladies smiled as they remembered their childhood, and their lives when they were once young girls with summer dresses and homemade curls! Fat men walked along the sands, believing their tummies were slim and muscular again. One man was as round as a ball, but he rolled as proud as a peacock, bare-chested, after his dog.

"Which one is the dog?" said a judgemental old cow as she sat behind her sunglasses in a deckchair and judged the world.

Seagulls flew back and forth trying to spot the sandwich eaters and particularly the child that was about to drop his lunch. Then it was a race between the dog and the gull for who got the meal.

Suddenly a wave knocked me off my daydreaming feet and swept me into the shore. Standing up, I ran to the dunes to warm myself in the hot sand.

After basking amongst the bikinis, and dreaming wonderful dreams, I walked like a peacock, as if I was trying to attract a mate! I think I must have been giving off the scent that I was only interested in the Gay coloured bird, though, because none of them flocked to see my mating dance!

After my dance through the dunes, I walked to the rocks on the left side of the cove. Here within the rocks was "The Dragon Pool"! My favourite rock pool in the world! The tide had just gone out past the pool, and this brought back golden memories of my childhood years. Several children waited eagerly, with their buckets and spades, for the tide to drop a little more, so they could dig and make sand castles, surrounded by little streams in the golden sand.

One young girl, about eight years old, said to me: "Excuse me Sir! Would you help me empty this big pool? I have a bucket and spade, and if you agree to help me, you can borrow my friend's bucket to help me empty the water out of the pool!"

Her excitement and anticipation was written on her face and I couldn't resist.

And I said, "Yes! I will help you empty the pool! But it's a large pool with gallons and gallons of water, so it's going to take a long time to empty!"

"How long?" she asked.

"Oh, about three hours!" I replied.

"That's alright," she said. "I've got all day!"

I noticed that some of the other children had buckets too. So, I said: "Who would like to empty the Dragon Pool, and catch crabs and fish?"

Everyone's hand went up, and now we had six kids ready to use their buckets!

One boy asked: "If I help, will we find the dragon who lives in the pool?"

"I don't know," I said. "But when my brother and I were your age, we did find the dragon!"

"Then I'm helping," the boy said.

"There are no such thing as dragons!" the girl who first spoke to me said.

"Oh, but there is!" I replied. "There are seahorses with dragon heads!"

"Oh… I hope we find one!" she said.

"But before we start, what is your name?" I asked.

"I'm Melody," she replied. "And these are my new friends that I just met on the beach!"

"I'm Kingsley, everyone, and I'm pleased to meet you all! Now, let's start emptying the dragon pool! "

"Kingsley!" Melody echoed back to me. "That's a strange name. But I like it!"

"I'm glad you like it. I've had it all my life!"

"Of course you've had it all your life," the boy said. "Your mum and dad gave it to you when you were born!"

Melody giggled, thinking the conversation very funny.

"Now let's organize how we are going to empty the pool! How many buckets do we have?"

Melody did the counting and said: "We have six."

"Okay, let's form a line everyone! Melody and I will fill our buckets from the pool, and pass them along to the rest of you to dump the water on the sand."

"Like form an assembly line in a factory?" the boy asked.

"Yes, that's right! And once the last person in the line has emptied the bucket, they must pass it back along the line, so Melody and I can fill it up again!'

"This is fun!" Melody said, as we filled our buckets and passed them down the line.

"We are making a river!" the boys shouted back.

"It's not going down very quickly," Melody said, trying to find her reflection in the now rippled pool.

"It *is* going down," I replied, "but very slowly! If you look carefully around the sides of the pool, you can see that the rock is wet where the water level is going down!"

Soon the other children began to get bored with the slow process, and I tried to switch the line around so that everyone had a turn at filling up the buckets from the pool. It seemed to work for a while, but the kids were soon bored again, and one by one, they left to make sand castles now that the tide had gone out some distance from the rocks. All except Melody!

She was determined, and she said to me, "You're not going to quit on me, are you?"

"No, I'm not," I said, "but we should stop and have lunch. "

"Okay," she said. "I'll run back to my Aunt and have lunch, and then I'll meet you back here!"

"Alright," I said. "I'm going to sit here and have my lunch at the pool!"

"Okay, Kingsley, see you soon!"

'What a wonderful little girl, and so full of life!' I thought, as I ate my cockles and Cornish pasty. The Dragon Pool had many fond memories for me! One could catch "gobies" in here – a small fish that lives in the rock pools inside the holes and crevices. Fraser and I once caught forty of them in one day, using a hook and line. And you can also catch rock and fiddler crabs with lines and bait!

The afternoon sun burned high and hot in the sky, and I hoped that Melody would have decided to go and play with her friends, rather than come back and meet me here at the pool. I could hear the cool waves calling me to come for a swim as I listened to the roar of the surf. But I felt I should wait for Melody! At least for half an hour anyway. I had promised to empty the pool with her!

"And I'm a man of my word!" I said aloud to a passing gull, who commented back: "You're a Caveman of your word!"

"Yes, I am, my feathered friend, and don't you forget it!"

Melody came back, re-energized after her lunch, and I figured we would soon be back to emptying the pool.

But surprisingly, she said, "Kingsley, can I talk to you? I'm feeling sad!"

"Feeling sad?" I echoed back. "And why are you feeling sad? And shouldn't you be talking to your mum and not a stranger?"

"Yes, but could I please talk to you, Kingsley?"

"Yes, alright then! What's bothering you, young lady?"

"I wish I had a boyfriend!"

"You wish you had a boyfriend?"

"Yes, all my friends do!"

"Well, how old are you? You are a bit young to be wanting a boyfriend, aren't you?"

"No, I'm 9! I'll have you know!"

"You're 9? Wow, that is practically a grownup!"

Melody, smiled, and I smiled back. "But I don't have a boyfriend," she continued, and her face began to pout again.

"Well, I know something," I said. "Somewhere there is a handsome boy, saying, 'I wish I had a girlfriend!' And he's about your age, too!"

"Really? Really, Kingsley?

"Yes, Melody, really!"

"And do you think he likes the name 'Melody'? My friend who has a boyfriend says that my name is stupid! And that's why I don't have a boyfriend!"

"Well, Melody, she doesn't sound like a very nice friend to me! Melody is a lovely name! And I met a girl once, when I was not much older than you. She made a melody in my heart!"

"Really, Kingsley?"

"Yes, really! And I loved her with all my heart!"

"Did you marry her?"

No, but I wish I had! She had to move away with her family to England. She loved horses, just like me! And we tamed a wild stallion together!"

"You did?

"Yes, we did!"

"My mum loves horses and so do I! But I still wish I had a boyfriend!"

"Well, let me tell you something that I have learned, Melody."

"What's that?" she said.

"Well, there is a special time, and season, to meet and fall in love with the right person. And, if we don't wait for that right time, we can make a big mistake and marry the wrong person!"

"I don't understand. I mean, how can you tell if it's the right time and the right person?"

"Let me see if I can explain. Okay, what season of the year is it?"

"Summer, of course!"

"And what comes after Summer?"

"Autumn, of course!"

"Well, what do you think would happen to Summer's heart, if *Winter* came after Summer, instead of *Autumn*?"

"Oh, that's easy! Summer would be cold and lonely. She wouldn't have a chance for her leaves to grow gold, and ride on the wind, and get to know Winter properly, before she gave Winter her heart."

"Well done, Melody! You are a wise girl, and a true poet!"

"I am?" She smiled.

"Yes," I replied. "What you just described happened to me!"

"Really?"

"Yes. I wanted to meet someone when I lived far away in Canada. The person seemed really nice and in lots of ways she was just like me."

"You mean like Summer?"

"Yes, Melody! That's sweet of you to think of me as Summer. I think I am warm like Summer. Anyway, the problem was, that we didn't wait long enough to really get to know each other! We didn't walk in all four seasons together, to give us the time to learn, grow and get to know each other as we should."

"You mean you didn't wait for Autumn and Winter to come?"

"Yes, that's right, Melody! And when the winds and rains

of Winter came, we were strangers, and we didn't stand together against the cold. We were two beautiful trees, but our roots didn't go deep enough together, and the wind blew us away!"

Melody listened intently to my words, and frowned.

"So, remember this, Melody: love is never in a hurry! And when the time is right, you will meet the young man who is right for you!"

"How will I know if he's the right boy for me? Even if we do walk through all the seasons together?" she asked softly.

"Well, first you have to feel a *melody* singing in your heart when you are together. "

"A melody – like my name!" She smiled.

"Yes, just like what your name means – music ringing in your heart!"

"Kingsley, can I tell you a secret?"

"Yes, if you like."

"*Music singing in my heart* is what my mum says my name means too! She said she named me after a song that a boy started in her heart when she was a young girl. That's why I want to meet a boy – it sounds so wonderful!"

"Thank you for sharing with me, Melody. You are such a special girl, for your mum and dad to have given you such a lovely name that suits you so perfectly."

"I don't have a dad! He left my mum when I was only two. And I don't remember him!"

"I'm sorry to hear that. And he missed out on having the most beautiful song in his heart! You!"

"Really?"

"Yes, really! You are very special, Melody!"

"I wish you could be my Dad!"

"Thank you! That makes me feel so special, Melody."

"Do you have a daughter, Kingsley?"

"Yes, I do. And, she is very beautiful too! Her name is Samantha and she's my princess!"

"Is she a real princess?"

"Yes, she is to me! And I call her Samantha, pumpkin, bride, cat, after a game we made up."

"I wish I could be your princess too!"

"You can if you like! You can be 'Princess Melody with a song in her heart'!"

"Wow, I'm a real princess!"

"You are!"

"Well, Melody, I must be going now to meet up with my brother. Don't forget what I said: When you meet the right person, you will feel a song singing in your heart! Walk with them through Summer, Autumn, Winter and Spring, and see if there is still a song ringing in your heart. And then when Summer comes around again, you will know that it is the right time, and the right boy for you!"

"Gosh, Kingsley, I'm going to tell my mum about you, and everything you said!"

"Thank you, Melody, for everything that you said too. And never forget that you are a real Princess!"

"I won't, Kingsley! And maybe I will see you down on the beach again, and we can finish emptying the dragon pool?"

"I'd like that, Melody. Bye for now."

"Yes, bye Kingsley."

"Oh, one more thing before you go, Melody. What's your mum's name? And are you on holiday?"

"Yes, my mum and I are on holiday with my Aunt. And my mum's name is Gay!"

"Gay! Did you say Gay?"

"Yes, my mum's name is Gay. And her name means *cheerful* or *merry*.

"Is she here on the beach?"

"No, I came to the beach with my Aunt Pearl. My mum was tired today, so she stayed in the caravan."

"Oh, I see. How long are you staying here on holiday?

"Mum said we booked the caravan for two weeks. And that tomorrow she's bringing me to the beach. Why were you asking about my mum anyway?"

"Because I once made a wonderful friend named Gay! And we fell in love! Gay Tripp was her name.

"Gay Tripp is my mum! Was she your princess?"

"Yes, she was!"

"Do you want to come and see my mum? My Aunt won't mind you coming to visit."

"I'll tell you what, Melody, when you get back to your caravan, ask her if she remembers a young man who once gave her a Celtic Cross necklace with a green birthstone in it."

"Okay, Kingsley, I will!"

"Oh, and if you want to try to empty the Dragon pool tomorrow, you can invite your mum to come. I will be here on the beach by 12 noon."

"Okay, Kingsley, I'll tell her! Oh, I can hear my Aunt calling for me.... Bye, Kingsley! See you tomorrow."

"Bye, Melody. Don't forget to ask your mum about the necklace!"

"Okay, I won't!"

My gosh! Was this really happening? Was Melody Gay's daughter? I felt shivers run up my spine. But it wasn't just excitement; it was a strange, indescribable 'knowing.' And I felt joy in my heart, that God had heard me and answered my prayers! It had to be my Gay! How many people are named Gay Tripp? I knew there was something about Melody that had drawn me to her! And I trembled with excitement all the way home to Fraser and Lynn's house.

I recalled what I had read in Gay's and Maggie's letters. Gay had gotten pregnant, and if Melody's dad wasn't in her life, then her mother would have probably kept her maiden name. Wow! I was so excited! At the same time, I felt that I didn't want to allow myself to fully believe it, in case it wasn't true, and I would be so disappointed.

"Come on, Kings!" I said to myself aloud. "Have faith! It *has* to be." And I prayed.

After an early supper with Fraser and Lynn, I headed off to bed. Tomorrow couldn't come fast enough! In my mind, I pictured Melody telling Gay about me, and about everything that had happened today. And I felt such hope!

Chapter Thirteen

The Princess and the Dragon

*F*raser and Lynn had already left for work by the time I got up. After a nice hot bath, I put on my best casual clothes, so that I would be ready to meet Gay. And I tried to imagine how she had reacted to Melody telling her all about me. I could see her in my mind's eye, getting flustered and that red blush coming over her face as she saw me! I pictured her trembling like me. I tried not to get too excited, but I felt like a school boy again. And I told myself it had been many years since we had seen each other, and things might not be the same; we might not have those same feelings. But my body and soul disagreed with me, as I trembled at the thought of seeing her face and being in her presence again. I always trembled when she was near! And it wasn't until she was in my arms that I stopped shaking. Once I'd held her and felt her love, I became a knight! And I could take on the world and win.

On my way to catch the bus, I stopped in at the Swansea Market as usual to buy my lunch. And today, I decided to have some breakfast in the market café. I wanted to say hello to David Griffith, who I had recognized when I'd first come into the cafe several weeks before. He knew my face from somewhere, but he hadn't had the time to ask who I was.

"Hello, David," I said. "I'm Kingsley! You used to be my Sunday school teacher when I was a boy."

"That's who you are!" he said. "I knew I recognized you from somewhere! But it was too busy for me to talk to you the other day. Hang on a moment, Kingsley, I'm going to get one of the girls to take over the line here, and I'll sit and have a coffee with you. What would you like with your coffee?"

"Oh, I'll have a Cornish pasty and an ice bun, Dave."

"You're having breakfast, are you?"

"Yes, I got up a bit late this morning, and I'm heading out to the Gower later. And I always come and pick up my lunch here in the market. So how are you doing, Dave?"

"Well I own and operate the coffee shop here in the market. It keeps me out of trouble and helps me pay the bills. I'm not at Linden Chapel in Mumbles anymore. My wife and I are pastoring a church in Fforest Fach. We have a large youth group, and I still enjoy preaching and teaching the Bible. How about you, Kings? You moved out to Canada, didn't you?"

"Yes, I did. And I live on Vancouver Island, which is quite lovely! 'Specially if you enjoy the outdoors as I do."

"Yes, you would love that, Kings! Camping and fishing and all that. And how about your family? I see your Dad and Brother once in a while in the market."

"Well, I have three wonderful children! A daughter and two sons! I went through a divorce a while back and that was hard. But I'm doing a lot better now. And it's great to be back on the Gower!"

"Yes, there's nowhere like it in the world, is there? No matter where we may wander, the Gower is always home! Anyway, Kingsley, I have to get back to work now, as I can see the girls are getting swamped with breakfast orders. Here's my number, and please ring so my wife and I can have you over for supper. We'd love you to come out to the church sometime, and see what God is doing in our congregation. Bye, Kingsley, I'll expect to hear from you soon!"

"Okay, Dave, I'll give you a ring soon. Bye now."

As I rode the bus out to Southgate, I felt excited and nervous! Would Melody's mum come with her today? And would she turn out to be Gay? I was experiencing this battle inside, trying not to have this complete expectation that she would be. Obviously, if she wasn't, I would be very disappointed. But I encouraged myself to put my trust in God.

And as I walked along the cliff tops to Pobbles, I felt more "joy" than any other emotion. For I believed it would be her! I had prayed so much, asking God to help me find Gay! And I felt peace within my soul now, knowing that He had heard my prayers and would give me my heart's desire.

When I arrived at Pobbles, the tide was well on its way out past the rocks. And there was Melody, and a bunch of other kids, already at work with their buckets, trying to empty the Dragon Pool!

"Well done!" I said, as I arrived on the scene.

"Hi, Kingsley!" Melody shouted out excitedly. "We already started emptying the pool! And you can borrow that bucket," she said, pointing to a red and white bucket on the sand.

"I'm quite impressed, Melody!" I shouted back. "You have everyone organized and working hard already. Well done everyone!" And, I picked up the bucket and took my turn in the line. I wanted to talk to Melody right away, about what her mum had said about the necklace. But I would have to wait until we all took a break. I couldn't stop this chain gang of buckets; if I did, I might never get them working like this again!

For the next hour or so, the kids and I worked hard filling the buckets and passing them down the line to the last person, who poured out the water onto the sand.

"Look!" I said, "we are making a stream all the way to the sea, and the water level in the pool has already gone down about two feet!"

"Yeah! "' everyone shouted excitedly, and they worked even harder.

"My arms are getting heavy," one of the girls called out.

"Mine too, mine too!" called out the other voices along the line.

"Time for a break," I said. "Let's rest for half an hour."

Once all the other children had left the pool, I was able to talk to Melody alone. "Did you get a chance to talk to your mum about the necklace?" I asked.

"Yes, I did! And guess what?"

"What?" I asked expectantly.

"She let me wear it! Have a look at it!" she said, lifting it from her neck and putting it in my hand.

Tears filled my eyes as I could see that it was the same necklace that I had given Gay, all those years ago!

"You're crying, Kingsley?" Melody said, watching my every expression.

"I'm just so happy," I replied with a smile, as I continued to examine the necklace.

"Is it the same one, Kingsley?"

"Oh yes, It's the same one alright. Look, it has the same green birthstone that your mum and I called "Evening Emerald"... we called it the green of the sea. Here, you better put it around your neck Melody so we don't lose it in the sand."

"Yes, then I'd be in big trouble, right?"

"Right," I said.

"Kingsley, come and see my Aunt, she wants to meet you. And, my mum gave her a letter for you."

"So your mum didn't come down to the beach with you?"

"No, my Aunt did. My mum isn't feeling well. Come on, Kingsley, come and meet my Aunt."

I walked behind slowly as Melody ran excitedly ahead to her Aunt. As I walked across the sands, it still felt like a dream to me!

"Hello, I'm Kingsley," I said, introducing myself to Melody's aunt.

"Pleased to meet you, Kingsley! I'm Pearl, if you remember? I'm Gay's sister. "

"Yes, I remember! It's been many years. It's nice to see you again. And how is Gay?"

"Not very well right now, I'm afraid. We lost our father to

a heart attack last month! And we are all still grieving. Especially Gay! She and Dad had been estranged for years. And now she feels guilty, and she hasn't had proper closure."

"I'm so sorry to hear of your loss! How is your mum? Helen, right?"

"Yes, that's right. She's doing as well as can be expected. You might know that her and my dad had been divorced for quite some time."

"Yes, I finally received Gay's letters. She had left them with Maggie in Penmaen, while I was away in Canada. I'm sorry that I wasn't here for Gay when she came looking for me!"

"Oh, Kingsley, you hadn't seen each other in years! And she couldn't expect to just show up on the Gower, and expect you to be here."

"Yes, but Mum loves Kingsley!" Melody said, having listened to the whole conversation. "And 'love lasts forever," she continued.

"Melody, it's not polite to interrupt peoples' conversations," Pearl said.

But in my heart, I rejoiced at Melody's words! And I said, "It's quite alright! Melody is right. Real love does last forever!"

A radiant smile appeared on Melody's face, and she said, "Come on Kingsley, let's get back to emptying the Dragon pool. And remember what you promised! The first seahorse we find, I'm going to put in my bucket, right?

"Right!" I said.

"Well, I guess you better get back to the kids at the pool," Pearl said. "And thanks for taking the time to play with Melody. You must be a real family man, Kingsley."

"Yes, I am. I have three wonderful children back in Canada."

"Oh, before you leave, Gay asked me to give you this letter."

"Thanks." I said. "It was nice talking to you Pearl. And please give my regards to Gay, and tell her I'm sorry for her loss."

I decided to wait and open Gay's letter this evening, when I would have some quiet time to think. As I continued to spend time with the children, I felt this 'great joy' in knowing that Gay was so close! And that I was actually spending time with her daughter, Melody, who was such a wonderful girl! I could see Gay as a young girl when I looked at Melody. And especially in her awareness and her passion for life.

Over the next hour or so, we reached within two feet of the bottom of the Dragon Pool. And I, as much as the children, became excited as to what we would discover.

I said to Melody: "Look, there are two little seahorses swimming around! Does anyone have a net?"

"Yes," one of the other girls said. "I have a butterfly net."

"Can you go and get it?" I asked. Meanwhile, Melody and I took our shoes and socks off and waded into the pool, while the other children sat around the side watching.

"What if a big crab pinches my toes?" Melody said with a concerned look on her face.

"They will be running away from our big feet," I said, "so, don't worry."

"Big smelly feet!" Melody continued and she started laughing.

When the girl got back with her butterfly net, I asked Melody to fill up one of the buckets with water, and hold it ready for me to put in the seahorses.

"Are they real dragons?" the other children shouted in excitement as I pushed the net around the pool after the seahorses. Finally I caught one and plunked it into Melody's bucket. Melody climbed out of the pool and raced with her bucket to show her Aunt the proud catch, and most of the other children chased across the beach after her. One little girl, however, stayed on the rocks at the side of the pool and pleaded with me to give her the next seahorse. And as I chased the remaining seahorse around the pool, I began to miss my own kids, and I wished they could be here with me. Being away from your family sure reminds you what is important in life, and I looked forward to phoning my children in the evening.

By the time Melody and the other kids arrived back, I'd caught the other seahorse. Which was just as well, as the tide was coming in fast now. The kids stayed on the beach watching the seahorses swimming around in the buckets. And I shouted out: "We only have about an hour left before the tide comes in again! Who wants to finish emptying the pool?"

"We're tired, Kingsley," they called back" "And, we've already caught the dragons!"

We had indeed. Let's just watch the dragons swimming in the buckets. And as far as I know, to this day, only my brother Fraser and I have ever emptied the Dragon Pool and found all its treasures within its waters!

♪❋

THE DRAGON POOL

There's a secret pool within the limestone rocks,
where Pobbles sea winds blow.
It's a place where my soul loves to come, in Spring,
Summer,and golden Fall.
And even in the cold of Winter,
on the Dragon Pool I'll call!
When the Atlantic breakers crash,
and the full moon smokes his stash of chilling mist,
The sands fill the pool golden,
and the dragon waters are shallow enough
for me to stand.
And I can hold hands with the dreaming dragons
As they breathe fire upon my enemies,
and consume them all.
When the moon is but a mermaid's fingernail,
and it shines a line upon the October 11th sands,
The pool is deep and mysterious again,
and it tells me stories whispered in the summer rain.

Where engagement rings on fingers swirl
the surface of your waters,
Where young girls kiss, and boys fish,
all within your magic circle.
Sailors' boots and seaweed glisten, but you must sit
and listen like fluffy the kitten.
Secrets, secrets are in your emerald depths where
I dive and swim and sing,
And you reveal a sacred hymn that only my soul can sing.
Dragon Pool, I carry you within.

© Kingsley Ross Hill

Slowly, this wonderful day grew to a close. And I walked Princess Melody, and her conquered dragon [Fire] across the beach to her Aunt.

"Aunt Pearl! Aunt Pearl! Look! I've caught the dragon! It's a real dragon! And I'm a Princess! Kingsley told me that I'm a real Princess, Auntie Pearl."

"I can see you've had a lovely time, Melody. But we have to leave now and meet your mum at the caravan."

"But what about my dragon? Can I bring it to show Mum? Please Auntie Pearl, please!"

Well, you better ask Kingsley if your dragon will be alright in the bucket all night. Because we won't be able to bring him back to the beach again until tomorrow."

"Can I, Kingsley, can I?"

"Well, as long as we put some fresh sea water into the bucket now, and you be sure to bring him back to the beach before lunch tomorrow, he will probably be alright.

So after filling up the bucket in the waves, I said goodbye to Melody and Pearl.

"Now you run along, Melody," Pearl said before I turned to go. "I'll be along in a minute."

"I just wanted to thank you, Kingsley, for spending so much time with Melody! She doesn't have a dad in her life, and now her granddad is gone, she just craves the attention of a father figure. She will be talking about this day for weeks!"

"I enjoyed it too," I said. "And please tell Gay that she has a real little Princess in Melody. Just like her mum."

Pearl seemed to look at me knowingly, like she could see into my heart. And she said, "Yes, I will tell Gay. Bye for now. I'm sure I will see you again soon."

"I'm sure of that," I replied. "Goodbye for now, Pearl." And I shouted out "Bye, Princess Melody." She had already started to climb the dunes.

What a full and wonderful day it had been, I thought, as I walked back along the beach to Pobbles. Then I climbed to the clifftop, and sat on the grass to read Gay's letter. When I opened the envelope, there were two letters. One was my poem that I'd written for Gay when I'd first met her at Penmaen Store. The other was a letter that she had written yesterday evening!

Dear Kingsley,

I'm sorry that I didn't come and see you myself today. After Melody came home and shared about the necklace yesterday, I knew it was you! The way she described you, and the conversation you both had about the seasons. It just had to be you! Please know that I can't wait to see you again, Kingsley! After all these years, I am also afraid! Not of you, of course, but rather of my life, and what you might think. When I think of you and I, I can't help but think of that Spring and Summer when we met . . . and fell so deeply in love! And there is so much to tell you. So much that I want you to know.

You have probably gathered from the letters that I left with Maggie for you, that my life has been in quite a mess for some time. And to top it off, my dad died last month! And I didn't get to tell him that I loved him before he died! And I've had a bit of a breakdown. My sister Pearl, whom you met and whom you remembered from before, is helping me with Melody right now, while I'm trying to cope. As soon as I feel up to it, I'll come and meet you, Kingsley.

Your "always Princess" Gay.

P.S. Do you remember when we wrote our names inside two big hearts as big as houses, that we drew on the beach?

I wept as I read her letter. First, because I could feel her pain through her words. But then my tears turned to joy! As I remembered us! And what we had shared! And I felt her love again, like a wave crashing through my heart, a wave that swept away time that had dared to come between this wonderful love that had been ours. Stronger than a love lavished upon an only child. Stronger than the driving winds and the cruel sea. Stronger even than death is our love!

Before going back to Fraser and Lynn's, I dropped in to visit my dad and Mary. Mary made us a cup of tea and we got caught up with the news. I decided not to share anything about Gay, yet. But I told them about Maggie and Heather, and how I'd got my box of treasures back, which included my Bowie knife and my throwing knives, that Dad had bought me on that Christmas day all those years ago! Dad reminisced as he drank his tea, and our times together and our memories echoed around the room And I was soon caught up with all the news – all that was important to our world! Then it was time to go.

"Bye Dad, love you. Love you too, Mary. And I'll see you on the weekend."

"Love you too, Kings. Have a good night."

And to top up a perfect day! Liverpool beat Arsesmell 3 to 1! Yes, that is the right spelling if you're a Liverpool fan! After a nice supper, and watching the 'match of the day' with Fraser, I headed off to bed.

Chapter Fourteen
Nan's Nan

I woke up with a song in my heart, as gay as the song thrush that was singing the sweetest song outside my window. As I looked in the mirror, I said to the man standing there: "Yes, Kings! It isn't a dream! You have found Gay!"

After breakfast, I walked into Swansea, as usual, and went to the market to buy my lunch. The cockle ladies already had a large container of cockles waiting for me.

And the missing-tooth woman said to me: "Here you are, Kingsley. They are all ready for you, love!"

As I approached the Welsh Cake ladies, they said: "Here's 10 warm ones right out of the oven!"

How I loved to be around my fellow countrymen in the market and to be known and appreciated! Having lived away for so long, I lapped up the friendliness of the Welsh people and held them close to my heart.

I got onto the #14 bus, and was soon on my way to Pennard. As I thought about yesterday's events, I wondered if I would see Gay today.... I could feel her in my heart, as I had done when we were young teenagers. But we were adults now, with so many life experiences that had helped to make us who we were today. I couldn't wait to start getting to know Gay as a woman!

When I arrived at the beach, Melody was already at the Dragon Pool and staring into her bucket as it stood on the sand. There were several other children there too.

I called out: "How's the dragon, Melody?"

"Oh, he's happy, Kingsley!" I could tell from Melody's big smile that she was happy to see me.

"Mum and I read him a story last night. But I think he's ready to go back into his pool now!"

"A good idea," I said. "He needs some fresh water and to be back with his friends."

Melody nodded. "Yes, he needs to play with his friends!"

And as the other children looked on, Melody poured 'Dudley,' as she had renamed him, back into the pool.

"Kingsley, will you take me to see the horses, now that Dudley is in his pool?" she asked.

"Yes, but we need to make sure it's alright with your mum or your Aunt."

"It's my Aunt who's here, Kingsley. We can go and ask her."

I was disappointed that Gay wasn't here, but I was excited to see what this new day would bring.

I reminded myself that I needed to be patient! And trust that there was a good reason why Gay and I hadn't met yet. And I remembered something that Maggie had shared with me on several occasions.

"Kingsley!" she'd say. "God's timing for things in our lives is always the right time! And waiting for Him is never in vain! As long as we trust Him, He will always come through for us!"

Pearl agreed to me taking Melody to see the horses and she thanked me for giving her some time to herself. "Here you are, Melody," she said. "Don't forget to take your lunch. And try to be back around five."

"Guess what, Kingsley!" Melody said as we started off.

"What?"

"My mum told me about her horse. His name was Blaze! And my mum said she won a big riding competition when she was a teenager. She has the trophy at home.

"I remember Blaze!"

"You do?"

"Yes! When I first met your mum, she kept Blaze in the horse stables in Penmaen. And sometimes she would let me ride him!"

"Wow, it's not fair! Both you and my mum have ridden a horse, but I haven't!"

"Your mum hasn't taken you riding yet?"

"No! But she keeps promising me that one day she will."

"Well, if she's promised you, then one day she will," I confirmed. "I'll tell you what. How would you like to come and meet a herd of horses that I know? Some of the mares have recently had baby foals!"

"Wow! Really, Kingsley?"

"Yes, really. And they aren't far from here; they're grazing in the Three Cliffs Valley."

When we arrived at the valley, there were the same nine horses I'd seen the other day, including four mares with foals. Melody was thrilled to see them, and she skipped around like a young horse herself!

"Can we name the foals, Kingsley? Can we?"

"Of course!" I answered. "They've been waiting for us to come and give them names! Every horse should have a name!"

"Just like people, right Kingsley?"

"That's right! And you know what? Your mum and I used to go around to the different herds of horses, and wait for the foals to be born so we could name them."

Melody, seeing how big some of the horses were, took my hand.

"There is nothing to be afraid of," I said. "As long as they know we aren't going to hurt them, they will be gentle with us. And one of the most important things to remember about horses is that they are very sensitive; they can actually feel how we are feeling!"

"You mean like if I'm happy or sad?"

"Yes, that's right! The best way to approach a herd of horses is to walk slowly towards them and talk gently to them. Now Melody, this is my friend Summer Cloud. She is a mare, and her tummy is still big because she has a little foal inside her."

Melody giggled quietly and whispered: "Is she really your friend?"

"Yes," I said, "come and meet her. And we don't have to whisper, as long as we talk quietly and don't shout."

I slowly lifted Melody onto my shoulders so she could pat Summer Cloud.

"Wow, she's so big!" Melody whispered. "And look at her big brown eyes, Kingsley!"

"Yes, and if you look carefully into her eyes, you can see how kind and gentle they are!

"I can see my reflection in her eyes!"

"Now that's very special! I was told once by an old man who lived out in the wild, that if you get close enough to a horse that you can see your reflection in his or her eyes, then that horse will be able to see you inside. And he can feel your mood, and what you are going through in your life."

"Wow, Kingsley! I can feel Summer Cloud looking into my heart! Why did you call her Summer Cloud?"

"Well, you can see that she is almost white, and I thought that the grey blotches on her sides looked like clouds! And I met her in the early summer. So, I thought Summer Cloud would be a good name!"

"I think it is!" Melody said.

"There is also something special about this mare," I continued. "She's Ruby's mare!"

"Who's Ruby?

"He's the leader of the herd – a big stallion!"

"Could I meet him too, Kingsley?"

"If he's around you can, but we'll have to be careful because he's a wild stallion. But let's go and look at the foals first!"

Melody got more and more excited as we approached the herd. She reminded me of myself at her age – with her sense of wonder and her passion for getting to know the horses!

"Here's a brown mare, Kingsley," she pointed out. "What do you think about naming her Chestnut?"

"A great choice!" I replied. "She reminds me of the beautiful brown and red horse chestnuts that we play conkers with in the Autumn."

"And look at her foal, Kingsley … she is a chestnut colour too! How about we call her Baby Chestnut?"

"I like the name," I said, "but what about when she grows up? She won't be a baby then, will she? How about *Little Chestnut*, because she has very defined features and will probably always be smaller than her mother? See how her legs are shorter than the other young foals? And they were born around the same time, certainly within a few weeks of each other."

"I like that name for her. She is very dainty, isn't she?"

"Yes."

"Can I tell you something, Kingsley?"

"Of course you can, Princess!"

Melody giggled and said, "I love being called Princess!"

"Well, you are a Princess, aren't you?"

"Yes, when I'm with you."

"Now I'm going to tell you something, Melody. And I want you to always remember this! No matter who you are with, or wherever you are, you are *always* a Princess!"

Melody looked at me and her smile seemed to reflect a belief in what I had said. Sometimes a look or expression can say a thousand words!

Melody took my hand, and said: "Come on, King, let's go name the other horses."

"Okay."

"Oh, and that's not what I wanted to tell you, King!"

"What is it then?" I asked softly.

"I wanted to tell you that naming the horses makes me feel special. Like I'm important!"

"Well, you are important!"

"I didn't feel important when my daddy left! I felt that's why he left. Because I wasn't important!"

"Princess, I want you to listen to me carefully! What I am about to tell you is very important!"

"More important than me being a Princess?"

"Well, it's *just* as important!"

"What is it, King?"

"Your dad leaving you and your mum was *not* your fault! It had nothing to do with you, Princess! But I know that you *feel* that it was partly your fault.

"How did you know, King?"

"Because it happened to me too! My mum and dad broke up and I felt like it was my fault!"

"You did, King?"

"Yes, I did. I lived with my dad, because my mum went away. But I know now that it wasn't my fault! And that's why it's important for you to understand that sometimes mums and dads don't get along, and one of them leaves, but it's *not* the fault of the child or children. Now I don't expect you to understand all this now, because you're a young girl, but one day you will understand things a lot more. *Now* you only need to believe that you are very special!"

"I do, King! You make me feel special! And I'm going to remember always what you told me!"

"You do that, Princess! Now let's go and see these other horses. Would you like to feed some of the mares?"

"Oh, yes! I would love to feed them!"

"Here you are! Now hold your hand out flat and keep your fingers together, so the mare doesn't nibble them. She wouldn't do it on purpose, but she might nip you accidentally if you don't keep your fingers still and flat. Look...like this!" I put a carrot in Melody's hand.

"It tickles!" she giggled, as the mare lowered her mouth and crunched up the carrot. "Her nose is warm, King! And I can feel her breath on my hand."

"Here's an apple! I have always found that apples are their favourite thing to eat. That's it; keep your hand still and your fingers together.

"She's crunching it, King. Look at all the juice! I think it's her favourite, don't you?"

"Yes, I do."

"Look, King! She has a red and brown coat. I think I'm going to name her 'Big Red' because she's the biggest mare in the herd! Now what shall we call her foal? How about Little Riding Hood, and then when she grows up, we can just call her Riding Hood?"

"A great name!" I said. "I like how you thought about her name still suiting her when she gets older."

"How about those horses over there? Are they part of the same herd, King?"

"Yes, they are just grazing a distance away so that there is enough grass for all of them to eat. How about this foal? He's bigger than all the others and he's running around a lot! And he's a baby stallion, so we need a boy's name."

Melody watched the frisky colt. "How about 'Silver Dancer'? Because he's running and dancing around his mother, and he has a silver coat?"

"Well done, Melody! I think that's a perfect name for him!"

"Well, it's almost lunch time," I announced. "Shall we go and visit Pennard Castle? From up there we can look down on the whole valley!"

We climbed up the sandy path to the castle. "Can you tell me a story about the castle?" Melody pleaded. "There must be some stories about a real castle!"

"Well, I do know one," I said, "and it goes like this:

This is a story that my dad told me, when I was your age. Once upon a time, there lived at Pennard Castle, a Great Warrior. Now many miles away in North Wales, there was a Prince who asked help from the warrior, to fight a battle against a powerful neighbour . The Great Warrior of Pennard Castle, did not bother himself to help the Prince. He demanded the hand in marriage of the Princes daughter, as the price to help the Prince. The Prince agreed , and gave his daughter to the Warrior to wed. So the Prince and the Warrior fought together, and conquered the Princes neighbor. After the battle was over, the Warrior of Pennard Castle held a great wedding feast. There was harping, wine and dancing, and the castle was filled with music and laughter! But at the height of the party, a dark cloud came driving up the Channel. Then another dark cloud, and another, until the whole air was filled with flying sand. All that night, the wind blew as strong as a hurricane, and when the dawn broke; Pennard Castle; with its church and village; were all buried in a golden winding -sheet of sand. No one escaped. And across the sea in Ireland, a whole mountain of sand had suddenly and mysteriously disappeared during the night!

~

"Oh, that's a scary story, Kingsley! I hope that we won't be destroyed by a sand storm!"

"No, we won't," I reassured her. "That was thousands of years ago and it won't happen again!"

Melody looked relieved. But she held my hand for a few minutes, just in case!

"Now before we go back to your Auntie Pearl, I want to show you one of the oldest wild horses ever to live on the Gower Peninsula! Her name is Nan's Nan, and she's the oldest mare in all the herds on the Gower. She's a grandmother to many of the adult horses! And a great-grandmother to many of the new foals!"

"Look, Kingsley, she has white whiskers and white fur on her face! And she walks really slowly."

"Yes, she is old and slow now. But she has much wisdom, like an old mother that has cared for many children!"

"Can I give her the rest of the carrots, King? She's old and she needs the food!"

"Here you are, Melody. Now don't forget to hold your hand still, and keep your fingers in close to each other. "

"I will." She giggled as Nan's-Nan gently took the carrots from her palm. "Nan's-Nan is my favourite horse, King! And do you know why she is my favourite?"

"No, I don't. Tell me why she is your favourite."

"It's because she is old and wise, and she has been a good mother in taking care of so many of the other horses!"

"I think that is a good reason for liking her the best, Melody! Good mothers and grandmothers are a wonderful blessing for those they love and take care of. I lived with my grandmother and she was the most wonderful Grandma to me. And I had a wonderful mare called 'Thunder Spring,' and she saved my life by keeping me warm in a cave after I got swept out to sea and almost drowned! She kept me warm all through the night while I fell asleep on her belly. Without her warmth, I would have died of hypothermia!"

"Wow, King, she was a real hero!"

"Yes, she sure was."

Do you think I could ride Nan's Nan, Kingsley? She is gentle and slow, and it would be easier for me to ride her than one of the younger and faster horses."

"I will have to think about it for a few days, Melody, and maybe there is a way you can ride her."

After spending the whole afternoon amongst the horses, Melody asked if we could walk up the sandy path to the castle again. "I want you to piggy back me down the path, and run as fast as you can, like in the story you told me about you and Fraser when you were boys!"

"Okay," I said. "But you will have to hold on tight! And we will only be able to run down once, because your Auntie Pearl will be wondering where we are!"

"Okay, it's a deal King!"

We reached the top of the path with tired legs. Melody climbed on my back and off we went! And I ran as fast as my legs would carry us. Melody shrieked with excitement as we bounced down the path, until my legs gave out from underneath me. We fell crashing and laughing into the soft sand.

"Again, King? Can we do it again, King? "

"Another time, I promise. But now we have to get back to your Aunt; otherwise she will be worrying and wondering what happened to us."

And as we picked ourselves up from the sand, I was like a boy again! What a wonderful time we'd had! "

"Look Kingsley, flowers!"

"Yes, aren't they beautiful? They grow in a little stream beneath Pennard Castle. The stream travels for many miles underground, and then it comes out underneath the castle and into the valley. These flowers are wild water Irises, Melody! And they only bloom in the middle to late summer, unlike the other Iris that blooms in early spring! Let's pick some for your mum? "I suggested. "I know they are her favourite flower! And the same colour as her eyes! Violet and blue!"

"You sure know a lot about my mum, King!" she cried. "You are right, she does have violet eyes! Can I pick the flowers, King?"

"How about we do it together, because you have to reach down into the bottom of the stream and dig under the pebbles to break the stem close to the root. Look, like this! That way another stem will grow up and flower again soon."

"Like this, King?"

"Yes, that's right! Just be careful you don't fall in!"

"Look King, I've got three flowers!"

"And I have four. So that's seven. Your mum will love these!"

"I know she will, King. I will tell her they're from both of us."

"King, can I ask you something?

"Yes, of course, what is it?"

"Do you love my mum?"

I was quiet for a moment. Melody continued to talk: "I know my mum loves you! Because she always told me the story of a boy that she met when she was a teenager, on the Gower. She said he was a Prince, and she was his Princess, and they fell in love. Sometimes when she talked about the Prince and all the things that he did, she would cry! You are my mum's Prince, aren't you, King?"

"Yes, I am!"

"Well, King, do you still love my mum? I know you do."

"Yes. I do! And I would like to get to know her again!"

"You mean walk through the different seasons together like we talked about?"

"Yes, that's right! And if there is a melody still singing in my heart, after we have walked the seasons together, then I am sure I will want to love her forever!"

"I hope you do, King! Because I love you! And if you can love my mum and get married, then you can be my dad!"

And fighting back the tears, I said, "I'd like that very much!"

After a minute, I said: "Now we better get back to your Aunt Pearl or she will have our guts for garters!"

Melody roared with laughter, and repeated 'guts for garters.' "That's so funny, King!"

"It's an old saying," I said, "meaning, we will be in big trouble!"

"You mean big do-do!"

"Yeah, big do-do," and we both laughed! "Come on Princess, let's get going."

"Yes, and I'm getting hungry, King!"

Suddenly, Melody reached out and took my hand, and she held onto me all the way back to the beach. As we approached her Aunt, I tried to let go of her hand, but she grasped it even tighter! For a few moments, I thought about what it would be like to have Melody as my daughter. For that's what she would be if Gay and I discovered that we still loved each other, and wanted to spend our lives together! Suddenly, Maggie's words were there in my heart:

"Take one day at a time, Kingsley!" "I will Maggie, I will! One day at a time."

"You really do have a Princess there, don't you, Kingsley!" Pearl said, seeing Melody holding tightly onto my hand. "Well, did you have a nice time with Kingsley, Melody?"

"Oh yes, Auntie Pearl! We had the best time ever! We got to name all the horses and their foals! And Kingsley is going to see if I can ride Nan's-Nan!"

"Nan's-Nan! Who's Nan's-Nan?"

"Oh, she's the oldest and wisest horse of them all! That's why she's called Nan's-Nan, because she's the Grandmother and Great Grandmother of all the other horses!"

"Well, that's wonderful Melody! I'm so glad that you had so much fun with Kingsley. But we have to go now. Say goodbye to Kingsley until Friday. And thank him for spending time with you today."

"Thanks Kingsley!"

"Why can't I come to the beach tomorrow, Auntie Pearl?"

"Because you and your mum have an appointment in Cardiff tomorrow! But I'm sure you will see Kingsley again on Friday or Saturday."

"Bye, King, and thank you. Hope to see you again soon!"

"Hope to see you soon too, Melody! And don't forget to give the Irises to your mum. Hold onto them tight as you climb up the dunes!"

"I will. I will, King"

"Thank you, Kingsley!" Pearl said. "It means so much to Melody, spending time with you! I haven't seen her this happy... well, forever! Oh, and as I mentioned earlier, Gay and Melody have an appointment in Cardiff tomorrow. But I'm sure we will be back down at the beach on Friday or Saturday. And before I forget, I need to give you this letter from Gay! Bye for now, Kingsley!"

"Bye Pearl! And see you soon. Bye Melody, I had a wonderful day with you!"

Kingsley Ross Hill

So I had another letter from Gay! I would read it on my way home on the bus.

Dear Kingsley.

Melody brought back her dragon with her last night, and she told me all about almost emptying the big rock pool. I've never seen her so happy, Kingsley! Thank you for spending such a special time with her! I want to ask you if you would like to meet on Saturday? I thought I would make a picnic, and we could have it up on Cefn Bryn and sit up on your stone, just like we used to do! I can't wait to see you Kingsley!

Love Gay

Such joy filled my heart as I read her letter! And I thanked God for answering my prayers! Only days ago, it seemed as if I had no way of ever finding her! But God made a way, through Gay's daughter whom I met playing on the beach. And I marvelled at the way God worked things out and planned all the details!

And yes, Maggie, I do remember that God often answers our prayers in wonderful and mysterious ways! And now I was meeting Gay on Saturday for a picnic!

Fraser and Lynn were out when I arrived back at the house. They had left me supper on the table. After supper, I decided to retire for the night. I was very tired, but also very happy! It was the end of another wonderful day! Thank you, God!

Chapter Fifteen

Evening Emerald

Thursday morning arrived, and Fraser knocked on my bedroom door. He was excited to have the day off and wanted to go fishing in the afternoon.

"That sounds great, Fraser! But before we go fishing, will you give me a hand taking my saddle to the Three Cliffs Valley? I want to put it on one of the mares!"

"Sure, Kings,"

"It's too heavy to carry it to Swansea and take it on the bus."

"We can take it with our fishing gear in the car to Penmaen. Then you only have to walk down the Burrows to the valley with it."

"Thanks, that will be great!"

After breakfast, we loaded up the fishing gear and the saddle, and headed off to Penmaen. It wasn't high tide until around 2 pm in the afternoon. That would give me the whole morning to try and get the saddle on Nan's-Nan.

"She's an old horse, Kings!" Fraser reminded me. "I don't think you will have much trouble getting the saddle on her back! Nothing like your wild stallion, Kings! He was as wild as the west wind, and as fierce as the north!

"As warm as the south, and like the rising sun in the east to me!" I replied passionately. "He was perceived as fierce by most people, and that was fine with me. Because no one knew him like me."

"I don't think we should take Nan's-Nan too lightly," I continued. "She can be pretty feisty, I'm sure! They don't call her Nan's-Nan for nothing!"

"Are you going to ride her yourself, Kings?"

"I might ride her to get her used to being ridden again, but I'm wanting to take a young lady that I met on the beach for a ride!" I still didn't tell Fraser about finding Gay yet, or that Melody was her daughter. I'd tell him on Saturday, after I'd seen Gay in person.

After parking the car at the top of the Burrows, I carried my saddle over my shoulders, while Fraser carried the fishing gear. It felt like old times, climbing down the dunes to the beach. I started to plan how I was going to get the saddle onto Nan's-Nan's back – without frightening her, and having to chase her all over the valley! I would feed her some apples and carrots maybe, while Fraser stood in front of her and patted her neck. Then, I'd try to gently slide the saddle onto her back! Easier said than done!

When we arrived in the valley, the whole Three Cliffs herd was there! Except for Ruby, who was probably galloping across the beach or standing on guard at his cave.

As soon as a few of the horses realized that we had food, we were surrounded by half the herd, including Nan's Nan!

"Let's save most of the food for her," I reminded Fraser, as we were hemmed in by warm tickling noses and nibbling teeth.

"Okay, Kings! Let's try and get the saddle on her now, while she's occupied eating the apples!"

Now you couldn't call Nan's-Nan a wild horse! Not compared to Great Thunder and his ongoing lineage! They were of a different heritage altogether. Nan's-Nan was more like an oversize Welsh Pony! and ancient in years for a wild pony. Nonetheless, I was sure that trying to put a saddle on her back was going to be a lot harder than Fraser or I could anticipate! And it was!

She was quite happy to have her head down in the carrots. But as soon as she felt me sliding the saddle on her back, her head came up instantly. She charged and bit Fraser on the arm!

"You nasty old cow!" he shouted. I roared with laughter! But that was until she turned and started to charge me!

"Run!" I shouted, and dropping my freshly polished saddle onto the ground, we ran across the valley to the river, as fast as schoolboys! Nan's-Nan chased us to the edge of the river, while Fraser and I stood with wet feet in the middle of the gently flowing stream.

Fraser turned to me and said, "Good luck getting your saddle on that miserable old cuss!"

"She's just spooked," I said, "and she'll soon tire at this rate! I'll run in and out of the river, and she will chase me and eventually tire out!"

"And I'll stay right here!" Fraser said adamantly. So, I ran back and forth between the herd and the river, until one of us would get tired! Nan's-Nan's stamina surprised me, and I started to fear that the first to tire was going to be me!

Fraser watched in amusement, while his wild brother ran with the horses. "You always were part horse," he shouted.

Finally, Nan's-Nan got tired and slowed to a walk; and I took a few moments to catch my breath.

Suddenly, my brother passed sentence, and said, "You're on your own now, Kings!" And he began setting up the fishing gear, still standing in the safety of the river. I guess that's what you call 'once bitten twice shy.'

So, I was on my own chasing Nan's-Nan around the valley. I lifted my saddle to my shoulders and walked after her. She trotted in front of me, stopping about every hundred yards to see if I was still following. Then, off she would go again. The saddle began to feel heavier and heavier, as the feisty mare continued her trot.

"Are you ever going to stop?" I shouted. "I only want to put a saddle on your back so a nice young lady can ride you. What's wrong with that? Any other horse would be happy for the chance! Can you hear me, Nan's-Nan? Did you hear what I said, girl? Come on, I'm getting tired of this!"

It was now that she changed tactics on me! Whenever she got about fifty yards ahead of me, she would stop and turn around, and wait until I was within about ten feet of her. Then she would show me her teeth as if mocking me and take off again!

After another fifteen minutes of what now seemed like a game we were playing, she allowed me to get within a few feet of her! Dropping my saddle on the ground, I approached her slowly and began to speak to her!

"Hello, old girl! I really need your help! There is a young lady who really wants to ride a horse. She has had a difficult time in her life for a few years now! She's lost her Dad, and more recently her Grandpa. The stallions would be too big and wild, and some of the younger mares might not understand what she needs. You have always been my girl; you are the eldest and wisest of all the horses! I was a young boy when you were born and I watched you grow up over the years. I need your mother's love and experience to help this young girl. Her name is Melody, and she's a wonderful girl who loves horses."

I picked up my saddle and stood right beside her. And to my surprise, Nan's-Nan stood still and allowed me to come right up to her! I fed her an apple and patted her neck.

"Thank you, girl," I said softly. She stood almost completely still as I lifted the saddle onto her back and did up the straps. "Thank you, girl, thank you," I continued to say. I looked into her wise old eyes, and then I knew that she had heard my heart!

"What did you say to her?" Fraser shouted.

"I was just honest with her," I replied. She responded to my heart! I even got the lead rope around her neck without any resistance, and led her to the river to drink.

Fraser was still watching with amusement. "How on earth did you manage that?"

"She didn't like the taste of you, mate!" I said, laughing. "She knew not to risk taking a bite out of me!"

It was time to start fishing now. While Fraser carried the rods and gear, I led Nan's-Nan down the beach to the surf. The tide was on its way in, a perfect time to start fishing. For the first hour that we fished, Nan's-Nan stood beside us with her eyes fixed out to sea. Could she see or sense something we couldn't? In my experience with horses, I was sure she could.

"What is it, old girl? What do you see?" Maybe she could sense the past and was remembering stories of this magical place that she was a part of! Or could she feel the future in her wise heart?

She sat down on the sand to rest. And Fraser, who had now forgiven her for biting him, came over to give her a pat.

"She's actually really gentle, Kings! I think we needed to approach her on her terms!"

"You're right, Fraser! She feels and responds to our feelings and emotions!"

Fraser and I caught three bass while Nan's-Nan rested on the sand. As the tide started to come in, each time coming a little closer to her, she stood up, and we started to walk back up the beach. I told Fraser I would stay a little longer to work with her, now that she was willing to help me.

Fraser grabbed our proud catch, and stooped to gather up our fishing gear. "How about we watch the footy on match of the day when you get back, Kings? I'll pick up a few cans," he said. "And please be careful trying to ride that mare!"

"I'll be careful, and see you tonight!"

For the next few hours, I walked Nan's-Nan, up and down the beach to the dunes and back to the singing waves that told us both stories! Soon the crashing waves were singing on high, and Nan's-Nan and I stood on the pebbles at the top of Pobbles Beach.

It was time for me to ride her to get her used to someone on her back, so that Melody could ride her tomorrow. My plan had been to walk her a lot and tire her out on the sand. I had certainly done that alright! She was walking slowly now, and she wanted to stop quite often to rest. It would be a good time for me to mount her from the beach, and I led her back down the pebbles to the flat sand. It shouldn't be too hard, I thought. She's a lot smaller than the big stallions.

I suddenly remembered Heather's instructions to me, from all those years ago! "You have to work with the horse, Kingsley, not against him! Be confident and talk to him. Let him smell you and get used to your voice. The horse will feel everything you're feeling inside and react to it! So be calm and confident. Not nervous, or he will pick up on your hesitation and make it difficult for you!"

"That's what I'm doing, Heather." I spoke out loud as if she was with me.

And that's what I did! I stood and faced Nan's-Nan and said calmly but sternly, "I'm going to climb onto your back now, Nan! I would really appreciate it if you would stand still and let me mount!"

At first, she seemed to give me a blank look, as if to say, "You have walked me the whole length of the beach, and I am too tired to argue." As I looked into her big gentle eyes, I realized that they were my shallow words, not hers. Now, In her eyes, I saw an inviting smile, which welcomed and invited me to receive the gift of her kind and wise heart!

I rubbed her neck and nose, and with only a little hesitation, she allowed me to put the bit in her mouth and attach the reins.

"Thank you, Nan," I spoke lovingly. "I know that you understand me and are going to let me ride you, aren't you old girl!"

I walked to her side, and reaching for the saddle, I pushed my foot into the stirrup. With one smooth movement, I pulled myself up into the saddle. Nan shied at first, feeling my weight on her back, and then broke into a trot.

"Steady, girl. It's alright, I know this is difficult for you too!" I was quite out of practice with my riding. I leaned forward, like I used to do when I rode Great Thunder, and patted the side of her neck, and with my other hand I grabbed hold of her short mane!

She soon slowed to a walk, being reassured, by my touch, that everything was alright!

"That's it, old girl! You are doing well, aren't you! Thank you for letting me ride you, Nan!"

I sat up in the saddle now and held the reins. Then I heard Heather's words again: "Hold them low and slack, Kingsley. As you're pulling gently on the reins, cue her with your foot at the same time, on the side toward which you want to turn!"

Nan immediately responded to my cue. And our connection was so strong; it was as if we had ridden together before! We did several wide turns to the left and then to the right, as she followed the cue of my foot. And we walked up through the dunes at Pobbles over to Pennard Castle, and then down into the Three Cliffs Valley to join the other horses.

Such wonderful memories walked through the pages of my mind as I remembered 'my great friend' Thunder! The years melted away and became *today* again in my soul! And my shouts of joy echoed again through the still valley! Horses' heads lifted from the river where they drank. Swallows darted in the light wind, as if doing a swooping dance to the sweet song of the skylarks that hovered overhead like watchmen over my sacred valley! And I was welcomed home!

Halfway up the valley, Nan appeared tired, so I dismounted and led her the remainder of the way.

"You're tired, old girl, aren't you? Well you can have a rest in a few minutes when we reach the other horses." Nan nodded her head in agreement and we continued. Once we were fifty yards from the other horses, I took off the bridle but left my saddle on her back, so I didn't have the challenge of putting it on her again tomorrow.

And I said: "I'll come back with Melody so she can ride you tomorrow." Nan trotted off to spend time grazing with the herd.

It had felt so good to be riding again, even if I was riding Nan's-Nan rather than a wild stallion! And so many memories of my days with Great Thunder came galloping through my mind again! Deep within my heart, I felt the spirit of my 'great friend!' I knew that he could feel me, where he was roaming, happy and free, over the great divide. And I shouted out on the wind, "I love you, Great Thunder! And I miss you, old boy!"

And just then a gust of wind blew over me! And I heard Thunder say: "I love you too, Kings!"

Before heading back to the Frasers, I decided to drop in at Heather's and catch her up with my news of finding Gay and her daughter Melody! I felt excited as climbed up the dunes to the burrows. I pictured Heather's face and her excitement as I told her my news.

Arriving at Heather's old farm house, I knocked on the heavy wooden door. "Just a minute," she called out. I stood for what seemed like a long time waiting, and finally the door thumped open. "Oh, it's you Kingsley! It's wonderful to see you! Now, come on in and tell me your news. "

As I walked in the door, she said: "I was just talking about you yesterday to my niece, up at the stables. Have you heard anything more about Gay? I've asked around in the village, King, and nobody seems to have heard anything about her."

"I've found her, Heather! I've found her!"

"You have? Where on earth did you see her?"

"Well, I haven't actually seen her yet. But I met her daughter, Melody, down on Pobbles Beach the other day!"

"You met her daughter?"

"Yes, it was amazing! I got talking to these kids down at my old Dragon Pool, and I had a long conversation with one of them whose name was Melody. Then she said that her mother loved horses and that her name was Gay! And I thought how many people are named Gay and love horses?!"

"Only one! And how did you communicate with Gay, if she wasn't down on the beach?"

"I sent a note with Melody, and in it I asked Gay if she had a Celtic Cross necklace with a green birthstone. And the next day, Melody arrived at the beach wearing it! And Gay also wrote me a note! Oh, Heather, I'm so excited! I didn't think I was ever going to find her!"

"And you ended up meeting her daughter first!"

"Yes!"

"Oh, Kingsley! I'm so excited for you! And this calls for a celebration! Can you stay for supper?"

"Yes, Heather, of course!"

"Well, you sit yourself down and I'll put on a pot of tea. Your face was glowing at the door, Kingsley, so I knew something wonderful must have happened! This is so romantic –Gay writing you a note, and her daughter wearing the same necklace that you had bought her all those years ago! Kingsley, this is meant to be! And I know that if Maggie was here, she would tell you the same! How wonderful!"

Over supper, I was able to share my heart with Heather. I told her all my hopes and dreams! And she listened, just like Maggie used to do.

"In some ways I still think of Gay just like I did when we were young, like it was the next week or month since we said our goodbyes. We're both adults now, Heather, having lived different lives, and we both have children. Could our love have transcended time and our separate lives? I feel it has, Heather! It's like a knowing in my soul!"

"You will know for sure after you have spent time together, Kingsley. And all I would say to you – is this: just take one day at a time. And don't put any expectations on each other! Remember that you have both had different lives and you have both had families. You'll need to get to know each other again! Maybe you'll fall in love all over again? I can't help but think so, Kingsley, given the way that you have found each other! It seems it's just meant to be!"

"Why don't you go on a trip around the Gower again, Kingsley? Maggie told me how you went around the Gower together!"

"Yes, I think that would be a great way to get to know each other again, Heather! We could even go camping!"

"You mean you can't expect her to live in a cave?"

"Oh, I don't know about that, Heather! A woman finds being carried off to a cave with a wild Caveman romantic, doesn't she?" We both laughed and I almost spilt my tea.

I spent three hours with Heather before catching the bus back to Fraser's. Before I left, she gave me a small parcel from Maggie. And said it was very valuable, and would I please not tell anyone where it came from. I gave Heather my word and took the parcel.

"What could it be?" I thought, as I rode along on the bus. I would wait until I got back to Fraser's before opening it. No, I was too excited to wait! So I opened it.

Dear Kingsley,

My husband gave me this when we first got engaged and I want you to have it!

As I am writing this letter, I am convinced that Gay holds a precious love for you that has never left her heart! In some strange but sure way, I have this knowing in my heart, that you will come home one day looking to find the woman whose love has never left your heart! Give her this ring, Kingsley!

Always have the courage to follow your heart, for out of your heart flows the wellspring of life!

I love you always, Kingsley! And I have prayed to our God, and asked Him to help you find what your heart is searching for!

Love Maggie

No words could describe how I felt when I opened the little blue velvet box and found Maggie's engagement ring with its emerald stone on it. Evening Emerald! And I felt like God Himself had put his arms around me! I thanked Him for helping me to find Gay and for giving me Maggie's engagement ring. And I asked Him to go before me, to be with me, as I asked Gay to come on a trip around the Gower. "Help her to say yes, God!"

By the time I got back to the house, it was too late to watch the match of the day. Fraser and Lynn had gone to bed. But there was a note on the table to tell me Liverpool had won their game!"

Chapter Sixteen
Friday's Child

I was up early and had breakfast with Fraser and Lynn. "Don't forget to keep Sunday free," Lynn said, as they headed off to work. "We'll be going out for a meal, and Dad and Mary will be coming too."

"Sounds great," I said, as they closed the door. But today was Friday! The day I would see Melody and take her for a ride on Nan's-Nan! And get another note from Gay, I hope! And I was soon on my way to catch the bus from Swansea.

The Pennard #14 finally arrived and I raced upstairs to sit in the front seat. I felt like a young lad again! I had always sat upstairs in the front seat of the double-decker when I was a lad. And today, I was just as excited! No, more excited!

"Why, are you as excited as a young boy?" the old lady behind me asked.

"I am indeed, Madam! I'm a 40-year-old boy!"

"And I'm a 75-year-old girl!" she echoed back.

"Then the world is as it should be!" said the conductor, laughing as he checked our tickets.

As we rode along the narrow lanes, I thought of Nan's-Nan, with my saddle already on her back. "I'm sure glad that I managed to get it on her yesterday!" I said to myself. "I think I'll take Melody up to the stables right away, and get her fitted with some riding wear! Hmm...I'm meeting her at the Dragon Pool at noon. I hope Nan's-Nan will still be in the valley when we get there. Sometimes the horses wander off to find a fresh grazing area and can travel a fair distance away. But there was plenty of grazing left in the valley yesterday, so the herd should still be there!

The bus arrived at Pennard Cliffs, and I walked along West Cliff Road to Pobbles. It was a glorious summer morning! Nature sang the most beautiful chorus that reflected back to me the hope and joy within my heart! As Maggie had shared in one of her letters, my life was part of a wonderful play, and God was the Director! I had been given a script to read and my heart recognized the lines. And even an engagement ring from Maggie to give to Gay! Was this all part of this 'great play' that I was starring in? I didn't know exactly how my part in the play was going to turn out, but I could trust the Director! He could see 'the bigger picture,' and he was putting all the intricate pieces of my script together. I thanked God for his directing!

My life had changed! Along with the people and circumstances in it! But amidst all the changes, with their joys and sorrows, victories and failures, this wonderful truth has always remained: "I, the Lord, do not change!" sayeth the Lord.

And this morning, I remembered God's love and faithfulness to me over the years, especially when I lived on the cliffs and beaches as a young man. My God did not change! He is the one thing that has remained constant in my life!

[Hebrews 13 vs 8, Jesus Christ is the same yesterday, today, and forever!]

My God does not change like the shifting shadows of the evening, when darkness approaches. Like the rising sun in the morning, you, Oh God, are sure and on time! For you, the night shines as bright as the day! Your attributes, oh God, are the same as in ages past. They sparkle in the night sky, and the guardians of the night proudly proclaim your faithfulness! And sing of your greatness! Your love, your power, your faithfulness and truth, remain unchanged! Lying evil men run away from your brightness. While good Godly men bask in your brightness and shine after you! You, oh Lord, are my secret place of refuge, where evil cannot touch me, but blows away like a dark cloud in the distance. You are my strength, and my faithful helper. My glorious sword of victory! Thank you for loving me with your 'perfect and everlasting love!'

I arrived at the Dragon Pool, and there was Melody!

"Kingsley! Kingsley!" she shouted, running to me and jumping into my arms. "I get to ride a horse today, don't I?"

"Yes, you do! But first, we have to go to the stables and get you a riding hat and a pair of boots."

"Okay let's go!" she replied, pulling my hands.

"I have to go now," she said to the other kids.

And we headed over to Aunt Pearl to tell her where we were going.

"Don't forget your lunch, Melody! Thanks, Kingsley, for taking her. All she talked about yesterday was the horses and how she got to name them all! Oh, and here's a letter from Gay!"

I thanked her and put the letter in my pocket. We left the beach and started our climb up the dunes to the Burrows and then onto the stables. When we arrived, Heather was there visiting with her niece, who now ran the riding school. I introduced Melody to Heather. And Heather took a special interest in her right away! She helped her try on different hats and boots, and even found her a riding jacket that fitted perfectly. This gave me some time to read my letter from Gay. I opened the envelope slowly.

Dear Kingsley,

Thank you for sending the flowers back with Melody on Wednesday. Irises! You remembered that they are my favourite flowers! Do you remember you once told me that they were the same colour as my eyes? And I blushed bright red? ("Yes, I remember," I said, and I smiled as I continued to read.)

         Kingsley Ross Hill

Yesterday was a very productive day, Kingsley! We went into Cardiff for the day, as you know. And my sister Pearl helped me to find a nice house for Melody and I to live in! It's bright and roomy, but best of all, it's within walking distance of my work and Melody's school!

I want you to know, Kingsley, that all Melody talked about yesterday was the horses! She so reminds me of you and me. Do you remember when we went to visit Thunder Spring in the cave? We fed her apples and carrots and brought her water from the river. ("Yes, I remember.")

And I understand that you and Melody are going to ride a horse today! I'm trusting you two to behave! And not to try to ride any wild stallions! I trust you with Melody, Kingsley. I hope you both have a wonderful day. I know you will!

About Saturday. I can't wait to see you! Let's meet at Maggie's old store and walk up to Cefn Bryn. And remember, you don't have to bring anything; I will make a picnic. How about we meet at 10 o'clock? See you there.

As I finished my letter, Heather and Melody came out of the tack barn. "Wow! Look at you, Melody," I said, seeing her face beaming from under her riding hat!

"She's all fitted out," Heather said. "Ready to ride a horse, aren't you Melody?"

"Yes, Heather, I am! And thank you for letting me use the riding gear."

"That's quite alright, Melody! And it was lovely to meet you! Now you make sure that Kingsley doesn't put you on a wild stallion!"

"I will," Melody replied.

"And I won't!" I answered Heather, laughing.

"Come on, Melody, let's go and find your horse!" And we walked back across the Burrows, and down through the dunes to the beach.

We found Nan's-Nan in the valley with the other horses. "You already have the saddle on her!" Melody exclaimed excitedly.

"Yes, I came and put it on her yesterday. Now, I'll tell you what we're going to do! I'm going to put the lead rope around her neck, and we're going to lead her away from the other horses so she doesn't get distracted."

I gently lifted the rope over Nan's head while Melody gave her a carrot.

I then gave the rope to Melody. "Now you talk to her in a firm and confident voice, and say: 'Come on Nan.' And pull slowly but firmly on the rope. Hopefully she will follow you!"

"Come on, Nan," Melody said firmly, pulling on the rope at the same time. And Nan turned and began to follow!

"That's it," I said. "Just lead her slowly and keep talking to her. She needs to get used to your voice!"

Once we were a fair distance away from the herd, I took the lead rope from Melody and got her to stand in front of Nan.

"Now, here's some more carrots to feed her. Now rub the side of her head gently – yes, just like that! And give her some nice firm pats on her neck, and keep standing close to her. That way she can smell you and get used to your scent. And that helps to keep her calm while you are talking to her. Now I'm going to give you the rope again, Melody. And I want you to lead her onto the beach. I'm going to walk behind, so that she can get more used to just seeing you."

"What if she runs and I let go of the rope?"

"It's okay if she does, and you can let go of the rope. But there's no reason why she should run! Just keep talking to her, and be confident; horses can feel what we are feeling on the inside."

"That's what my mum says, King!"

"Alright Melody, keep leading her out onto the beach, and in a few minutes, we can stop and help you climb into the saddle."

"Oh, I think I'm going to be nervous, King! What if she bucks me off?"

"Now you listen, Melody! There is nothing to be afraid of! I rode her yesterday myself! This is what I want you to do. I want you to stop pulling on the rope and see if she stops."

"She stopped, King!"

"That's good! Now you keep standing in front of her and pat her on the neck. Here's a few more carrots to feed her."

"King, look! She's pushing her nose into my jacket!" Melody laughed.

"That's great!" I said. That's her way of saying hello and getting used to your scent! Once a horse recognizes your scent, she will never forget it!"

"You mean Nan will always remember me, King?"

"That's right, she will never forget you."

"That's really cool, King!"

"It is, isn't it! And that's why we must always be kind! Because horses, just like us, remember who is kind and who is unkind to them!"

"That's like in my class at school, King. I remember who is kind to me, and who is mean. And I don't want to sit next to someone who doesn't like me and is mean to me."

"That's right! So, you can see how important it is to be kind, can't you?"

"Yes, but what about the bullies in my class? We have one boy, Mark Price, and he's a real bully. My mum said to be nice to him three times. And then, if he's still mean after that, to kick him in the balls!"

Melody and I looked at each other and roared with laughter!

"Quiet," I said. "We might frighten Nan! But I agree with your mum! There is no place for bullying! And if Mark Price ever

lays a finger on you, you have my blessing to kick him in the balls!"
We laughed again, and Nan's-Nan neighed!

"She agrees with us, King!"

"I think she does!"

"Now, let's get you riding on her back, shall we? Come here and stand with me at her side and I'm going to help you mount."

"No, King, I don't think I can do it!"

"I'm sure, you can, Melody!" I reassured her. "Do you remember when she pushed her nose into your jacket and sniffed your scent?"

"Yes, it tickled!

"Well, that was her trying to tell you that she's your friend!"

"Well, if she's my friend, then I'm sure I can!"

"That's the spirit, Melody. You just have to be confident and trust! Remember Nan feels everything you're feeling inside!"

"Yes, I remember, King."

"Now, I'm holding the lead rope, so you are not going anywhere, are you Nan?" I said, in a strong confident voice.

"Now put your left foot in the stirrup, like this, Melody, and I'm going to give you a boost up, by pushing on your right foot like this. Now we are going to try and do this in one smooth movement. That's it. Keep your foot in the stirrup. And as I push underneath your right foot, I want you to hold onto the front of the saddle, and pull yourself on."

"Like this?" she cried.

"Yes, just like that! You're on, Melody! You're sitting in the saddle!"

"Look at me, King! I'm sitting on top of Nan's-Nan!

"You are, aren't you! Well done, Melody!"

"Now let's go for a walk, shall we? I want you to sit up straight in the saddle, and I'm going to lead you across the beach! We won't try and trot, because she needs to get used to you first. The reins are for you to guide her in the direction you want her to go."

"No, don't make her canter, King! I've watched my mum canter, then gallop, and she goes really fast!"

"We're just going to walk her today, Melody. She needs to get used to you being on her back. We must remember that even though she is gentle and used to being around people, she's still a wild pony! We have to go slowly with her. If she feels comfortable, because she knows that we respect her feelings, then she will give us her trust! Just like with humans, trust must be earned!"

"I understand, King! It's just like getting to know someone. It takes time to really get to know what they are like!" "That's right, Melody! I couldn't have said it better myself!"

Melody's face lit up underneath her riding hat. "I'm glad that you're my friend, King!"

"And I'm glad that you're my friend too!"

As we walked across the sands, I said a quiet prayer to God, thanking him for helping me to get Melody safely onto Nan's back, and for the fun she was already having! She looked so happy and proud. Nan's-Nan was the perfect horse for Melody to ride. We walked all the way to Oxwich Beach and back!

While we were on our way back to Pobbles, we heard the thunder of hooves behind us! And it was Ruby on his afternoon gallop! And Nan was uneasy for a minute or two, while Ruby thundered across the sand in front of us. Then when he approached his cave, he slowed to a trot and stopped at the entrance.

"Wow, he's a fast stallion, isn't he?" I said to Nan, trying to calm her down.

Melody was calm on her back, and she said: "It's alright, Nan! Ruby won't hurt us. He's just going for his gallop!" Nan soon calmed down, and we continued our way along the sand.

And Melody said: "One day I want to ride a horse and gallop as fast as Ruby!"

"And it will be exciting," I assured her.

"Can we go and visit Aunt Pearl, King, so she can see me riding Nan's-Nan?

"Yes, and then we can have our lunch," I said, feeling hungry.

As we approached Pearl at Pobbles, Melody shouted: "Look at me, Auntie Pearl, look at me! I'm riding Nan's-Nan!"

"So, this is the famous Nan's-Nan," Pearl replied.

"Yes, she's called Nan's-Nan because she's old and wise!"

"That's great Melody, and you are riding her so well!"

I helped Melody to dismount onto the beach, and we sat and ate our lunch with Pearl.

"Why is Nan just standing still and watching us, King?" asked Melody.

"She's tired, and probably hungry too."

"Here you are, Nan," Melody said, feeding her half of her sandwich.

"Looks like you have a friend for life, Melody," Pearl said.

"I think she does," I echoed.

After lunch, Melody and I walked Nan back to be with the herd in the valley. "Why can't I ride her back?" Melody asked.

"Because she's tired and needs to rest!"

"Yes, she can't get too tired, King, can she? Otherwise, I might not be able to ride her again!"

"That's right Melody! It's important to know when a horse needs to rest."

Before getting too close to the herd, I made Nan stand still while I showed Melody how to undo the saddle straps and slide the saddle off Nan's back. I took off the lead rope, and we both said: "Goodbye Nan! We will see you again soon. "

"And thank you for letting Melody ride on your back," I added.

Nan neighed gently and nodded her head.

"Look, King, she's acknowledging what we said!"

"She is, isn't she! Horses are very intelligent animals!"

We walked back to Pearl, and it was time for Melody to go.

"Bye, Kingsley!" she said, rushing over to me and giving me a big hug! "Thank you for helping me to ride Nan's-Nan!"

"Yes, thank you, Kingsley," Pearl said. "We will see you again soon. I understand you will be seeing Gay tomorrow? I hope that you both have a wonderful reunion and time together!"

"Thank you, Pearl! I replied.

And I began my long walk back to the bus. It wasn't really that long, but my legs were tired from all the walking across the sand; they felt heavy as I climbed the dunes and walked along the cliff-tops. But in my heart, I felt light and happy! It had been such a wonderful day! And tomorrow, I would be meeting Gay! And I read my letter again as I rode on the bus.

Chapter Seventeen
A Picnic on Cefn Bryn

I raced to the shower, having slept in! Of all the days to sleep in, it had to be today! I put on my best casual clothes. We would be walking and picnicking – so you don't need your Sunday best, Kings, I said to myself as I stood in front of the mirror.

Locking the door behind me, I headed off to Swansea to catch the bus. But I'd just missed one! And there would not be another #14 for 45 minutes! I quickly calculated the time, and I realized that with the walk along the cliff-tops and climbing up the dunes, I wouldn't be able to meet Gay on time! We were meeting at Maggie's old store in Penmaen at 12 noon. There must be another bus that could get me to Penmaen village on time? I asked one of the bus drivers who had just arrived on another Swansea bus.

"Yes," he said, "if you catch the #18 Rhossilli bus, it also goes to Penmaen. There's one in 25 minutes and it will get you there at 11:50."

"Thanks!" I said, relieved. I had 25 minutes before the bus left. So I decided to go into the Swansea Market and have a cup of coffee at David Griffiths' cafe. I didn't need to buy my lunch today as Gay was making us a picnic!

David wasn't at the shop, he had gone to visit someone at one of the other businesses in the market. I sat and had a coffee alone. Saturdays are the busiest day of the week in the market, and the place was buzzing with people already. I'm glad I'm not queueing up for welsh cakes today, I thought. There must be fifteen people in line! It was always worth the wait, of course – once you bit into that lovely warm cake! After finishing my coffee and downing an ice bun, I headed off to the bus.

I was on my way to see Gay – after more than twenty years! What would it be like, I thought, to see her today? What would she look like? Would she still have her warm, fun-loving personality? Or would the years have scarred and jaded her?

In my thoughts of her, in my far-away home on Vancouver Island, I'd always pictured her as being much the same, with just a few changes as she had aged. As, indeed, I had aged! But maturity can be something lovely! Especially when you can love somebody in all the fullness of it! At least, that's how I felt inside! I had all this wonderful love and life experience to lavish on somebody! I hoped and dreamed it would be the same for Gay!

It's interesting how, when we have been away from people we love for a long time, we imagine them as being the same as when we left them! As if in some strange way, 'that time' would leave them unchanged! Or maybe change them to be even more appealing to us than in our past memories!

But the truth is, I really didn't know what to expect, other than this perfect and mature version of my "beautiful Princess"!

So many are the tides that have come in, and washed over the times and places where Gay and I walked and loved! Yet in my soul, these precious memories are alive and awake, like singing mornings! And I feel her love in my heart, as if it were only yesterday when we stared into each other's eyes, and caressed our souls in a way that we would never do again with another human being! Oh, I could write poems, sing songs of the precious love that we found, but this poet would only run out of lines.

I remembered Heather's advice from yesterday. Try not to have expectations, Kingsley! Or at least have realistic ones!

How can one not have expectations, when one's soul 'shouts out' in passion! And when the biggest and most powerful wave has swept across the beach of our soul, with hopes and dreams. Is this not real? Of course, it is! And to deny it is death!

Love reigns supreme over all else! When you find it, you must embrace it! And hold it fast and not let it go! Ride on its back like a wild stallion, and don't fear its power! For love is life! And it's meant to be lived in all its colours and passions! For God Himself is love! He showed me that a long time ago, when I lived on the cliffs and beaches of the Gower Peninsula. And no wave can wash it away!

And as far as living in 'reality,' my shouting soul say's this is the only reality for me!

I know that Heather was only hoping for the best for me. Not wanting hurt or disappointment to visit my heart! But I will be myself and see what unfolds today. Of course I have to be passionate! And follow my hopes and dreams, and find love again! I have to learn the longings and yearnings of my soul, and reach for them.

Our human soul knows what it is missing. Maybe some hearts would settle, and deny the lies of compromise, and sacrifice their own hearts. That, my friends, is not the genuine article; it's a counterfeit! I will not settle or compromise, by not seeking and finding what I know is there!

God has given me "promises" in his Word! And I am claiming them!

[*Matthew 7, vs 7 and 8, Ask, and you shall receive, seek, and you will find; knock, and the door will be opened to you. For everyone who asks receives, and he who seeks finds, and to him who knocks it shall be opened.*]

The bus arrived in Penmaen village and stopped close to Maggie's old store. And there was Gay! Dressed in a lovely blue summer dress that was clinging to her beautiful figure! Her hair was still long and flowing, as I'd so often pictured it, and now she had blond highlights that shone in the sunlight. And her eyes were still that beautiful violet, and they sparkled as she looked into mine!

"Kingsley!"

"Gay!"

We both spoke at the same time, and Gay had a bright rose blush on her soft white skin, and there was trembling in my voice. We both tried to speak at the same time again, and there was nothing else to do but laugh! Which soothed our nervousness.

"I'm Kingsley," I said jokingly, and reached out to shake her hand.

"And I'm Gay," she replied, giggling, and she shook my hand.

Then I gently pulled her towards me and hugged her tightly! "Oh, Gay! Is it really you?"

And trembling in our embrace, she said: "Kingsley, is it really you?"

"It is," I whispered, as I breathed in the lovely scent of her long, flowing hair.

"And yes, it's me," she whispered back, giving me a gentle kiss on my cheek. And we held each other for the longest time, as the weeks, months, and years that we had lived separately flowed through our caressing fingers into each other's souls, as we became one again!

"Oh, my King, I've missed you so much!"

"I've missed you so much, too, my Gay!"

And it was just like it had been all those years ago! We were together again! And our souls sang a song, and its chorus we knew so well!" There was no need for words! Our hearts did all the talking.

"Do you remember?" I whispered.

"Yes, Kingsley. Our hearts are talking, aren't they? "Kingsley. I've missed you, and I don't know what to say!"

Slowly, I let go of our embrace and looked deep into her eyes that shone with tears and love.

I kissed her tears. "There is nothing you need to say."

"You are so beautiful," I said, running my fingers through her soft hair, and feeling my own tears leave my heart and roll down my cheeks.

She kissed my tears away with her warm, soft lips. And the whole world stopped! And my soul began to sing! I vowed not to wash my face again, not until she gave me another kiss! Just like I had done when we'd first met!

"I've made us a picnic," she said, smiling.

"May I carry your basket, and escort you up the Bryn?" I asked. She gave me her hand and we walked.

"Kingsley, do you remember how we would walk, and then stop and look into each other's eyes?"

"You mean like this?"

"Yes, like this," she whispered. And I cupped her face in my hands and we fell deep into each other's eyes!

We held hands all the way to the top of Cefn Bryn, only letting them go to climb over the large stones and to cross the singing streams. Our hands would reach out and find each other again. Oh, to feel her hand in mine; her fingers gently squeezing and caressing, and melting the years away! My heart believed again that she was mine! Oh, my Gay! I never want to let go of your hand again!

As we walked, we spoke in silence, our souls understanding each word!

Then Gay broke the silence. "Well, my Prince. Would you like to climb up on top of Kingsley's Stone, and have our picnic up there?"

"Yes, my Princess! From there we can look out across our Kingdom, and see the "Gower of the Hills."

"The Gower of the Hills," she echoed. .

"Yes, the Gower of the Hills is a place apart! It starts at Loughor. When you stand by the ruin of the Norman Castle on the little hill of Loughor and look to the north, you realize that you are in a new land. The village of Loughor itself, was once the Roman fort of Leucarum, guarding the river crossing. The Normans followed the Romans into the Gower of the Hills, and nineteenth century industry came to the area. But there is no question that once you are at Loughor, you are well out of the Gower Peninsula."

"Oh, Kingsley," Gay said, "I love hearing you explain about the history of our land! It's like listening to you read to me!"

"Thank you," I said. "I've always felt passionate about all of the Gower, where my father and I roamed. He gave me such a gift in teaching me so much! Look, Gay! You can see from where we are sitting, the Loughor Estuary, winding its way northward into the hills."

"Yes, I can see it! And it looks silver with the sun reflecting on it, and with the grey shadows of the hills behind it! Are those hills the "Gower of the Hills?""

"Yes, they are, and up there are some of my most sacred places! There are ancient ruins and castles, with stories crying out in the wild winds, where kestrels hover and ravens dance. There are secret valleys with villages and farms, and little chapels that stand on lonely hills. That was the area that was first swept by the last great Welsh religious revival! It was at Mariah Chapel, at Loughor, that the revivalist Evan Roberts started this celebrated spiritual fire-storm that spread across all of Wales! If you look out from here when it's high tide, the Loughor Estuary looks like a magnificent lake rather than a part of the wild sea. Once I sat up here under a full moon and a red sunset. I could see the whole estuary sparkling like a big ruby ring!"

"Will the girl you marry wear a ruby ring, my Prince?"

Yes, she will, my eyes answered back.

"Oh, Kingsley! You've got to bring me up here on a full moon!"

I will, my heart answered back. "I will!" And I put my arm around Gay's waist as we ate our picnic upon my stone. I continued to tell her about the Gower of the Hills.

"Tell me more," she said, "tell me more!"

I felt so grand, sharing the stories of my exploring and adventures with her!

"Is there a special castle that you have spent time exploring on the Gower of the Hills?" she asked.

"They are all special! But there is one, in particular, that has reached out and talked to me! It's called 'Castel Meurig'! Castle

Meurig stands on the highest point in Gower of the Hills, at 1,226 ft. There, in the heart of the high hills, is the one spot on a clear day where you can see over the full extent of the official Gower. If you look to the south, you'll see a flash of the sea, which shines like a permanent flash of lightning breaking through the clouds. And you can also see the line of Cefn Bryn where we are now, and also Llanmadoc Hill, running out into the winding Loughor Estuary. Eastward lies the deep trench of the River Tawe and the dark mountains of the Central Coalfield, Gowers Barrier."

You can see all the landmarks from up there, and even make a few of your own! All the lonely little villages curve up towards you, like little children running to their father! You want to pick them up in your arms like God, and hold them as your own!

"Oh Kingsley, will you take me there? I want to share it with you!"

"I'd like that too," I said, holding her more tightly.

We spent the whole day and evening on Cefn Bryn. Just walking and talking, and sharing our hearts. And Gay told me, in detail, about her life. And just before the night clouds walked across the horizon wearing their black capes, we climbed back up on my stone, where I recited a poem that I'd written when I'd lived on the beaches and in the caves.

♪❋

TWILIGHT STILL

When the sun tilts and sizzles into the sea,
all nature watches, as still as can be.
The sparrow hawk moves his head from side to side,
and says, look!
The sun's going into the sea!
There is a time before the darkness
but it is after the day's brightness

Kingsley Ross Hill

when my soul stands still,
Twilight Still.

The sun, she lays down her head
still glowing through her blankets
upon the western sky. She is still
before she dreams in the shadows.
Twilight Still.

The sleeping hours of the day
have been lived and have gone.
They lie still in my memory song,
Twilight Still.

The night clouds they come,
wearing their silent silver gowns,
and the meadowlark is quiet below.
I watch as the moon races the silence
Over the hill, and it is now that my soul knows
It is Twilight still,
Twilight still – Twilight still.

© *Kingsley Ross Hill*

After I finished reciting my poem, we looked out across the Loughor Estuary, where the tide had now come in, making the whole estuary look like a lake!

It was then that Gay said to me: "Do you remember when we said goodbye to each other, and I asked you to send your love with me, otherwise I couldn't go?"

"Yes, I remember, Gay. Like it was only yesterday!"

"Well, Kingsley. Your love did come with me, and it's never left my heart! And I came looking for you, and I couldn't find you," she cried.

"I know," I said. "I read your letters that you left with Maggie. And you have found me now, my love! And I have been waiting for your love to come back to me, Gay! And we've found each other again, haven't we?"

"Yes, Kingsley, we have! And I still love you so much!"

"I love you too, my Princess!

"Where do we go from here, Kingsley? I can't lose you again!"

"You won't," I assured her. "We are going to take one day, and one season, at a time, and everything will work out. We just have to have faith!"

We walked back down the Bryn by moonlight, and then rode the bus to where Gay and Melody were staying at the caravan site in Reynoldston. The same bus would take me back to Swansea.

"When can I see you again?" Gay asked before getting off the bus.

"I have a family commitment tomorrow," I said. And Gay had a commitment to visit her mum on Monday. So we arranged to meet at the same place on Tuesday, 10 a.m., at Maggie's old shop.

"Bye, my Prince," she said, kissing me.

"Bye, my Princess, see you on Tuesday!"

Chapter Eighteen

Hearts in the Hills

*I*woke up Sunday morning as if I was in a dream. Only it wasn't a dream! We had found each other again! And although I wanted to see Gay again as soon as I could, these next two days would give me a chance to think and plan. All I knew was that Gay would be returning to Cardiff in three weeks to go back to her job, and Melody would go back to school. And in just over a month, I would be returning to Canada, to my work and life there. Only I didn't want to return without Gay! My heart shouted out to me: "I don't want to lose her again!"

Suddenly, there was a knock on my bedroom door. It was Fraser, excited for us to start our day. I'd have to think more about Gay and I tonight when I had some more quiet time after our busy day.

"It's 9 a.m. already, Kings" my brother said.

Nine a.m.! Wow! I'd sure enjoyed a long sleep of sweet dreams about Gay!

"We're picking up Dad and Mary at 10 a.m.," my brother continued, "and Lynn has made us a great breakfast!"

"I'll be right down," I said, and I quickly got dressed. At the breakfast table, Lynn shared that Dad had said he would take us anywhere I wanted to go!

"That's great!" I said, as my cup of hot tea and a rare cooked breakfast slowly woke me from my sweet nighttime dreams. And I felt very touched that this Sunday was going to be so focused on me! Where I wanted to go and what I wanted to do. The truth was I didn't really care where we went so long as we were all together!

And I just felt so happy and excited about Gay and I! My hopes and dreams were starting to come true!

"So where do you think you would like to go, Kings?" my brother asked. "Dad said he would take us anywhere as far as West Wales!"

"Where would *you* like to go?" I asked. "I'm just looking forward to spending the day with all of you, and connecting with everyone again."

"How about we ask Dad?" I said. "He'd be pleased if I asked him to take us where he'd like to go...."

"Good idea, Kings! He will be happy if you do that," both Lynn and Fraser answered back.

My dad was much like me in his sense of adventure, and in his interest of history and culture. And especially archeology – going out on adventures to find treasures from the past!

When I was a boy, when most of my classmates were running around playing cowboys and Indians, or pretending to be part of the American Civil War, I was out with my dad, using metal detectors over ancient battle fields of the Romans and Normans and Saxons! My dad drew actual maps of where he thought these battles had taken place. We found Roman coins by the dozens, and medieval swords and helmets and shields! Dad even found a Saxon battle helmet that was almost in perfect condition! There were so many artifacts that we had to bury them in the bottom of the garden, so that the authorities wouldn't come and confiscate them, in the name of the Queen. She has enough treasure, don't you think?

My dad and I went further back than the Normans and Saxons even. We found cavemen and animal remains, in the caves around where we lived, that went back to prehistoric times! My greatest finds that I can share with the public are a Saber-toothed tiger's tooth and a throwing spear with a flint point that I found in one of the caves. And the other greatest find, which nothing else compares with, is an ancient manuscript wrapped in animal fur that

I found when I was 12 years old. My father took it away, and said he would give it back to me when I was old enough to appreciate it.

So back to the present time, I will ask dad where he would like to go today. And with his interest in history and culture, I can be sure that we will be going somewhere interesting.

After breakfast, we headed over to Dad's house, and he was already warming up the car when we arrived. And his partner Mary had packed one of her great picnics.

Yes, it was going to be a full and exciting day!

"Well, Kings! Where do you want to go, eh?" asked my dad. "That's how that lot speaks over there, don't they, Kings, eh?

"Yes, Dad! They can't speak the Queen's English over there!"

"No, I gather they can't, Old Son!" We both roared with laughter.

It was great to be enjoying Dad's humour again! I realized how much I had missed it!

"Well, old chap! You haven't answered my question yet. Where would you like to go in this fine land?"

"Well, I've thought about it, Dad. I'd like *you* to choose where we're going. I'm just happy to be spending time with you!" And then Mary squeezed my arm in approval, while Dad turned away for a minute so he didn't show his tears.

He turned around again and said, "Gower of the Hills! Let's go to the Gower of the Hills!"

My heart was thrilled as I heard him say Gower of the Hills; it connected him and I in a special way! Dad and I had a great history of father and son experiences up in those hills.

As we drove along, everyone wanted to hear about my experiences with the horses. Fraser had told them of my adventures riding Nan's-Nan.

"So, you're taming an old mare, this time, are you Old Son? Rather than another wild stallion?"

"Yeah, there won't be another horse like Great Thunder, Dad! He was one in many lifetimes! And he's ridden on a wave to a distant shore now. But his spirit still chases the wind from Pobbles to Oxwich Bay!"

The narrow road began to climb to the foothills and we were surrounded by such haunting beauty that it called out to me, deep within my soul.

I answered its call: "Yes! I hear you! I am as Welsh as the rolling hills!"

And I could feel the excitement in my father's voice as he talked of times and discoveries past. And today, like me, he anticipated finding new adventures.

I wrote my father a poem from my heart!

♪✳

MY FATHER'S HEART

In my father's heart, I am kept as a treasure!
Safely protected by his love and pride!
And he brings me out on those cold and miserable days,
and I warm his heart and make him smile like the laughing sun.
He celebrates with me my successes,
and encourages me not to fail!
And when I do, he finds a way to lift me up,
and again I find the strength to pull up my sail!
And when I see my father's smile,
and the pride sparkling in his eyes,
I can sail out on any tide, and jump the waves of the storm!
And on any shore that I may land,
I am safe and secure to be who I am!
I never have to run and hide, because I have been
taught at my father's side.

© Kingsley Ross Hill

We continued to wind our way up and up, into the singing Gower of the Hills. A new adventure was upon us.

For several miles now, I had observed the River Tawe, from where I sat in the honoured front seat of my father's car. The most sacred seat! Given to the Clan Member of our family who had most recently been away and missed! We all took our turns sitting in the sacred seat of my father's car, as we returned home from our wanderings in the outside world. Our outside world was anywhere beyond the deep trench of the River Tawe and the dark mountains of the Central Coalfield to the east, where our culture and traditions might not prevail.

My father always told me, "When you know and understand where you came from, you will never lose yourself in a place where your heart doesn't live!" I have found this to be true.

And whenever I have been away to where my heart doesn't live, I return home safely to the Gower. I know that it has been my father's love and pride watching over me, protecting me. His love is as tall as the Camarthenshire Vans – the pillars of the north.

We now reached the village of Felindre, and Lynn and Mary needed to pee.

"They shouldn't have drunk all that tea," my father said. "Sorry, Love, you will have to find a tree!"

Behind Felindre runs the River Lliw, which cuts back into the moors that rise northwards to their highest point. Dad stopped the car again on the moors as we visited a herd of wild ponies. Lynn and Mary fed them part of their picnic lunch, while Dad, Fraser and I kept our lunch for ourselves.

The ponies were used to people stopping and having their lunch. One or two of the mares looked at my brother and I like expectant dogs waiting for their treats. Fraser and I had to push them away as we guarded and ate our salmon sandwiches, and our Welsh cakes that Mary had lovingly packed into brown paper bags that even had our names on them.

The ponies were as friendly as I'd seen in any herd. I had a vision of Gay, Melody and I naming them. I would have to bring them up here.

Up here in the hills, I desired to share with my father my new hopes and dreams that had been born since finding Gay. Dad looked at me, knowing that I wanted to talk. But we weren't alone, so it would have to wait.

It was time we were on our way again, my father said, and we all got back into the car. And a horse almost came with us; I had to close the door on his nose.

The road now took us to the wide-open spaces of Mynyddy Y Gwair – the Mountain of High Pastures. Up here, the green and rolling meadows were so splendid, that you couldn't help feeling like one of God's children. At any moment, you think you might see God Himself walking over one of the hills to meet you! And today, in a way, He did! He met me through my father, who stopped the car and asked me to follow him.

"The rest of you stay around here," he said. "I want to talk to our Kings alone," and I followed my father up to a lonely hill.

All the hills look solitary up here! Even when standing with each other! But this hill was surrounded by four other hills, each one guarding a different direction. Like protecting Angels, they cut off the breeze so that dad and I stood in a still and silent place.

Quietly we stood together amidst the silently shouting hills. It was as if my father and I waited within our souls for them to be silent. Then my father said what he always said when he wanted me to share my heart.

"Well, boy?" And he would say no more, not for hours, until I spoke.

I remained silent for a while, examining the thoughts of my heart. Then I spoke. And I told my father of my broken life, the painful sting of loneliness and strife. And he listened and thought. And then he listened and thought some more. And the hills were listening too.

Then he said: "'You needed to come home, boy, and heal your heart. The Shepherd still has a great plan for you." That was the only time I heard my father talk of God! But that was enough! Because, my father had heard my heart!

This opened the door for me to talk to him about Gay and how I'd found her again. And of Melody, and finding the seahorses in the Dragon Pool; something my dad and I had done when I was Melody's age.

He said only five words, smiling: "That is a wonderful plan!"

And I said: "I love you, Dad!"

And he smiled again. And I walked back to the car with my father, with his approval of my plans, and I stood tall again, like a man!

We spent the rest of our day exploring Penlle'r Castell, which means 'The Summit of the Place of the Castle.'

We walked over the complex of mounds and ditches, which is all that remains of the old stronghold – which the Welsh call 'Castell Meurig,' Dad reminded us.

But even though little remains of Castell Meurig, its ghosts run free and ride the strong winds that blow and tell the stories of where the castle once stood. Today, my father and I looked out together at the view from the highest part of The Gower of the Hills!

And Dad said: "We must soon be going, as the ghost soldiers of Castell Meurig will be soon returning."

"Come on, let's get out of here," Mary said, half frightened at my father's words. And we made it back down to the car without seeing a ghost.

We drove back down from the eastern boundary of Gower that runs along the River Tawe southwards towards Swansea. I was reminded of a fond boyhood memory as I stared at the Tawe's dark and murky water.

"Why is the Tawe always muddy brown, Dad?" I would ask, and he would say that it was the colour of Wales, with its coal, rain and soot.

And my brother Fraser and I would catch eels in its muddy mouth in Swansea, where it spat into the sea. And we would mail any miserable neighbour an eel through their letterbox if they dared to be less than friendly. One day, Fraser and I mailed old Mrs. Voisey three eels for frowning on such a lovely day! And she was soon knocking on the door of our house, all ready to give my father the news of our transgressions. It was a while before she stopped talking, and my father couldn't get a word in edgewise. Then she finally stopped talking, as Fraser and I listened behind the door.

And my father said: "Yes, I shall talk to my boys, and tell them that next time you would prefer a hamster rather than an eel!"

We were now approaching the outskirts of Swansea again. Lynn reminded us that we were eating out tonight.

"Where shall we have supper?" my dad asked.

"How about the Indian Curry House?" I said, knowing it was Dad's and Fraser's favourite. We enjoyed a nice meal there, and we finished our evening with a famous Joe's Ice Cream! (The best ice cream I've ever tasted, I must add!)

It had been a wonderful day connecting with my family. And especially the time I'd been able to share with Dad! He seemed to always know my heart! Even when we hadn't seen each other for so long. By the time we got back home, I was tired and I headed off to bed.

Chapter Nineteen
Monday's Dreams

Fraser and Lynn headed off to work, and I was glad to have the day to myself with nothing planned. I needed to do some thinking about my hopes and dreams regarding Gay. After breakfast, I walked into Swansea, as usual, and bought myself a lunch in the market, and then I had a coffee in David Griffith's café.

"Hello, Kingsley!" David said to me from across the room. " I meant to call you on the weekend. Would you like to come over for supper on Friday night?"

"Would it be alright to bring someone?" I asked. "It's not definite, but I may have a friend with me." I thought I would ask Gay to come with me if she was free.

"Yes, of course," David answered, writing down his address. "If you come over about 6 pm, that would be great!"

"Okay Dave, I'll look forward to it!"

"So, what are you up to today?" he asked.

"Oh, I need some solitude today, some time alone with God, to do some thinking."

"Always a good thing, Kingsley! We need to be alone and be still to hear God's voice!"

"Yes," I replied, "we do."

"Looking forward to seeing you Friday. Bye for now, David, and don't work too hard."

"I won't," he said with a smile, and I headed off to catch the bus.

I decided to catch the #18 Rhossilli bus and get off at Port Eynon. I could spend the day at the beach and visit the village. And then walk back along the cliff-tops to Pennard, and catch the #14 back into Swansea. I had my day planned!

It was a beautiful day as I rode along the narrow lanes to Port Eynon. There was but one cloud in the sky, in the shape of a sea monster on the horizon. And, I was glad that I'd brought my swimming shorts; I'd go for a swim in the afternoon, I thought.

I got off at the first stop in the village and began to walk down the hill. Port Eynon was always a place where time seemed to stand still! Today was no different. The past greeted me with the present, and the three of us walked down the road. Pastel-coloured stonewashed cottages, in lemon, rose and light blue – even the white ones seemed to glow in the morning sunlight, I thought, like happy pearls. On their wooden windowsills, the summer flowers called out to the new day.

And I shouted back: "Good morning!"

"Who is he talking to?" a woman said to her dog as they walked past.

"Good morning to you both," I answered back, and I continued on my way.

It was 11 a.m. Still early for Port Eynon, even in the summer! But as I wound my way through the village to the sea, I could hear, in the distance, the excited shouts of children who had come with their buckets, and spades, and dreams to dig in the warm sand – everything they needed to build their world! As for me, I was heading to the bay to build my hopes and dreams, and they included the most beautiful woman in the world – my Gay!

I passed by the general store and there were fresh cut flowers in a bucket. I bought them to put on Maggie's grave. I would be passing right by the churchyard on my way to the beach. How I wished Maggie were still here to talk to! But at least I knew where she was! She was united with her beloved husband in Heaven. When I thought of them together again, I was happy for her, for I knew how much she had missed him.

I paid for the flowers and headed to the church. As I placed the flowers upon Maggie's grave, I stood for several minutes just remembering this wonderful lady who had blessed my life in so many ways! And I began to talk to her: "Oh Maggie, there is so much to tell you! I've found Gay! And we spent the day together on Saturday! And you were right in what you said in your letter: Gay still loves me. We shared the most beautiful time together, up on Cefn Bryn. And you know what, Maggie? I still love her too! In some mysterious way, I think I've always been waiting for her love to come back into my life. She told me that my love had never left her heart. Oh Maggie! There is so much to think about, and to try to plan in my life!"

In these few minutes that I talked to Maggie, I heard again the words that she had so often said to me: "Kingsley! Go and share whatever is in your heart with God in prayer! He knows, understands, and cares! Just go and acquaint Him with your heart's longings, and He will give you His peace, and the assurance that He has heard your prayers, and He will answer you because you put your trust in Him! You just have to believe in faith, that He has heard you! And He has."

So, I knelt at Maggie's graveside and poured out my heart to God.

Dear Lord,

I pray that you will work everything out for Gay and I, so that we can be together! I know that I've only spent one day with her, Lord, since we said goodbye all those years ago! But I still love her, Lord! And I want to love her as the woman and mother she has become. I believe that she loves me too, Lord! I want to ask her to come on a journey around the Gower with me, so that we can really get to know each other again! It seems to me that with how everything has worked out, only you could have put together the incredible circumstances that allowed us to find each other again —my meeting Melody and having a special connection with her, and then discovering that Gay was her mother. And Maggie's letters and Gay's letters. And Maggie having left me her engagement ring for me to give to Gay. I don't believe that any of this is coincidence, Lord! Surely it is you already answering my prayers! And I know, oh God, that I haven't lived a life that has been pleasing to you over the last several years. Please forgive me. Hear my prayers! I need you so much! I need your help to work everything out, Lord! Please give me your peace, and the assurance that you have heard my prayers!

And as I finished praying, I had such a sense of God's presence. It was like He put His arms around me, giving me His peace and assurance that he had heard me and would answer my prayers! And I thanked Him for His peace that was now in my heart!

"It's nice to hear a young man praying," said a voice that made me jump. I looked up to see an elderly woman placing flowers on a nearby grave.

"Yes, I need God's help," I exclaimed.

"Well, He hears our prayers," the woman said. And I walked away assured of what I had asked for.

It was early afternoon now, and the sun felt warm upon my face as I arrived at the beach. It was about half-tide and the beach sang with the sounds of summer. Children made sand castles, and dug trenches all the way to the laughing, hand-shaking waves. There were families making sand boats, eagerly awaiting the story-telling sea to take their ships to the faraway lands of their dreams. Such wonderful memories filled my heart and mind as I remembered the boats of yellow sand that my mother, father, and brother and I made on those summer singing days long ago when our hearts were one!

Suddenly, a bee buzzed and brought me back from yesteryear. I saw dogs taking their owners for walks, and they looked much alike. Especially the fat woman and the poodle; they both barked as they walked by. Men hid from their wives and the sun, from behind newspapers and dark glasses, while they watched the bikinis go by.

And there in the car park, a coach full of grannies arrived. They were wearing gay hats as big as flying saucers to keep away the sun. And a few old men, who had lived as long as the grannies, set up coloured deck chairs all in a row. And an old granny said: "My gosh, you old buggers are slow!"

A young boy, who had a kite but no wind, ran until he was puffed. While his sister, who looked like Princess Anne, dropped her ice cream in the sand, and a seagull swooped down from the sky and squawked "I'll eat that second hand!" And the girl cried loudly while her sunburned mother tripped her way back to the ice-cream selling store, and asked for some more, before her little girl's tears washed all the sand from the shore.

And a Dad pretended to be playing with his dog as he watched Raquel Welch go by. "What can I do to catch her eye?" echoed back the only cloud in the sky, who apart from that, said neither hello nor goodbye!

And an old lady said to another, who was knitting another colour in the jealous sky, "I'm sure the cloud is friendly and will allow the sun to walk on by!"

The rollers were swelling now out on the tide, and rubber rings and coloured things took boys and girls for a ride. Mums and dads walked hand in hand, and splashed their feet in the healing sand, and life felt good again, and they put off their divorce until after the weekend! And it felt so good in the warm sand!

Teenage lovers like puffed up peacocks also walked tall and hand-in-hand, believing that their first love, like Pennard Castle, would always stand.

The wind woke up now, and blew up the sand, and an old lady held on to her hat with one hand. Her husband in the deckchair looked up to see if he was still damned, and he wasn't, because she reached out with her other hand, though she had to look twice as her eye was full of sand.

"Don't rub it, dear, just hold my hand." And the man flung his newspaper, which sailed with the kite, and the boy ran with the wind until out of sight. And I said, "Good day to you all!" and carried on with my plight, and the dark cloud moved on and the whole world was alright!

I walked down to the ocean waves and headed towards Horton Beach on the far side of the sands, where I would find some quiet and solitude.

Tomorrow I would see Gay again! I began to get as excited as the boy with the kite! I thought about how nice it would be to have a picnic with her at Pobbles tomorrow. We could swim in the sea. And if she brought Melody, we could make a sand boat and travel to places near and far! After our lunch, we could go and find the horses in the valley. And maybe climb up to Pennard Castle in the evening and watch the sunset. Oh, I felt so happy and excited! My heart flew higher and higher than the boy's kite, until I was as high as the skylarks; I sang with them of my hopes and dreams. Then, at the close of the day, I would ask Gay if she would come on a trip around the Gower with me.

Well, I'd made my plans for the day. I prayed and asked God to bless them! I remembered Heather's words: "Just take one day at a time, Kingsley! The rest of the days will follow as they should!" And what good advice this is – to live and embrace the day at hand.

After my meditation and prayers, I headed back to the busy summer singing side of the beach. I changed into my shorts and went swimming in the sea. The breakers were getting bigger now, and the larger swells pushed them into the excited shrieking children and adults. I tended to do my shrieks of excitement on the inside – unless there was no one on the beach of course!

After diving in front of several waves, I managed to catch a big one, which swept me right into the beach! I always find it exhilarating to body surf on a wave. As I stood up in the surf, smaller waves crashed into me, and I could smell the scent of suntan oil, riding on the breeze that blew over the bikinied sun worshippers on the dunes. As the waves continued to crash into the shore, the smell of salt and sea made the beach feel fresh and new again! Yesterday's sandcastles disappeared, making room for today's new dreams! Including mine! I thought of bodysurfing with Gay, and Melody playing with sea monsters while riding on my back. As I stared up into the sand dunes, I saw beautiful girls lying in their beds of sand. I dreamed of lying there with Gay, and being kissed by her and the sun!

Seagulls circled and then cheered as lunch time appeared. Boys and girls opened their egg and tomato sandwiches to inspect them, while gusts of wind blew sand into salads and hair. One boy shouted, "He had ham in his bun!" And his sister complained and said, "Mum, there's mustard in this one!" "Oh, give it to me," she said, "and you can have mine!" And then she turned back her head to her conversation with the sunshine!

Up on the hill, the wind blew through the laughing pine, who shouted down, "Summer, Summer, you're all mine!"

And I shouted back, "No, no, Summer is mine!" And then the wind stopped blowing in the happy pine, and he bowed his head and sat still in the sunshine. And then I thought, Summer can't all be mine! I will share it with you, Mr. Pine!

And the wind blew, and he started shouting again. "Yes, let's share," he said. "You can have the sunshine and I can have the wind."

"It's a deal," I said, as I walked up the beach to beat the seagull to my bread.

"Are you having your lunch?" a dog said.

"Yes, and are you a thoroughbred?"

"I don't think so," his owner said. "The cat died so I got him instead!"

"I see," I said. "Now if you will excuse me, I'll lay down my head in my sand bed."

After my lunch, I lay in the dunes amongst the bikini flowers, who had painted their nails as colourful as rainbow showers, and the minutes turned to hours as I dreamed out to sea, and poured a cup of mermaid and lemon grass tea.

I walked again to the far end of Port Eynon beach, which is really Horton Beach. But Horton always seems to live under the shadow of her sister's sand dune figure and golden sunshine hair, where most people come and put down their resting chairs.

I climbed up from Sister Hortons' beach to the clifftop, and then walked to Oxwich Bay. From Oxwich, I walked across the sand to Pobbles, and then on up to Southgate village to catch the bus.

It was 9:00 pm when I arrived back to the house. Lynn had left out a supper for me, and after a visit with the telly's Coronation Street in the living room, I took my tired head off to bed.

"Good night, Kings! See you in the morning! Yeah, good night Fraser and Lynn!"

Chapter Twenty

Capture the Princess

Well, it was Tuesday morning, and I wanted to look my best for meeting Gay! I showered and washed yesterday's sea from my hair. As I glanced in the mirror, at my tan and muscles, I looked pretty good! But on the inside, I felt nervous as well as excited! I knelt at the foot of my bed to pray, and asked God to be with me, and to go before me and prepare this special day! I thanked him again for bringing Gay and Melody my way!

"Help me, Oh God, to know what to say!" There were Heather's words again: "Kingsley! Just relax and enjoy the day!"

I didn't stop at the market to pick up my lunch today. Gay had said that she was going to bring a picnic to the beach. As I rode the bus, it was becoming a beautiful summer day, with blue sky and only a gentle breeze in the tops of the trees. A perfect day for the beach!

I got off the bus at Pennard and made my way towards Pobbles along the West Cliff path. When I reached the cliff top that overlooked Great Thunders' cave, I stopped and peered over. There was Ruby, standing guard outside the cave! What a magnificent animal! But compared to my stallion, Great Thunder, he and any other stallion would be second best! Great Thunder had had his time as King of the sands. Ruby was most likely one of Great Thunder's grandsons. I watched Ruby for a while from the cliff top. I could see his hoof prints in the sand going from both directions; he had been on his run from Oxwich and back.

What a heritage, I thought! Generations still stand guard at old Thunders cave! And I was there when Great Thunder first stood outside. And I began to understand more and more, that all my experiences living on the clifs and having my horse family, was all part of God's wonderful plan, and making me into who I am today.

I continued my way along the cliff top to Pobbles. When I arrived, the tide looked about half way out, which would be ideal for building a sand boat on the beach before the tide came back in again. As much as I would enjoy having Gay all to myself, it would be fun to have Melody with us and all build a ship together. I'd have to wait and see.

Climbing down to the sands, I looked around for Gay. There were quite a few people on the beach already, but I could not see Gay or Melody. So I sat on a rock and fixed my eyes on the distance, as they would be coming from the direction of Three Cliffs. There seemed to be no one coming from the distant sands. All I could see was Bell Rock that stood like an Island in the yellow sand.

I waited for about twenty minutes, and then I could see someone in the distance wearing something green or blue. And as the figure got closer, I could see that the person had a child with them. I was reminded how I used to watch for Great Thunder coming and going across the sands; today it was for my Gay and her daughter.

My heart began to beat faster as I could see more clearly now. The woman had long flowing hair, and I recognized Melody's build, with her fair hair, and the blue and white bucket that she was carrying. I decided to walk towards them and meet them. Melody recognized me from a distance and started running towards me.

"Kingsley! Kingsley!" she shouted in excitement and ran into my arms. "Can we empty the dragon pool today? Mum said we can if it's alright with you?"

"That would be fun," I said, "but have you ever built a boat on the sand? The waves come crashing into the boat, and you swim the seven seas?"

"A pirate ship?" Melody exclaimed.

"It can be any ship you like," I answered.

"Mum! Mum!" Melody cried. "Can we make a pirate ship on the beach? Kingsley said I can make any type of ship I like!"

"A pirate ship?" Gay echoed back, as she arrived at the happy scene.

"Yes," I said, "and you're the Princess we are going to catch!"

"I am, am I?" she said, with the most radiant smile. Then she kissed me gently on the cheek, while Melody watched in momentary silence.

What a welcome, I thought.

I held Gay tightly in my arms. "Look Melody, I've been caught already!" she laughed.

"Come on, you two," Melody called, "let's get started building our ship."

"Let's put our beach stuff and picnic down first," Gay said.

"That's right," I said, "we have to claim our place on the beach, before some pirates come and claim it first!"

"She's so excited already!" Gay exclaimed.

After we claimed our place on the beach, I helped Melody to mark out the shape of our ship on the sand. Then we started digging a trench with our bucket and spade, just like my mum and dad had done with me. Gay changed into her bikini and watched as she sunbathed.

"It's important to dig a trench first," I shouted in excitement. "So that it breaks the waves before they come crashing into the ship's wall." Melody and I soon had a trench dug around the shape of our ship and now we could build our wall.

Gay called out, "Let's have our picnic now, and then I will help you build the walls."

While we ate our picnic, Gay told me the news as to how her time in Cardiff had gone on Thursday. She had been able to secure a new place to live for her and Melody. It was close to her work and to Melody's school. And her mum, Helen, had finalized a deal on buying a house close to where Gay and Melody were going to live. It had indeed been a fruitful trip! I shared with Gay the wonderful time that I'd had with Dad and my brother, up on the Gower of the Hills.

Gay looked so lovely. As we shared more of our hearts and lives, I realized she was still as beautiful on the inside as she was on the outside! My heart sang within me, as I recognized her more and more.

After we finished our picnic, the three of us started to build the walls of our ship. Gay and I shaped the walls, digging the sand with our hands inside the ship, while Melody ran back and forth to the edge of the waves and dumped buckets of wet sand for Gay and I to sculpture. Our vessel was taking shape.

"We have about another half an hour," I said, looking at the tide that was coming in quickly now. "One more bucket of wet sand, Melody, and then you climb into the ship with your mum and I. We must make the walls tall and thick before the waves reach us." It was all very exciting for all of us!

"The waves have arrived at the front of the ship, Mum and Kingsley! The waves are pirates!"

"Quick!" I said, "Let's all work on the front of our ship and make the bow walls the thickest. The bow of the ship is the first to break into the waves and the fighting pirates."

Gay then stole a kiss from me and whispered in my ear, "You can kidnap me anytime you want, Kingsley, my pirate Prince!"

And I whispered in her ear: "I intend to, Welsh Princess!" And I kissed her gently on the cheek.

"Kingsley! Mum!" Melody shrieked. "We are almost surrounded by waves!"

"Quick, keep digging," I said, as parts of the wall started to crumble into the waves. And we patted sand onto one part of our ship and then the other.

"Look, look!" Melody shouted. "We are surrounded by pirates!"

And we were. We were now a ship on the high seas, having used all the soft sand within our vessel to reinforce the walls.

"We are going to sink," Gay said. "Let's get ready to abandon ship!"

No sooner had Gay finished speaking those words when a large wave crashed over the side of our ship, turning it into a swimming pool. Both Gay and Melody shrieked as the cool waves swirled up to our waists.

"Okay, everyone," I said, "let's hold onto each other tightly, and on the next big wave, we will jump into the sea and abandon ship! Okay? Jump!" And in we went. Melody climbed onto my back and pretended I was a pirate fighting turtle. I pretended to be a pirate fighting Prince, as I held onto Gay's waist.

"Have you come to rescue me, my Prince?" she asked.

"Yes, I have!" And I took her arm and piggy-backed her onto the beach, while Melody swam around us shouting at the pirates. When we reached the shore, only one wall was left of our gallant ship 'the Good Ship Gower.' And we watched as the pirate waves reclaimed her back into the sea.

Melody's friends now arrived and she went off to play near the Dragon Pool. Gay and I lay on our towels while the sun warmed our bodies. "That was so much fun, Kingsley," she said.

"It was, wasn't it?" I said, turning onto my side and looking into her lovely eyes, which welcomed me deeper and deeper, like the wild sea, into her soul. And we spent the next hours, which seemed like a lifetime, looking into each other's eyes. There was so much to say in our silence, and not to say but just to know. Our hearts did the talking as through each other's eyes we could see the past, present and future.

"My heart is safe with you. I love you, Kingsley," her words affirmed to me.

"I know," I said, "I feel it within my soul. My heart is safe with you too, Gay. I love you too!"

We didn't have to understand how the details would work out in our lives. There was this wonderful "knowing" that our love was growing, and all we needed to do was to grow with it and everything would work out.

I told Gay about my friend David Griffiths and his invitation for us to go to his home for supper on Friday evening. Gay was sure that Pearl could watch Melody and she agreed to come.

Gay, Melody and I spent the whole day together on the beach. In the evening, we went up to the Three Cliffs Valley and spent time with the horses. Nan's-Nan recognized Melody and I right away, and walked over to visit us. Gay said that she was the oldest horse she had ever seen in the wild and was appropriately named Nan's-Nan. Melody fussed around the foals like a mother, and she showed Gay their various markings and told her how we had named the foals the other day.

And, this evening there were two more fouls with the herd. Melody named the baby stallion 'Manely' because he had such a large mane for a young horse. He was a lovely grey stallion. And I told Melody he would surely grow up to be a great leader – and the protector of the herd one day.

Gay and I watched as Melody repeated to the foal what I'd said to her.

"Hello, Manely," she said. "One day, you are going to be a great leader and the protector of the herd." And she asked Gay and I if talking to Manely would make a difference in his life. And did he understand her words?

"Oh yes," we chimed in together. "Words are very powerful, and they can help us believe what they say, and to live out our destinies."

Later in the evening, we all climbed up from the valley to Pennard Castle. On the northwest wall of the castle that overlooks the valley is 'the room,' as my brother and I call it. This part of the castle was added on sometime after the original walls had been completed. You walk through the arch-shaped entrance to find you are secluded within four high walls. Of course, there is no roof now, but the feeling is one of being in a castle room. This evening, Melody took Gays hand and mine, and then led us into a familiar place that our hearts instantly remembered. And it felt like it was yesterday once more.

During that special summer that we had spent together we lay in each other's arms and watched the night sky. And tonight, our castle room transcended time and space as our souls remembered. We reached out to one another again, and Gay and I held each other tightly.

And Melody said: "You are the Prince and the Princess of the castle!" And we were.

And I said to Melody: "You are young Princess Melody!"

"Did you hear that, Mummy?" Melody asked. "Kingsley said that I am a Princess!"

"Yes, I heard, Melody. You are my Princess!"

Melody danced and twirled in her flowered summer dress, and Mr. Pennard Castle echoed: "You are a Princess indeed."

"Who wants to hear about a special game that my brother Fraser and I used to play when we were boys?"

"I do, I do!" Melody and Gay shouted together.

"Well, the game is called 'Normans and Saxons'! We would get a group of friends together and have a battle! We made swords out of wood and used the tops of metal garbage cans for shields. And we made bows and arrows, and throwing spears, out of tree branches from the woods. Sometimes when we were cutting our arrows and spears, we found fork-shaped branches and we made sling shots out of them. We shot small stones at each other."

"My favourite part of the game was when we had girls playing with us. Then we changed the name of the game from 'Normans and Saxons' to 'Capture the Princess.' The object of the game was to divide the knights, which were us boys, into two groups. We fought bitter battles to capture the Princess, who was one or more of the girls! If there were two girls, for example, there would be one Princess per group of knights, and we would fight together against the other team to capture and kidnap their Princess, who was then taken to this room. If there was only one girl, then she ran and hid. And the team that was first to find her in the castle grounds got to keep her as their possession, until the other team came and conquered us, and took her away. We fought many bitter battles against each other, using spears, bows and arrows. And sometimes slingshots. Sometimes we got bad injuries. I threw a spear into someone's leg once and he needed five stitches! I felt really bad about that."

Melody's eyes filled with wonder as she looked around the room, half expecting to see a knight as I continued to tell the story.

"The Princess was taken and kept in 'this room' as a prisoner. She was guarded, to keep her from escaping, by a knight who stood over there, at the arch entrance to the room. Once the battle was over, the Princess got to choose a knight of her pleasing from the team that had captured her. So, we knights fought very bravely for her favour. The chosen knight became a Lord, and he got to kiss the Princess all alone in this room!"

And Gay whispered in my ear, "You can capture me anytime, Kingsley! And I will choose you to be my Lord and Master."

I whispered back, "I will capture you right now!" and Gay blushed and giggled.

Melody said, "Let's play 'capture the Princess' right now!"

Gay looked at me, and then at Melody, and said, "Okay let's play! So, Melody, you run and hide right now, and Kingsley and I will come and try to find you!"

"Close your eyes," Melody shouted, and she ran off to hide.

Gay and I were in no particular hurry to find Melody. We walked hand in hand within the castle walls, stopping often to look into each other's eyes and kiss.

"Oh, Kingsley," Gay whispered. "Melody and I are having the most wonderful day! Thank you for making it so special for us. I feel like I have the family I have always dreamed of when we are together!"

And as Gay shared how she felt, I felt that God was also allowing me to see what it would be like to have Gay as my wife and Melody as my daughter. And my heart was excited!

"Where do you think Melody is hiding?" Gay asked, after kissing me again.

"Oh, I couldn't tell you! Because when you kiss me like that, I lose all sense of direction!"

Gay giggled and kissed me again.

"Hey, you two!" called a familiar voice. "Come and find me, and stop kissing! You have to capture the Princess before you can kiss!"

Gay laughed. "Now we are in trouble. Where do you think she is?"

"I bet she's doubled back on us," I said, "and gone back to the room."

Gay and I snuck up quietly towards the castle room. And there she was, crouching down against the far wall.

"Found you!" Gay shouted. "Now it's your turn to find Kingsley and I."

We played our version of Capture the Princess within the castle walls until the night clouds came to capture us, with their swords of the night and shields of darkness, and all was still within our sacred castle and in the valley that had fallen asleep below.

♪✻

WHEN EVENING SHADOWS FALL

A POEM

When evening shadows fall
The soul that is at peace,
may contemplate the passing of the day.
The shadows of the tall trees reach
long upon the ground,
As they converse with the dipping sun,
whose warmth has faded
like a kiss of not too long ago.
Not as a memory that vanishes around

winters corner, not to be thought of again.
Our human hearts can become still,
and ones soul reflect on the warmth or cold within,
where passion and desire shout in joy or
sorrow like the crashing sea against the iron
rocks of Fall Bay.
For me, my soul is warm and glowing,
though the sun has gone below the green hill,
where the daffodil bulbs rest and
dream of the coming spring.
When the evening shadows fall.
An owl hoots from deep within Three Cliffs woods.
And old Mr. Pennard Castle and me, we understand, you see.
And the lonely wood pigeon in the valley
makes his last call, and Cefn Bryn,
shouts down and says, I think he spoke for us all.
When evening shadows fall.
The wind breathes cooler,
and Gay's kiss is more warm,
before the night clouds make their
march across the sky, and remind our hearts,
that it's a long time till dawn.
I once thought the night clouds march was cruel,
as they came and stole away my day.
But not so now, now I have your love to
keep me warm.
When evening shadows fall.
The Killy Willy stream, seems to wind slower,
as his waters twist and turn and
reflect the silver moon who shouts back
"look at me, I'll be there soon.
I'll meet you at the end of the sky
for a cuppa tea in my sun room."
A flap of wings and the owl is hunting,

Kingsley Ross Hill

and won't return to his hollow tree,
until the orange dawn.
Can I hold your hand, my love, and keep you warm.
Yes, Kings, let us sing our song until dawn.
Hold me and kiss me, until the new morn.
Oh, how I love it when the evening shadows fall,
and I wake up in your arms in
the morning chorus call.

© *Kingsley Ross Hill*

"The stars are starting to show themselves to us," said Melody. "It's like they're continuing our game of hide and seek in the heavens."

Then she asked, "Does God play that game too?"

And I said, "I'm sure He does!"

We all lay on our beach blankets upon the soft sand in the castle room. Gay lay to my right, her soft scented hair covering part of my face and she held my hand with gentle caresses. Melody lay snuggling up to me on my left, and with the shining stars above us, my soul shouted, "I am a complete and happy man!"

After we finished watching the night sky, I walked Gay and Melody back down to the valley. By the light of the moon, we climbed up the dunes and across the Burrows to Penmaen. There I rode the bus with them to Reynoldston, where they were staying in the caravan. Before Gay got off the bus, we arranged to meet again the next day, and go to visit Heather in Penmaen.

Chapter Twenty-One
Hello Mrs. Tripp

I met Gay in Penmaen village, as arranged, and Gay's sister Pearl had taken Melody for the day. We walked through the village to Heather's house and on the way we bought her some flowers at Maggie's old store. Maggie's store would never be the same without her, both Gay and I agreed, and we felt her absence as we paid for the flowers.

"Time waits for no one," Gay commented. "Except for us!" we both said at the same time. And indeed, God had waited for us, and worked out time and circumstances in our favour. I thanked him in my heart, for His sovereignty and his perfect timing in working things out in our lives. For it seemed like only yesterday that I had struggled with my faith in believing that God would somehow help Gay and me to find each other again. But He did! And in doing so He answered my deepest prayer!

[Romans 8 vs 28, And we know that all things work together for good to those who love God, to those who are called according to His purpose.]

Gay knocked on Heather's heavy wooden door, and I heard Heather call out again: "Just a minute, I'm coming!" Heather was thrilled to see us! And she said we'd arrived at the perfect time! "Come in, you two, I've just put on a fresh pot of tea."

For the next few hours, Heather brought us up to date on the Gower news, especially for Gay, who hadn't seen Heather since coming to the stables almost twenty years ago, looking for me. What was so remarkable for Gay and I was to understand, in greater detail, the series of events that had taken place for her and I to find each other again! In Heather's words, it was nothing short of a miracle! Letters written and left over twenty years ago! Gay and I having families on different continents! And yet we had experienced 'something,' as Heather called it all those years ago. But Gay and I knew what the bond had been, and still was. Even after all this time, it was 'love!' A God-given love for each other that had endured in our hearts.

"Well, I am just thrilled that you have found each other!" Heather said. And then she reminded us of how Maggie had prayed for us both, every day for over twenty years!

"God answered her prayers and our prayers!" Gay and I shared, taking each other's hands and looking into each other's eyes.

"I can see that you love each other," Heather proclaimed.

By the time we got caught up with all the local news, it was supper time, and Heather asked us to stay and eat with her. Which we were very happy to do.

After supper, Gay and I caught the bus to Port Eynon, so we could visit Maggie's grave together. The flowers I'd taken the other day still looked fresh beneath her headstone. We sat and reminisced about our experiences with Maggie. And Gay shared with me how Maggie had encouraged her, on the two times she had come looking for me, not to give up; and to leave the letters with Maggie, hoping that I would eventually come to see her.

"Maggie would always tell me to share my heart with God and tell Him exactly how I was feeling! I didn't think that God would be that interested in me, but Maggie told me that He was! So that's what I did Kingsley; I told him everything. It's what kept my faith alive, believing that one day I would find you again, Kingsley! The love of my life!" and she began to cry.

"I held her in my arms and told her that my love had never left her! "I've carried you in my heart, Gay! Through all the seasons and years since we've been apart!" Then I began to weep too. Gay kissed my tears away and said, "Our love is so deep and true!" And we knelt and prayed together, thanking God for his faithfulness, for answering our prayers and helping us find each other. And there at Maggie's grave, our 'doorway to heaven,' as Maggie had called it, Gay and I professed our love for each other!

And we said out loud: "We love you Maggie, and we believe that you can see us now, because as you often said, there are windows in heaven!"

We were in the first week of September now, and the days had been getting shorter. But the sunshine remained, at least for now. As I thought about asking Gay to come camping around the Gower with me, I hoped we would have an Indian summer well into the end of the month. And I had to remember to ask her to come with me on Friday night, when we went over to David Griffith's house for supper.

Meanwhile Gay asked me if I would like to come with her and Melody to visit her mum in Cardiff, and to see where she and Melody were going to live.

"Mum wants us to come and have dinner with her in her new place."

"I'd be delighted to come with you," I said.

Gay had rented a car for the last month of her holidays in Gower, and we were able to drive up to Cardiff.

By the time we left Port Eynon, it was getting late in the evening. We decided to call it a night and be ready for an early start in the morning.

"Bye, Gay," I said, as she got off the bus at Reynoldston. "Say good night to Melody for me, and give her a hug!"

"I will, Kings! I will pick you up in Swansea in the morning." And I rode the bus home to Fraser and Lynn's for an early night.

Gay and Melody picked me up in the morning, as planned, and we were soon traveling along the motorway towards Cardiff. Cardiff is fourty miles from Swansea, so we would be there in about an hour and a half. As we drove along, I thought of the last time I had seen Gay's mum. It was a lifetime ago, and yet I remember it like yesterday! She pulled up in her car and took my Gay away to England to live! My heart broke! Today I was going to see her in very different circumstances, and as a mature man!

I remembered something Maggie had said to me when I was tempted to elope with Gay, rather than have her mother take her away. She said if I eloped with Gay, I would lose the respect of Gay's family, and things would not work out for us in the long run. But if I did what was right, in the sight of God, then God would work things out for us in His perfect time. And sitting here next to Gay today, I was sure glad I had listened to Maggie's wise counsel. Her words had been good and true!

On our way we stopped in Bridgend for a snack and to stretch our legs. Melody and I found a bakery.

"I see you two can find a bakery!" Gay laughed.

"Yes," I replied, "that's most important!" And we bought an ice-bun each and something to drink.

⁓

After our break and a short walk around the town, I offered to drive the rest of the way to Cardiff.

"Are you sure you can remember how to drive on the right side of the road?" Gay teased.

"Yes," I answered, "if I can drive with those lunatics in Victoria and Vancouver, then I can drive anywhere! I'll just do what I did when I first went out to Canada."

"What's that?" Melody asked, intrigued.

"You just follow the car in front of you and hope they are going to the same shopping centre as you are!"

"And then you get lost," Gay added.

And Melody laughed.

"Yes, get lost," I replied. "Some of the best places I have found in life have been when I've been lost!"

Melody laughed again.

"I want to get lost and go somewhere special," Melody shouted.

"There is still twenty miles to go before we reach Cardiff," Gay said. "That gives us plenty of time to get lost somewhere!"

"We're going to get lost! We're going to get lost!" Melody sang. And with our new song in our hearts, we followed the car in front of us, so to speak.

The sign read 'Welcome to Cardiff.'

And Melody said: "We're almost there, Kingsley!" and we soon pulled into Gay's mum's driveway. Helen had bought a flat on the outskirts of the city, in a very nice area.

Helen met us at the door and greeted me with a handshake and a smile.

"You remember my mum, Kingsley...." Gay said.

"Yes, of course I remember," I said, "Hello, Mrs. Tripp, it's nice to see you again!"

"Oh, please call me Helen, Kingsley! It's nice to see you again and do come in, all of you!"

And we went inside to a ready-made cup of tea and home-made biscuits. Helen then gave us a tour of her new place, and it was indeed a lovely place, and a lot bigger than it looked from the street. She proudly showed us the three bedrooms and two bathrooms, and it had a nice balcony off the living room that got the afternoon sun. Gay then went into the kitchen to help her mother make lunch, while Melody and I played a rather "make up your own rules" game of monopoly in the living room.

Helen and Gay soon called us for lunch, and we all sat 'round the kitchen table. Helen asked me about my life, and my family situation in Canada. I shared about my children, and my work as a Pastor and Counsellor on Vancouver Island.

Then she said something that pleasantly surprised me. I thought that she was going to talk about the difficulties that Gay and I would have to face if we planned on trying to make a life together. But she didn't. Instead she talked about the spring and summer that Gay and I had spent together, before Gay moved to England.

"Kingsley, my husband and I were so concerned that you and Gay were going to elope, once you knew that we were going to move away. But you didn't, Kingsley. You were a respectful young man! And I want to tell you that whatever you and Gay decide to do with your lives, you have my support!"

Fighting back the tears, I said thank you to Helen. "Knowing that we have your support means a lot to me. And I was very sorry to hear about the loss of your husband."

"Thank you, Kingsley! As Gay has no doubt told you, we got divorced some years back. But his death is a great loss to all of us!"

After Helen had finished talking, my mind flashed back to that conversation that I had with Maggie, or should I say that she had with me. I had thought about it earlier in the day when Gay and I knelt down to pray at Maggie's grave. Maggie said: "If you and Gay run away together, it will only turn Gay's mother and father against you. And you will end up losing respect for each other. If you do the right thing, God will bless you. And if things are meant to be, God will work everything out in His good time."

"Oh, Maggie! How your words have come to pass! I have the respect of Gay's mum and even her blessing on our relationship. And God sure is working things out for us, Maggie!"

The conversation now turned to Gay and I, and how we had finally found each other again. I shared with Helen how I had first met Melody on Pobbles Beach, and that she was wearing the necklace I'd given to Gay.

Helen said, "Well, normally I would be surprised by something like that happening, Gay told me about you finding her letters all these years later, when you went to Maggie's old store. But to be honest, Kingsley, I'm not at all surprised! It seems clear to me that you and Gay were always meant to be together!"

Gay smiled at me from across the table, and then started to cry. "Oh, Mum!" she cried, "you don't know what those words mean to me! I've loved Kingsley all these years!"

"I know you have, Gay," she said. "And you have my blessing in planning a future together!"

I said, "Thank you Helen! I love your daughter with all my heart, and Melody too."

"And me too, Grandma!" Melody shouted in excitement. "Kingsley loves me too! He said that I'm a real Princess! He helped me ride on a horse named Nan's-Nan."

"I could have told you that you're a Princess," Helen replied. "And I must come and see you ride this Nan's-Nan sometime! And how did the horse get the name Nan's-Nan?"

"Oh yeah, Kingsley and I think that Nan's-Nan is the oldest horse in the world."

We all laughed.

After lunch, all of us managed to squeeze into Helen's car, and she took us to Cardiff Bay. And as we walked the seafront, Helen took my arm, while Gay and Melody walked beside us. In these few minutes in time, I knew within my soul that I had found what I'd been looking for, all my life: a family of my own!

After our walk along the bay, we spent some time in the old part of Cardiff Town, where my uncle owned an antique shop. The shop was closed, so I couldn't introduce anyone to my Uncle Andrew. Helen took us out for fish and chips on the dockside, and we enjoyed a wonderful family time together. Then after I'd told Melody a mermaid story, it was time to go.

By the time we got back to Helen's flat, it was 8 p.m. Time we headed back to Swansea. But before we left, I asked Melody to come with me to the shop down the road.

"What are we going to buy?" she asked, as we closed the door behind us.

"Wait and see," I said. "It's a surprise!"

At the store, I said "Now you can pick out some flowers for Grandma."

Melody picked out a large bouquet of wild flowers, to which we added some ferns and baby's breath.

"Why is it called 'baby's breath'? It doesn't have bad breath!" Melody laughed.

The shopkeeper wrapped the flowers in coloured paper and a bow, and Melody carried them proudly back to the house to give to her Grandma. And with a thank yous and hugs from Helen, we were on our way back to Swansea. We had intended to go and see Gay's new place, and to drive by Melody's school, but it was getting late and Gay wanted to get back to the caravan so Melody could go to bed.

Shortly into our journey back to Swansea, Melody fell asleep, which gave Gay and I time to talk about how we were feeling. It was a wonderful family time that we had shared, and a continuing affirmation that God was uniting Gay and I. It was very romantic as we approached the city lights of Swansea holding hands.

And Gay said: "I never want to let go of your hand again, Kingsley! My mum really likes you, I can tell!"

"I'm glad" I said, "I think she is indeed a lovely lady!"

"Thank you, Kingsley. She is!"

As Gay dropped me off at Fraser's, I reminded her of our supper invitation the next night, at my friend David's.

"I'll be here to pick you up at 6 p.m.," she said.

"Okay, Gay, I will see you tomorrow evening.

"Bye, Kings, see you tomorrow."

Chapter Twenty-Two
Good Friday

I enjoyed a nice sleep-in on Friday morning and then a hearty breakfast of eggs, sausages and toast, and, of course, some HP sauce on my bangers!

After breakfast, I walked down the road to my father's house like a teenager in love!

"A 40-year-old teenager in love?" asked a passing gull.

"It doesn't matter how old you are," I said, "as long as you are in love!"

"That's true! Oh, how I love a romantic!" he said, and flew off towards the bay.

As I approached my father's house, I crossed the street so I could look into his upstairs window, where he usually sat in his lounge chair looking out on the street. It was the place where my father started each new day –his 'lookout seat.' A bit like mine on top of the Great Tor, when I lived in Leathers Hole on the cliffs!

I crossed the road again and rang the doorbell. When I opened the door and went inside, I heard his voice call out, "Who goes there! Friend or foe?"

"Friend!" I shouted. "It's Kings!"

"Kings!" he replied, his voice excited. "Come on up, Kings! What's new in the world, old Son? Have you tamed any wild stallions lately, or robbed Jonesy of his milk money?"

"No, Dad!" I laughed. "But I've found the woman of my dreams! Gay Tripp down on the beach!"

"By Jove, Gay Tripp! That's the girl you used to ride horses with, and live in a cave, isn't it? Wait, you lived in a cave, and her mother had something to say about her living there with you if I remember correctly?"

"That's right, Dad, She's the woman of my dreams! And I've found her again after all these years!"

"The woman of your dreams?" echoed Mary's voice coming from the kitchen.

"Yes, Gay Tripp!"

"Mary! You remember her?" Dad said. "She came and stayed with our Kings in Leathers Hole, until her mother stole her away to England! What did you do with the mother, Kings? Tie her up in the cave?"

Both Mary and I roared with laughter.

"No, Dad," I answered. "And her mother has given us her blessing now. I went and visited her yesterday up in Cardiff, with Gay and her little daughter Melody."

"Well, jolly good, old Son! So, she's the one, is she? You've managed to tame her, have you? Or was it you who needed to be tamed? Oh, that's right, you can't be tamed, only trained!

"I'll tame you in a minute!" Mary said to Dad, bringing us both a cup of tea. " So, tell us all about it Kings! You met this girl again after all these years?"

"Yes, Mary, and I'm going to ask her to marry me very soon!"

"Good God, Mary, did you hear that! Our Kings is in love and he's going to ask her to marry him."

"That's great, Kings!" Mary said, "Congratulations!"

"Yes, that's great, old Son," Dad continued, "and I'm very happy for you!"

"Thanks, Dad and Mary!" and we drank our tea.

"Would you like another cup?" Mary asked.

"No, thanks," Dad answered, bringing in a bottle of sherry. "Our Kings is getting engaged! This is something to celebrate!"

Mary brought in some crackers and cheese, and the three of us celebrated.

"You always loved that girl, didn't you, Kings?"said Mary.

"From the moment I saw her," I replied.

"I'll drink to that!" Dad said. "It's not often you meet the love of your life, is it, Kings?"

"No, it isn't, Dad. Especially when you have lost her once before!"

"Yes, indeed! Cheers!"

And as I drank my sherry, I thought about how I had never really lost her! She was just waiting for me to return to her, and with God's help, I had.

After my celebration with Dad and Mary, I walked into town. And I continued celebrating by going into Swansea Market to buy some welsh cakes and cockles, and my favourite dessert – a custard slice! I just wanted to keep celebrating!

Once I'd bought my lunch, I walked over a new bridge that crossed the Mumbles Road to Swansea Bay. The old 'slip bridge,' as I had always known it, had been taken away since my last visit to Wales. It was one of the few changes I'd seen in this beloved land of mine, where time could still stand still! Further along on my walk, I came across the 'slip bridge' again! They hadn't taken it away! They had just moved it to its resting place, as it sat proudly reminiscing about its history at the side of the walking path to Mumbles.

I climbed down the stone steps to the sandy beach. As I walked along Swansea Bay, I bumped into more memories than I could share in a whole day. I was living out new hopes and dreams today.

Tonight, Gay and I would go over to David Griffith's house for supper. Tomorrow was Saturday, and Pearl would have Melody, and we would have the whole day alone. I wondered if it would be the perfect day to give Gay Maggie's engagement ring and ask her to marry me? I wanted to get married outside Great Thunders' Cave on Pobbles Beach, as I considered that my family home!

So yes, I'd ask Gay to marry me tomorrow, and I'd give her the ring in the grounds of Pennard Castle! I began to get so excited and I danced my way along Swansea Bay, singing out that I was getting married.

"What do you think?" I shouted out to a flying seagull.

"Oh, I don't know, wild boy! We seagulls all get married on Gull Rock, you know!"

"Yes, I know Gull Rock! My brother Fraser and I go fishing near there at Eddy Tuckers Cove! Do you know it?"

"Yes boy, I've seen you there! Catching mackerel, and salmon bass in the summer air!"

"I'm Kingsley, Mr. Gull," I shouted.

"Pleased to meet you! And I know who you are! You're one of the Hill Brothers – the oldest one – who rode the wild stallion across the sands!"

"That's right, Mr. Gull!"

"You don't have to call me Mr. Gull. I'm Charle to you, wild boy! And, my wife's name is Sylvia."

"Well, I'm pleased to meet you, Charle! And I have a great friend back in Canada who is also called Sylvia, and she's a great painter!"

"I saw you dancing along the beach. Is it some kind of mating dance?"

"Kind of. Only I haven't asked her to marry me yet!"

"What! And you're dancing as if she's said 'yes' already? Well, you're a cocky wild boy, aren't you?"

"Yes, I am! But I'm sure in my heart that she will say yes!"

"You are, are you? That's nice to be so sure about something like that in your life! You should be a preacher or a teacher, or something."

"I am. I'm a Pastor back in Canada, Mr. Gull, I mean Charle! And I have God in my life to help me do my work! And I am so thankful for that!"

"Well, Bless me, Father! You're a preacher as well, are you boy! We gulls don't need a preacher! We know that God made us, and that He feeds us on every tide! Only you humans are confused about God, and who He is!"

"You're right, Charle, you're right! What do you think about me having my wedding outside my cave on Pobbles beach? I know Gay would like it! And her daughter Melody would love to be a flower girl down on the sands!"

"Or a ring bearer? You didn't think of that one, did you, wild boy?" the gull cackled.

"No, I didn't. Thank you!"

"Was Melody the little girl you were emptying the Dragon Pool with the other day?"

"Yes, that's right, Charle! My only concern is Gay's mother, Helen! She's a real lady you know! And she might not appreciate traipsing through the dunes and down to Pobbles in her heels!"

"Oh poppycock! It's your wedding, isn't it? And you can cry if you want to! And she will cry too if she breaks her shoe!"

"That's a great song, Charle, I'll remember that one!"

"You will, will you? Then just tell her mother to take her fancy heels off and walk in bare feet like the rest of us!"

"You're right, Charle! It is my party and I'll walk bare foot if I want to!"

"Well it's been nice talking to you, wild boy! But I'm heading to the Gower now, and I'm meeting Sylvia on Gull Rock for some romancing! And it's not my wedding, so I'll fly if I want to! You'd fly too if it happened to you!"

"Well, bye, Charle! It was really nice talking to you. And thanks for the advice on my wedding plans! I will get married at my cave, and please drop by if you can."

"I'll do that, boy! And congratulations!"

By the time I'd walked the length of Swansea Bay, I was sure of my plans. I knelt on the sand and asked God to bless them and to continue to direct my path.

[Psalm 32 vs 8, I will instruct you and teach you in the way you should go; I will counsel you with my loving eye upon you.]

Kingsley Ross Hill

When I stood up, I noticed there were footprints before me on the sand, and I watched as the incoming tide washed them away! And I thought about life! and how short our time is here in this world! As the fresh, clean sand re-appeared from the receding waves, I was so thankful for the blessing that God had given me – a new start in my life with Gay, Melody, and Helen. Years ago, on this same beach, I had watched with a broken heart as the sea washed away the last of Gay's and my footprints! But now we had the fresh new beach for the rest of our lives to make footprints together! And no matter what big waves and storms came upon us, our footprints would always be side by side on the sand. Thank you, God, for speaking to me through your sand and sea!

After a full day of walking the horseshoe of Swansea Bay, I headed back to Fraser's to get ready for my evening date with Gay. She would pick me up at 6 pm, and then it was only a short drive to David's house, in Gowerton.

Gay arrived on time, and she looked so beautiful! Her long flowing hair hung over her shoulders, and she wore a green and grey Celtic lace dress, with the Evening Emerald Cross. I could smell her delicate but distinct scent, which made me want to pull her gently towards me and hold her. So, I did! I put my arms around her and held her closely as she let her body relax in my embrace. After holding her tightly for what seemed to be a lifetime, I placed my hands upon her waist, and kissed her gently on the back of her neck. Gay turned her face and met me with a wet lipstick kiss. Our eyes met, and we beheld each other's souls in an embrace that we never wanted to end!

"I love you!" she whispered, and my voice was an echo of hers.

"Would you like me to drive?" I asked, walking her around to the passenger side of the car.

"Yes, Kings!" she said, as she lifted her dark green heels into the car. Gay was also the perfect height for me – five inches shorter. And with her three-inch heels, she was two inches shorter. The perfect height for looking into each other's eyes!

As we arrived at David's house, I told her again how beautiful she looked in her green and grey dress that brought out her always sparkling eyes – eyes that could change my breathing with a glance. She blushed! – making her face even more radiant, like the rising sun at dawn.

We held hands and walked up the driveway like a Prince and Princess! And we were! As I rang the doorbell, we stole a quick kiss. Gay rubbed the lipstick off my face with her handkerchief, just in time before David and his wife came to the door.

"Come in, Kingsley." David said. "This is my wife, Jackie!"

"Nice to meet you" I replied.

"And this is Gay."

"Pleased to meet you, Gay!" said David. "I've known Kingsley since he was a young boy in Sunday school at Linden Chapel in West Cross."

"It's called Linden Christian Center now," Jackie added. And she led us to the living room, where we shared a bottle of red wine.

It turned out that David and Jackie had left Linden Christian Center about ten years before.

I recalled a lesson David had taught me when I was 9 years old. It was a teaching on Heaven and Hell, and David described both places.

"I can remember saying to you, David, that I wanted to go to Heaven and not the other place. And I was so relieved when you told me that Jesus loved me, and that he had died on the Cross to pay the penalty for my sins! All I had to do was to believe what He had done for me, and ask him to come into my heart and be my Savior, and then I didn't have to go to hell!"

David was thrilled that I'd remembered what he'd taught me so long ago!

[John 3 vs 16, For GOD so loved the world, that He gave HIS only begotten SON, that WHOSOEVER believeth in HIM should not perish, but have everlasting life.]

As we sat at the dinner table, Gay openly shared her family story with David and Jackie. They listened with sincere interest and empathy as Gay continued to share about the loss of her father. And she told them about her and me, and the love that God had given us for each other.

And through Gay's words, God helped me to see deep into her heart; I felt my love for her growing stronger and stronger.

⁓

After supper, David and Jackie took us for a drive to Mumbles Pier. We bought Joe's Ice Cream before walking out onto the pier.

"You can't beat Joe's Ice Cream, can you, Kingsley?" David exclaimed.

And we all shouted to the salty surf: "No you can't!"

It was a lovely night out on the pier as the light began to fade. People's lights were flicking on in their homes around the bay. The lights were always welcoming for anyone out at sea, or for people looking across the bay. Swansea Bay is shaped like a horseshoe, and it was becoming a horseshoe of lights reflecting on the still water of the bay.

"It's so romantic!" Gay whispered in my ear, as we walked behind David and Jackie, and we stopped every so often to admire the view and kiss. It was nice to be walking with another couple, I thought, even though David and Jackie were a generation older than us. They were young at heart and full of wisdom! David, being a Pastor, had a love for people, and both David and I worked with youth – me, as a counsellor and Pastor back in Canada; and David and Jackie ran the youth group at his church in Swansea. It gave David and me lots to talk about, and, it was also evident that Gay and Jackie had made a good connection.

Jackie invited us to come to their morning service on Sunday, and to bring Melody to be in the Sunday school too. We gladly accepted.

Before our evening ended, I talked to David about my plans for Gay and me. He said that he and Jackie would help us in any way they could. I felt that I had been given a mentor in David, and I praised God in my heart for bringing David and Jackie into our lives at this time, when we needed direction and guidance.

We ended our night with a cup of tea at the café beside the pier, and we all agreed that we'd spent a special evening together.

As Gay and I left David and Jackie's home, we talked about our plans for the next day. Deep in our hearts, the cry of the future could be heard! A future that we wanted to spend together! And before we drove away, I took Gay's hand and prayed to God to go before us and to be with us, as we walked into the future together!

"Go before us, Lord, we pray! And even though we don't know how everything can be worked out for us to be together, You do! Help us to have faith and to trust you, Oh God!"

And after our prayer, we had peace that He would work things out for us.

"Pearl is watching Melody for the day tomorrow," Gay said. "She's taking her shopping for school supplies. As Pearl doesn't have any children of her own, it's something I share with her, and she loves it!"

"That's really wonderful," I said. "I'm learning more in my life, through my relationship with my brother Fraser, about how important family is! And being able to share what we have been blessed with in our lives, with each other! Except for you! I don't want to share you! Except with Melody of course, and your mother and Pearl!"

Gay blushed and laughed, and then she kissed me on the cheek! I was a happy and contented man as she dropped me off at my brother's house.

"Wait!" I said, before kissing her goodbye. "Will you meet me at Pennard Castle at 10 a.m. in the morning?"

"Pennard Castle?" she echoed. "I thought we were going shopping and spending the day in town?"

"No, meet me at the Castle, Princess. It's really important! Then we'll go into town in the afternoon."

Gay was quiet for a few moments, and then she asked: "What are we going to do at the castle?"

"I'm sorry Princess, but I can't tell you that!"

Now she was blushing and smiling, and she said: "Okay my Prince! I will meet you at the castle at 10." She then pulled me back into the car to kiss me.

"Kingsley! I don't know why we are going to meet at the castle.... I am nervous and excited."

"Me too," I said, looking deep into her beautiful eyes.

"Good night, Gay," I said, giving her one more kiss and pulling myself out of the car.

"Bye, Kingsley. See you tomorrow!"

And as my head hit the pillow, I thanked God for the perfect evening. Tomorrow, I would ask Gay to marry me!

Chapter Twenty-Three
The Castle and the Ring

efore leaving the house, I made a treasure map for Gay –
so she could search for her ring! We were meeting at the
castle at 10, and I wanted to get there at least an hour before she
arrived. I managed to catch a bus that got me to Southgate Village
by 8:30 a.m.; and by the time I walked across Pennard golf course
to the castle, it was 9 a.m. I had an hour before Gay arrived.

It was a beautiful autumn morning with a crispness in the air.
The skylarks hovered and sang in the sky above me, telling stories
of their spring and summer days. A song that I could now sing with
them! Because my beloved Gay – the woman with the sunshine in
her hair – had come back and brought spring to my heart.

I had arrived back on the Gower having forgotten the song
I used to sing! But now it was back! And I sang with the skylarks
and I danced with the kestrel!

"You're singing again, boy! And dancing!"

"Yes, Sir, I am!"

"Good to see it, boy! Carry on."

"Yes, Sir, I will!"

I had wrapped Maggie's ring, in its little blue box, with
brown paper and then tied it with a string. Now I dug a hole in
the rocky ground underneath the archway in the castle wall. It was
where Gay and I used to stand together and watch the quiet valley
below. Sometimes we saw the horses drinking from the river or just
standing in the cool, flowing water under the warm summer sun.

Today the valley was silent, as if waiting with me in anticipation, to hear what Gay would say when she found the ring! But

the skylarks still sang in the cloudless sky, and as they flew lower, their song seemed sweeter and sweeter, as if they, too, were waiting! And they were, of course!

My love would be coming soon, I thought, as I walked around the castle walls – the walls within which the secrets of the ages are kept! And sometime today, our secrets would be whispered in the wandering winds and inside the castle walls.

Now I climbed up onto the castle walls, as I had done when I was a boy, waiting for someone special to arrive. And I heard again, on yesterday's winds, my mother's call: "Kingsley and Fraser, come down from the castle walls, before you fall and hurt yourselves!"

And today I called out to the wind, and said, "No mum, I can't come down! I am waiting for my love, for she is coming to see me!"

And then a wind blew down from heaven, and she said, "Oh, I see! Congratulations, Kingsley, my boy!"

♪✳

SONG OF GAY

I could see now in the distance my love coming towards me!
You, my love are so precious!
Come now and kiss me with your tender lips!
Yes, kiss me over and over again!
Like falling rain on a parched land,
let your kisses rain down on me and refresh me
like the springtime!
Pour your love in a crystal glass and let me drink of it!
For your love is sweeter than the finest wine.
And how fragrant is your scent
that travels before you, as your arrival is announced on
the gentle breeze!
Oh, come to me, my darling!

Your body excites me, as your dress swirls
and your hair dances, as your bare feet walk silently
towards me upon the wild grass.
Your name is like a fragrance, a bottle of perfume just opened,
and your radiance is like the rising sun!
You are the song that is sung over a thousand hills!

How lovely are your creamy cheeks that wear
your morning blush!
And your necklace of Evening Emerald! –
that sparkles like secret promises waiting to be discovered!
How beautiful your slender neck, that I will smell and kiss,
and I will string jewels around it.
And I will make you earrings of gold and sapphire
that shine like your eyes, the light of your soul!

How beautiful you are, my darling! How completely lovely!
Your eyes are like calling doves, and like a waterfall,
I fall inside you, and I see my own soul as I dance with you!
You are my spring bluebell on Pennard Hill,
and the lily of Three Cliffs Valley!

© *Kingsley Ross Hill*

My love was almost here now, and I climbed down from the wall of the castle and ran to her as to the summer sun! She threw her arms around me and held me tightly like her knight who had been away in battle! I stroked her face and kissed her! She blushed like a morning rose, her eyes saying things that words could not! Her look of excitement and expectancy wrote the first poem of our day!

I asked her to sit down and I told her a story.

"There was once a Prince who loved a Princess, and they shared the most wonderful love in all of Gowerland! But the Princess was taken away from the Prince in his youth! Which left the

Prince feeling like a part of him was missing, and the hole in his heart could not be filled! For a long time, the Prince came back to the castle, hoping and praying that one day his Princess would return!"

(I could not hold my tears as I told the story of my heart! Gay wept too, but feeling her love and strength, I continued.)

"The Prince had something special to give to the Princess! But because the years went by and she did not come back, and he hid his special gift on the castle grounds, and he tried to carry on with his life. The Prince was then given the wonderful gift of a wild stallion, the wildest stallion in all the land! But still he could not forget his Princess, for the Princess's love lived in his heart! And every time he looked at his saddle, he was reminded of her love, for the Princess had given the Prince her saddle, her most treasured possession, before she went away! His love and longing went out to her. And she had taken his love with her and kept it deep within her heart!"

"One day, with his broken heart, the Prince left for a faraway land, and he thought surely now I can forget her! But he found that no matter where he went, or what he did, he couldn't get her love out of his heart!"

I began to weep again, as I felt my love for Gay rising in my heart like the sun.

Gay also cried, and she continued the story.

"While the Prince was away in a faraway land, the Princess returned twice looking for her Prince! For she felt in her heart that a part of her was missing! A part of her that she could no longer live without! And the Princess, not being able to find her Prince, wrote letters to him, and she gave them to the Prince's friend Maggie, who promised to give the letters to the Prince if he ever returned to the Gower."

Now it was my turn again, to continue the story.

"And one day the Prince came back from the faraway land, in search of his Princess, because he could not live without her love! After praying to God to help him find her. The Prince found the two letters from her. Maggie, before she died, had given them to the Prince's friend Heather. After reading the letters, the Prince realized that the Princess still loved him and was searching for him. And his heart was happy, and he stayed, and he searched for her!

I stopped talking now and looked into Gay's weeping eyes. And through her tears, I could feel her love radiating out to me.

"I love you Gay, so much! I have never stopped loving you!"

And she replied: "I love you too, Kingsley, with all my heart! And I have carried your love with me since the day I went away!"

We hugged and kissed, and hugged and kissed, as our tears of joy mingled together and ran down each other's cheeks. Gay dried my eyes with her hair, and I kissed her salty tears away!

"You taste like the ocean today," I said, and we both laughed.

"Now close your eyes," I said, and I put the treasure map in her hand.

"What is it?" she asked excitedly.

"It's a treasure map," I answered. And Gay began to follow the clues on the map while I followed slowly behind her.

"Aren't you going to help me?" she said, glancing back.

"No, keep looking and you will find it!"

She finally stopped at the archway in the castle wall, overlooking the Three Cliffs Valley.

"This was our favourite place!" she said, looking back at me. "And on the map there is an arrow pointing down at this spot!"

I didn't say anything; I just smiled.

"What do I do?" she said, looking down. "I don't see anything!"

"You have to dig for treasure," I said, and I handed her a stick to dig with. She began to dig in the hard ground.

"Try over here," I said, putting my hand over hers, and moving the stick over about a foot from where she had started digging. "The ground is soft here," I said, taking the stick gently from her hand. "Try digging with your hands."

She knelt and started to dig in the softer ground. "It's really soft here," she said excitedly. "Like there is something buried here!" She looked up and our eyes met, and she pulled the brown paper package from the ground.

"What is it, my Prince?" she said in a soft voice, and a pink blush suddenly covered her face. "Oh, Kingsley, I'm so excited! What is it?"

"Let's sit here in the archway overlooking the valley, and you can open it!" I replied.

Gay sat on the edge of the archway, and I sat behind her with my legs around hers. She leaned back upon my chest, and I smelt her hair and kissed her neck.

"Aren't you going to open it, lovely lady?" I whispered gently into her ear. "We must be quiet, because all the Princes and Princesses of the past are with us, all around us, listening and waiting for you to open it, my Princess!"

"Oh, Kingsley! This is so romantic! I wish this moment could last forever!"

"It will," I said," as I pulled her head back gently to meet my kiss. And our tongues danced as we tasted the centuries of Prince and Princess kisses that had expressed love within these castle walls!

"My love, open your present!"

"Yes, my love, I will!"

As I held my arms around her waist, she untied the ribbons and bows that decorated the brown paper. And there within the folds of the parcel, was the royal blue velvet box.

"Oh my gosh, Kingsley," she whispered, looking back at me with a look of love that made my heart skip.

"I love you, Gay, and this is for you to keep for forever and a day!"

"Forever won't be long enough, Kingsley," she said, turning her head to kiss me again. And when we both came up for air, we both said at the same time, "We are going to need that extra day – the day beyond forever!" and we both laughed.

Then Gay opened the velvet box, and found the ring! And she cried tears of such joy!

"When I was a little girl," she said, "my mum brought me here once. And I stood where we are sitting now, and I dreamed that one day I would meet a real Prince and fall in love, and he would make me his Princess! And I remember my mum telling me that Princes and Princesses lived here not in the present day, but long ago! But since I met you Kingsley, I know that they still live today! You are a real Prince, Kingsley! And I love you with all my heart!"

Gay pulled the ring out of the box and saw that the stone was Evening Emerald!

"Kingsley, it's the same colour as the stone on my Celtic cross that you gave me! And it represents our special times when we walked in the emerald evenings of our youth!"

As I listened to Gay's words, I celebrated in my heart! And I felt Maggie's spirit with us, celebrating our love! I pictured her face smiling from heaven, and my mother smiling as well, for she had gone to heaven too, just a few years ago!

"Who are you talking to?" Gay asked.

"To Maggie and to my Mum," I answered. I know they are with us! There are windows in heaven!"

"Yes, I know, my love! I can feel my Dad with us too!"

"What are they all saying, my love?" I asked.

"They are saying that you are Orange and I am Indigo!"

And we both stood up in the archway and shouted across the valley together: "These are the colours of our love, you know. I am Orange, and you are Indigo!" And we kissed and said, "Yes, my love, I know."

I then held Gay's fingers and gently took the ring from her palm. As I knelt down on the ground, our eyes never left each other. And I said, "Gay, will you marry me? You are my true love! The love of my life! And I will love you forever and a day!"

And she smiled and cried, and her face lit up as radiant as the sun. And she said: "Yes, yes my love! You are my forever love! And I don't want to live another day without you! And nor does Melody! She loves you dearly, Kingsley! We both love you!"

And she shouted out on the wind. "Yes Kingsley, I will marry you, my Prince!"

And I slipped my ring upon her finger, and it was a perfect fit!

"How did you know my size?" she asked, beaming.

"God knew; He measured it!"

"Yes, Kingsley, He knew the perfect size!"

We spent the rest of the day at Pennard Castle and waited to watch the sunset – which had been our favourite thing to do in the days of our youth. Tonight, we walked and held hands as a mature man and woman. And we talked of our hopes and dreams and spending a lifetime together.

And I asked Gay, now that we were engaged, if she would come on a camping trip with me around the Gower.

"Yes, Kingsley!" she said excitedly. "I'll ask if Mum will take Melody. I know she will be happy for us! I will ask her tomorrow, when Melody and I spend the day together with her.

"It will take us about eight days," I said, "if we take our time exploring the Gower."

"That would be perfect," Gay replied. "That will still give me three or four days to get ready for work again in Cardiff."

Gay and I watched the most beautiful sunset from our castle.

"Do you remember the sunset that God gave us, the night before I had to leave for England, Kingsley?"

"Yes, I remember."

And this sunset was even more beautiful, we agreed, because we didn't have sadness in our hearts, only Joy. We named this new sunset 'the sunset of God's promise' because it represented our future together! From this sunset forth, each new sunset would write upon the skies the stories of our love and our life together.

The Gower Peninsula is called 'the land of the setting suns.'
And tonight, the orange glow of the sunset lit up Gay's long, flowing
hair, and made it shine like the colours in the western sky.

"You look so lovely, my beloved! With your sunset hair, and
your Evening Emerald ring!"

As I walked Gay back down to the valley, and up to where she
had left her car in Penmaen, I asked her if we could pick up Melody
to take her to get a Joe's Ice cream, overlooking the bay. Then we
could tell her our news. For she was such a part of us finding each
other again. Gay was happy that I wanted to include her in our
special evening and tell her of our wonderful plans.

"I know she will be so thrilled, Kingsley! She loves you, and
she wants so much for you to be her dad!"

And I felt such joy in my heart, and I thanked and praised
God for his blessing as we walked along!

When we arrived at the caravan in Reynoldston, Melody
was very excited that she didn't have to go to bed, but instead was
going out for a Joe's ice cream. She raced into my arms and gave
me the biggest hug.

We were soon on our way to Swansea, and we went for
a walk along the promenade before having our cones. It was a
lovely night as the welcoming lights of the city reflected out across
the bay. And as Gay held my one hand, and Melody the other,
I felt such a profound sense of belonging and family, something
I'd never experienced before. At least, not in the wholeness that
I felt tonight.

After we'd walked for a distance, Gay spoke up.

"How would you like it if Mum and Kingsley got married,
Melody?"

"Really? Really?" she answered ecstatically. "Then I would
have a real dad?"

"Yes, Melody, you would" I said excitedly.

"That means I would have a dad like the other kids in
my class?" she continued. As I listened to her words, and more

importantly listened to her heart, I was reminded of the awesome responsibility, and the awesome blessing, that was being presented to me! At Melody's words, Gay looked at me with complete trust that I would take care of her and Melody, as a husband and father.

"When are you getting married Mum and Kingsley? I mean Dad. I mean, is it okay to call you Dad, Kingsley?"

Gay looked at me with a blushing smile, and I said, " Yes Melody, I would like you to call me Dad!"

"I know when you two are getting married, Mum!"

"And when's that?" Gay replied.

"It's when you and Dad have walked through all four seasons together! Then you can get married. You will know you are with the right person once you have walked through winter, spring, summer and autumn together."

Gay looked at me in wonder, at Melody's words! Then I shared with her how Melody and I had had this wonderful conversation about relationships, when we'd first met on the beach at the Dragon Pool.

And I said: "Yes Gay! Melody has a lot of wisdom. She understands how important it is for two people to take their time in getting to know each other. The seasons represent the different times and experiences that we need to go through, to really know and understand each other."

As I spoke, Melody had the biggest smile on her face, and she said, "See Mum, Dad says I'm really smart! And do you know what? Dad and I have already walked two seasons together – when we first met before in the spring and summer! So now you have to walk the autumn and winter together before you get married!"

Gay and I looked at each other and laughed, and I said: "Yes Melody, we can get married in the spring!"

"Hurray!" Melody cried. "Spring is my favourite time of year, when all the foals are born!"

"Me too," I said. And Gay said that was her favourite season too.

We walked for another half an hour or so, and then drove back to the caravan. Gay and Melody sat quietly in the living room while I called Gay's mum on the phone in the kitchen, and asked her permission to marry her daughter.

Helen was quiet for a while, and then she spoke up: "Yes Kingsley! I give you my blessing! I know how much you love my daughter and care for my granddaughter, Melody! And if my husband were alive, he'd give you his blessing too! And Gay has always loved you, Kingsley; she's never stopped loving you. And I've watched you with Melody, and you will make her a wonderful father! And Kingsley, one other thing! Thank you for calling and showing me the respect to ask me.

"Thank you too, Helen!" I said.

Gay and Melody now came into the kitchen, and Melody asked if I could put her to bed and tell her a story tonight. So I did.

I told her my story of when I had slept in my cave at Bacon Hole. How I went to sleep in the warmth and light of my fire, as it danced pictures on the walls of my cave. And how I dreamed of emptying the Dragon Pool and finding seahorses, with whom I rode the sea and found sunken ships with treasure. Melody's eyes flickered as she lost her battle to stay awake and drifted away to dream the rest of our story.

It was getting late and time for me to go. Gay drove me to the bus stop and waited with me for the bus to arrive.

"I will see you on Sunday," she shouted. "Melody and I will pick you up for church. And meanwhile I will call Mum and ask her if she can have Melody on Sunday afternoon, and we can have our trip around the Gower."

David and Jackie had invited us to come to their church on Sunday, and there was also a Sunday school for Melody. I also had something special that I wanted to ask David – I wanted him to marry Gay and me in the spring! And I would ask him on Sunday.

Gay and I weren't seeing each other tomorrow, which was Saturday. That would give me a day to think and pray, and spend some time with Fraser.

Saturday morning arrived, and "No, yesterday wasn't a dream! It really happened! Gay said she would marry me! And I am going to be a dad to Melody!

Fraser and I watched the football game, as usual, and then after breakfast I told him and Lynn my news. And they were so happy for me! And Fraser said, "We must go out and celebrate tonight with a meal!"

After watching Liverpool win their game against Spurs, Fraser and I headed out for a ride on Guzzi! Guzzi is a 900cc, shaft drive, piece of engineering brilliance! Made by the Motto Guzzi motorcycle company in Italy. No "Jap crap" for the Hill Brothers! Wow, what a bike! Sleek, fast, stylish Italian design, with great handling to boot! And I had fond memories of my motorcycling days as we rode along the country lanes and left every car in the dust behind us. Fraser is a great rider, and I felt safe riding behind him. I reminisced about the 21 motorcycles I had owned, loved, and lost, before buying a car.

And I remembered riding my Triumph Tiger through the village with the police in hot pursuit! All my friends were cheering me on in my rebellious madness! Oh, how vain my life was then! But, by the grace of God, I am still here! And, needless to say, motorcycling is still in my blood!

We stopped at Illston Combs in Park Mill, a favourite boyhood haunt for Fraser and I. And this morning on our walk, I received encouragement and support from my brother. Much as I was certain, and joyous, about my decision to marry Gay, there were significant challenges ahead of me: my having to go back to Canada, and Gay and I having to make the decision about where we were going to live. Would I come back to Wales to live? And have to travel back and forth to visit my own beloved children in Canada? Or would Gay and Melody come to Canada to live, once we were married?

Fraser has this wonderful gift of taking life as it comes, taking everything in his stride. And not having to understand all the various details as to how something was going to come together or work out. He often said that he had no real faith, but I always begged to differ. For God spoke to me powerfully through my brother!

"It will all work out," he said as the silence fell between us. "When the time comes for the decision to be made as to where you will live, you will have peace and clarity, and you'll know what needs to happen!"

Just like Maggie would so often say: "Trust in the Lord with all your heart, and do not lean on your own understanding. Acknowledge Him in all your ways, and He will direct your paths."

And when we finished our walk, I felt grounded, and confident of the present and the future. Fraser also shared with me about how my faith in God, and seeing Him at work in my life, had encouraged him. And we both shared how pleased our mum would be for us now. Her two boys both trusting in God and experiencing His blessing in their lives! That had been her prayer for us, before she left for heaven, two years ago.

I also talked about my excitement about being a father to Melody. I knew from the experience of fathering my own beloved children that fatherhood is one of God's greatest gifts to men. And now I was going to be a Dad to a girl who had never known what it was like to have a real dad in her life. What an awesome privilege God was entrusting to me! And I prayed for His wisdom and guidance, to be the best Dad I could be, to all my children. And the best husband I could be for Gay!

Before Lynn and Fraser and I left the house to go and celebrate my news, Gay phoned to say her mum had agreed to look after Melody in Cardiff while Gay and I went camping and exploring around the Gower. I was thrilled at the news, because I felt that this time together was something that would help to ground us in our relationship before Gay headed back to her job in Cardiff, and I headed back to Canada.

"It will be like going on a honeymoon early," Fraser said.

"Yes, it will!" I replied excitedly. We will really need the time to connect before having to be apart for some time.

Now we headed out to the restaurant to celebrate. Fraser and Lynn proposed "Steak by Night" in Swansea. Dad and Mary had gone down to Devonshire for the weekend, and wouldn't be back until sometime on Monday. And I thought about how pleased they would be as I told them my news about Gay and me.

The waiter came and took our orders. And I ordered steak with Yorkshire pudding and veggies. Fraser had recommended the Yorkshire pudding. And it was, as he said, a meal the size of a medium size plate, with a cavity in the middle full of homemade gravy! And the steak and house sauce. (My mouth is watering while I write, dear Reader; could you pass the pepper please?)

Lynn had dressed to the nines, and Fraser wore his suede jacket and leather tie, only worn on the most special of occasions! It was great to see them enjoying themselves. If any couple had something to celebrate, they did. They had been married for over eighteen years.

After our meal, we headed out for a Joe's Ice cream. Really, no night out in Swansea would be complete without it! Not in our family anyway!

We were carrying on a tradition that had started with my Grandma and Grandpa, then my mother and father when Fraser and I were young boys. I was doing well this week! A Joe's Ice cream last night with Gay and Melody; one with Fraser and Lynn tonight; and oh yeah, I'd also had one with David and Jackie on Friday!

"Maybe I should take a day off!" I pondered. "No! Not on your Sundae! (Get it Reader? Not on your Sundae?)" Laughing, I remembered: "Oh yeah, it's Saturday isn't it!"

After having Joe's ice cream again, I could not bear the thought of going back to the Dairy Queen in Canada. Absolute rubbish, compared to Joe's.

We ended our evening with a walk along the seafront, and then headed home.

"Goodnight, Kings! And congratulations on your engagement!"

"Thanks Fraser and Lynn for a great evening. See you in the morning."

Chapter Twenty-Four

Sunday the Sabbath

*G*ay and Melody arrived to pick me up for church at 9:15. The morning service was at 10:00, and as we arrived at Mount Pleasant Church, David and Jackie were there to greet us at the door. Jackie took a special interest in Melody and showed her around the Sunday school, which Melody was excited to attend.

Once the regular Sunday school teacher arrived, Jackie introduced her to Melody, and Gay and I headed upstairs to the main church sanctuary. We talked to David until the service was about to start; David was preaching at the evening service tonight, so he had booked a guest speaker for this morning. Gay and I sat in the pew, about three rows back from the front. Gay looked so beautiful this morning in her blue velvet dress, and her white stockings and heels. And a white cashmere sweater that felt as soft as her flowing hair. I felt so proud as Gay took my arm.

After a lovely praise and worship time, in which the music team and congregation sang some of the traditional Welsh hymns, both Gay and I commented to each other that we felt the presence of the Holy Spirit around us and throughout the building! The guest speaker also talked about love. And it was one of those sermons that felt like it was custom-made for me! And Gay felt the same way! It was like God was putting His arms around us and affirming our plans to spend our lives together, and in particular, affirming what the commitment of love really means!

After the service, David and Jackie invited us over to their place for lunch. And at the dinner table, Melody kept sharing how much she had enjoyed Sunday school. And Jackie gave her a Children's Bible.

"It's even got pictures in it, Mum and Dad!" she said excitedly.

Both Gay and I shared with David and Jackie how we had enjoyed the service, and how we had strongly sensed the presence of God. This was encouraging to them, as they had been praying specifically for God's Spirit to fill the church.

As our conversation went on, I asked Gay if she felt comfortable with me talking to David about our wedding plans. And asking him if he could marry us. She agreed, so when Jackie and Melody were playing a game after lunch, I talked to David while Gay was present. He was thrilled that we had asked him, and he said that he'd be honoured to marry us, even down on the beach!

But there was a problem with the timing. He and Jackie would be going away on a mission trip, and they would be gone for almost a year! That would be too long to wait, both Gay and I agreed. We wanted to honour God by not living together before we were married. We wanted His continued blessing on our relationship.

Then David said something that changed things in an instant! He said he could be available to marry us over the next few weeks, before he and Jackie left for their trip. Gay and I had envisioned having our wedding in the spring, after I'd been back to Canada. But we said we'd pray about it and let him know within a few days.

In the evening, Melody spent time with her Aunt Pearl, while Gay and I went for a walk.

"What do you think?" I asked. "I don't want us to feel rushed in any way, and we both want to honour God!"

Gay shared that she felt a special connection with David and Jackie, and especially with how they had received Melody.

"They didn't judge me as being a single Mum, which has been my experience in a lot of 'so called churches.' I would really like David to marry us!"

"I would too," I replied. And I took Gay's hand and led her in prayer, as we asked God's direction and guidance in making our decision.

∽

After our prayers, both Gay and I sensed God's presence and peace within our hearts, and we continued our walk, enjoying His creation around us. As we walked back to the caravan, God impressed on our hearts that we should ask David to marry us in just a few weeks. Gay shared that it would help to give her security and strength to have us become 'one' in God's sight, before I went back to Canada. I felt that it would also strengthen me, and help keep me focused while I was so far away.

"Kingsley, my love! I lost you once and I never want to lose you again! I want to get married, Kings. I want us to be able to make love as a husband and wife when we go on our trip around the Gower."

I held her in my arms and assured her that this was what I wanted too! And we ended our walk by praying, and thanking God for his peace and assurance, and we were grateful that He was with us and directing our paths.

∽

Once we arrived back at the caravan, I called Helen and asked her if we could go ahead and marry within the next few weeks. She thanked me again for showing her respect in our asking and gave us her blessing.

On Monday, I phoned David and we arranged the wedding date for a week from Saturday. That's not this weekend but next, I thought, as the date sank in.

I went over to Dad's house in the evening and told him and Mary the news. They were surprised at how soon the wedding would take place. But they were thrilled for us, as were Lynn and Fraser. And I marvelled at how God had caused everything to work out and fall into place.

♪⁂

A PSALM OF KINGSLEY

In You, O Lord, I have put my trust;
And I have never been disappointed.
You have given me my hearts desire,
and my hopes and dreams,
you have kept them safe within your heart,
and embraced them as your own!
You inclined your ears to my prayers,
and answered my cries for help.
You are my place of safety;
my high tower where the enemy can not reach.
My heart praises you,
for the marvellous things you have done!
You, O Lord,
are my greatest joy, and the strength and power of my life.
You travel
before me and prepare the paths I walk on.
I see your footprints ever before me along the way.
You guide me with your eye upon me, and
I am always in your thoughts.
Your faithfulness sours high above the clouds,
and your love engulfs me!
Protecting me from every side.
The sword of the Lord fights
for me! And he puts a garrison of peace
around my heart, even as the battle rages on.
The one who guards my soul, does not sleep or slumber;
but is at my right hand always.
I will tell the world, O Lord, of "the great and
mighty deeds you have done!"

© *Kingsley Ross Hill*

For the next several days, Helen and Mary helped Gay and I with our arrangements. And David and Jackie became like mentors to us. I met with David four times before the wedding, and he shared his wisdom and life experience with me, which was such a great help as I prepared to join my life to Gay and Melody.

Melody was thrilled that she was going to be the ring bearer, and also a bridesmaid with her Aunt Pearl. And I asked both Dad and Fraser to be my two best men! And we would have the wedding outside Great Thunder's Cave, or our "family cave," as Gay and I now called it.

Dad and Mary helped to pick out a suit and tie with an aqua blue shirt, which was the theme colour of our wedding. Helen and Lynn helped Gay and Melody with their dresses. It was amazing how everything came together in a spirit of friendship and fellowship, considering that some of those involved, like Lynn and Helen, had never met before. It was more evidence of God's presence and favour.

A week before the wedding, David and Jackie invited everyone over to their house for a special dinner. Gay and I felt so blessed and our hearts overflowed with thanksgiving and praise to our God.

One of the highlights for me, prior to the wedding, was to go over to Penmaen Stables and invite Heather to attend the wedding. She was so excited that we were having the ceremony at Great Thunder's cave! She remembered the day that I first rode, and thundered across the sands!

"You are as wild as your stallion, Kingsley," she said. "And you are marrying the most beautiful woman in the land, aren't you?"

"Yes, I am Heather," I replied. "And I love her so much!"

"I know you do Kingsley, and she loves you. You were always meant to be together! Maggie always said you were, and that one day you would find your way back to each other. And you have! Congratulations Kingsley! I am so happy for you! And if you wait here for a minute, I have something I want to give to you, and you needn't say anything to anyone!"

Heather disappeared into a back room for what seemed like a long time. And then she came back into the living room and handed me a small box.

"You can open it now," she said excitedly. It wasn't often that I'd seen Heather excited, and it was usually when one of her students did something particularly well in her riding school.

I opened the box to find the most beautiful gold ring, with three flashing diamonds on it!

"It was my wedding ring, Kingsley, and I want you to have it!"

I didn't know what to say; I felt so overcome with emotion. First it was Maggie's Evening Emerald engagement ring, which Gay treasures. And now this! Heather was giving me her wedding ring!

"It's been cleaned and polished like new, Kingsley. And I want you to have it to give to Gay on your wedding day!"

I couldn't hold back my tears any longer, and I wept with joy!

"Thank you, Heather! Thank you so much!"

On my way home, I stopped off at the post office to buy some flowers. I then caught the #18 bus to Port Eynon, where I visited Maggie's grave. I knelt and prayed to God as I remembered what Maggie had shared with me in her letters.

"You were right, Maggie. God did have a wonderful plan all along! And He did see the big picture! And he brought all the pieces and players together, Maggie. Just like you said he would. So much didn't make sense at the time, like when I missed Gay, and your letters, when I was away in Canada. But your words spoke to me all these years later, and God did join all the scripts in my life's play together, Maggie. And guess what? I'm getting married! God worked it out so Gay and I could meet again, and His timing was perfect! Do you remember telling me about God's perfect timing? Well he did it again, Maggie!" I cried.

Chapter Twenty-Five
Wedding Bells Across the Sands

The day of the wedding arrived! September the 19th, and it was a low tide at 3 pm, so we decided to have the ceremony at 2 pm at the cave. Fraser and Lynn had gotten me up early, and Dad and Mary were going to drive us to the car park on Pennard Cliffs. David and Jackie would meet us at the car park at 1 p.m., and from there, the seven of us would walk along the cliff-tops to Pobbles Beach.

Gay, Melody, and her family would walk down through the Burrows and across the sands from Penmaen, and meet us at the cave. Heather would arrive on horseback, of course, and was riding down from the stables with her niece.

It was a cloudless afternoon on Pennard Cliffs as we met at the car park. I stood tall and proud in my new suit that Dad and Mary had bought me. And Fraser and Lynn had got me an aqua silk shirt and brown tie, which worked beautifully with my brown herringbone suit.

"You look like a handsome Prince, coming to claim his Princess," Mary said. And indeed, that's what I was doing as I waited for David and Jackie to arrive.

"This is my first wedding on a beach!" David shared with Dad and Mary, as we walked along the cliff tops. And in the distance, Cefn Bryn wore an appropriate wardrobe of brown ferns about his waist. And a grey rock belt, old red sandstone shoes, and a blue-sky bow tie above.

"So, glad you could make my wedding, Mr. Bryn. We go back many years, don't we?"

"We do indeed, wild boy! And now you're a Knight of the Gower! I wouldn't miss your special day and I understand you're getting married at your family cave?"

"Indeed, I am, Mr. Bryn. Indeed, I am!"

As we walked down through the dunes to Pobbles, the tide was about three quarters of the way out. And the sun sparkled on the rippled sea, like the diamonds in the ring that I would soon be giving my Gay!

"It is of the purest gold and rare in design," the jeweller said, when I'd taken it to be sized.

"That describes my lovely Gay," I replied. "She is of the purest love, and so rare that she is one of a kind. And the three diamonds on the band represent Gay, Melody and I! And our new family that our vows would signify us to be, on this most special day!"

When we arrived on the sands, I lifted my eyes to the west. And in the distance were four figures, with one being smaller than the others. It had to be Melody, with Gay, Helen and Pearl beside her. As they got closer, I could see the coloured dresses they were wearing. Gay's was aqua and white with a crown of wild flowers in her hair – that Helen and Heather had picked from the last of the summer smiles that grew along the burrows. And Melody wore a dress similar to her mum's with aqua and white. She also carried a bouquet of Autumn Iris, which reminded me of the purple colour of Gay's eyes.

Suddenly a wave of emotion rolled over my soul, as the reality of our sacred day sank in! I was marrying the true love of my life! The one I did not want to live without. And she came with a young daughter, who I was growing to love. And within minutes, I would become the Dad she so needed in her life. I also had another mother, whom I highly respected, and who would be a strength and resource to our family.

Dad and Mary were here too. How wonderful to have my

Dad as my Best Man, and Fraser as my Groomsman. And Heather, who now arrived on horseback with her niece riding a smaller horse at her side. It was Heather who had trained me to ride Great Thunder. And Pearl who looked beautiful as she watched over her sister with a tender and protective smile. And David and Jackie, who had become mentors to Gay and I, as well as becoming wonderful Christian friends.

And yes, I was the happiest and richest man in all of Gower Land!

"You are a true Knight of the Gower, Boy!"

"Yes, Sir, I am!"

"Well done, Boy!"

"Thank you, Sir!"

Gay and I stood in front of the entrance of our cave, and Melody was to the left of Gay.

"Before we start," I said, "I'd like to honour three members of our family who couldn't be here today. But their spirits are, and they roam the Gower wild and free. "

"First, there is Great Thunder! My beloved stallion and friend, who taught me so many of life's lessons and what it meant to live free. And today, I stand where he used to stand, outside our family cave.

"I would also like to honour Thunder Spring, who saved my life in this cave when she kept me warm through the night, so that I didn't die of hypothermia after being swept out to sea.

And, Little Thunder, who became Roaring Thunder, after winning his first fight with another stallion. He was Great Thunder and Thunder Spring's son. I was there when Thunder Spring gave birth to him in this cave. This sacred place, dear friends and family, is Gay's and my family home," I said.

"And mine!" Melody shouted out boldly.

After my words, people looked around, as if expecting something to happen. And it did! Just as David was about to start the service, the stallion I'd seen running the sands when I'd arrived on the Gower in the Spring, came galloping towards us! People watched in amazement as he slowed to a canter, and then a trot, and then stopped and stood on the right side of the cave. Suddenly, I had another best man, a stallion. Welcome, Autumn Dancer!" I said.

Melody giggled, and Gay smiled and whispered quietly: "We are all here now."

"David, you can continue with the service now," I turned and said.

David began reading from the Bible in 1ˢᵗ Corinthians 13: 4-7

Love is long-suffering and kind. Love is not jealous, it does not boast, does not get puffed up, does not behave indecently, does not look for its own interest, does not become provoked. It does not keep any record of wrongs. It does not rejoice in unrighteousness, but rejoices with the truth. It bears all things, believes all things, hopes all things, endures all things. Love never fails.

I'd read the verses several times before, but standing here today with the love of my life, the words came alive within my heart like never before. As David read, "love is long-suffering and kind," Gay and I fell into each other's eyes. And suddenly there was only us. As God's sacred words were illuminated in our hearts, I had a vision of our marriage, of Gay and I being patient and kind to each other, through all the years and seasons of our lives. And I could feel my smile like the sunshine radiating from my face, as I felt the love and joy of my heart and Gay's love reflecting back to me.

"I love you," she whispered.

"I love you too," I whispered back.

And as David stopped talking, Melody shouted out, "My mum and Kingsley love each other! And, I love you too, Kingsley. You are my daddy now!"

Autumn Dancer neighed.

Everyone shouted "Hurray!" And the sparrow hawk dived,

the sun smiled, the sea roared, and Pennard Castle sighed. For our love had nowhere to hide.

May I have the rings, David now asked. And Dad, walked over to him, and handed him the beautiful ring that Heather had given me. It was on a little cream silk cushion that Mary had made. Melody, now left her mothers side, and walked over to David, and handed him Gays ring for me, which was also on a little cream coloured cushion. Her face beaming like a little bride herself. As Gay and I turned to look at one another to say our vows, I could not describe how "wonderful" I felt inside! She was indeed, the most beautiful woman in the world to me! And her face and eyes were radiant with love for me! Her dress, and her hair were perfect! And when she smiled, oh, this poet ran out of rhyme! Suddenly, I breathed again, as David, said, Kingsley and Gay, repeat after me. I was first to say my vows, and I also read Gay a poem. Gay now wept with tears of love and joy, as she listened to my words, and then repeated her vows to me, after David. I then read a little poem that I had written for Melody. That's my poem, she said loudly! See, I told you that I was a real princess!

After we had made our vows, and I had finished reading Melody her poem, Gay and I walked hand in hand to the sea, leaving everyone behind us at the cave. And as we reached the waves, Autumn Dancer, thundered past us, and I shouted, thank you for coming old boy!

∽

It was interesting that apart from today, 'our wedding day,' I hadn't seen Autumn Dancer since the first time I walked the beach, when I had just arrived in the spring. Ruby was the only other stallion around. Sweet memories gently turned the pages of my mind, as I remembered Great Thunder and felt his presence with us.

"And Gay said, "I know our horse family can see us. They are celebrating with us right now."

"I know," I replied, as I felt Gay's eyes and her spirit travel deep into my heart. "I love you Gay" was all I could say.

We reached the waves, and I held her in my arms and kissed her. And we danced in the tide. Best friend and lover was the song of the sea around us. And we splashed and played and laughed, and as Gay jumped on my back, the white train of her dress rode on the waves behind us like a dancing mermaid.

I lifted my eyes to see Melody walking down the sands towards us.

"Come on, little Princess!" I shouted. Melody took off her sandals and started running.

"Yes, come on, Melody!" Gay shouted.

And Melody ran straight into my arms. I lifted her up and swung her around in the waves. Then I lifted her up onto my shoulders and the three of us walked across the beach in the waves.

And the seagull said overhead, "You are a rich man, Kingsley Hill."

I shouted back, "I am indeed, Mr. Gull." Oh, its you, Charle, thanks for flying by! I wouldn't have missed it, he said. Congratulations, wild boy! I must be off now, got to meet Sylvia on Gull Rock. Bye Charle.

And Melody said: "I'm glad that you talk to seagulls, I do it all the time."

And Gay replied: "Now, I have two of you who talk to animals."

I giggled and Melody laughed.

David and Jackie were putting on a small reception for us at their church. After Gay, Melody and I had changed out of our wet clothes, we headed back to the car park. As we left the beach, Autumn Dancer galloped past and Melody shouted, "Bye, and thanks for coming to the wedding!"

"Yes, see you soon, Autumn, old boy," I said. And I knew in my heart that he was one of Great Thunder's descendants!

What a perfect wedding!

We arrived at Mount Pleasant church, and David and Jackie had gone out of their way to make it so special for us. Gay cried as she saw the whole church decorated with ribbons, flowers and balloons.

"Look, Mum," Melody said, "the ribbons and balloons match your dress and Dad's shirt. And look over there!" she continued, taking both our hands and leading us over to the most beautiful cake.

"Look, Dad, we are all on the cake! There's you and Mum, and there's me!"

"You're right," I said. "The figurines represent the three of us." And I said to Helen and Heather: "What a wonderful idea! They represent our family. Thank you for the cake."

"It's made Melody's day, having her figurine on the cake," Gay said to her mum and Heather. And it had. I watched her take the hand of everyone there, and one by one, she led them to the cake and pointed herself out.

And again I felt God speaking within my heart, of the wonderful blessing and responsibility He'd given me, in being a Dad to Melody.

I also felt my mum with me in spirit as I examined the cake. It had a thick layer of marzipan and sweet icing on top of the dark fruitcake. My favourite!

"Oh Mum, I miss you so much! But I know there are windows in heaven. And you can see me right now and how happy I am. One day I will see you again. Say Hi to Grandma and Grandpa for me, okay?"

Heather overheard me talking and we shared the moment.

"They are with you, Kingsley," she said, "rejoicing with you."

"I love you, Mum," I continued.

"I love you too, Kings. Congratulations!" she whispered.

After Gay and I cut the cake, Melody served all the guests, and the smile on her face grew larger and larger, as people told her that she looked beautiful in her lovely blue dress. David played his guitar and Jackie sang us a wedding song. The whole church was full of joy and music. Wow! Gay and I were so blessed! The whole wedding and the reception were perfect.

Dad and Fraser got up and told stories of how I used to stampede the wild horses through the neighbourhood, and race motorcycles through the village with the police in pursuit. As I looked across at Gay's mum, she grinned and bore it.

And I said under my breath: "Well done Helen, what a sport!"

Gay overheard me speaking and said, "What were you saying about my mum?"

"I was saying you should offer her another glass of port."

And it was Mary's turn to talk now. She shared how I'd ridden my stallion Great Thunder through the church yard and scared the priest! She said that she was so glad that I'd turned out alright in the end!

Helen took another sip of port from her glass and almost tripped over her high heels. The defining moment now arrived as Helen took the mike. I closed my eyes and waited for her to say that 'one word' that all bridegrooms fear their mother-in- laws will say at their wedding: 'Help!'

But Helen didn't shout for help. Instead, she welcomed me into her family, with tears in her eyes, and she spoke of how happy I'd made Gay and Melody since coming into their lives. She even told the story of how Gay and I had met and fallen in love all those years ago.

"There could never have been anyone else in this life that Gay could love as she loves Kingsley," she said. "You are the perfect man for my daughter, Kingsley. Welcome to my family."

Heather looked at me and laughed. "Are you feeling relieved?" she asked.

I heard Maggie's voice in my heart say, "Aren't you glad that you didn't elope now?"

And I whispered back with a smile. "Yes, Maggie I am. And thanks for coming."

"Oh, I wouldn't have missed it, Kings!"

Gay took the mike now and said, "I'm sure glad that King turned out alright in the end too. But I always knew that he was alright. I do like the wild side of my Prince! He has brought a whole new meaning to 'sweeping a girl off her feet'! It's on the back of a wild stallion I go, and over the hills and far away!"

At her words, I stood up taller in my suit and tie. Melody stood up now and Jackie adjusted the mike to her height. She told everyone that she and I had another horse now, Nan's-Nan. "She's called Nan's-Nan because she is the oldest horse, the great mother of all the horses."

And Heather nodded her head and clapped in approval, which was followed by the rest of us. Melody smiled and took a bow, and her face was beaming as Helen helped her down from the stage.

After the reception, Gay, Melody, and Helen and I went back to the caravan for the night. Then Helen would be taking Melody back to Cardiff to start school, and Gay and I would be leaving on our trip around the Gower.

Helen gave Gay and me her room, while she and Melody shared the other one.

"Good night, Melody!"

"Good night, Helen or Mum!" I smiled, having acquired a new Mum.

When Gay and I opened the door to the bedroom, there were candles and flowers, and a bottle of champagne with a set of beautiful crystal wine glasses. Cards and gifts covered the couch. As we looked around the room, we felt overwhelmed with the blessings that had been bestowed upon us!

I poured Gay a glass of champagne.

"Truly this was the most wonderful day of our lives," we both exclaimed. We drank a toast to God and to each other. I had married the love of my life! I could write a book describing the beauty and romance of our wedding night. But I will just say that all the years and months, and the seasons and days, and even the hours and minutes, that we had been apart, were united tonight as our souls became one."

♪✳

OUR LOVE

A POEM

"I am the spring crocus blooming on Cefn Bryn,
The lily of the Three Cliffs Valley." (Gay)

"And you are like a lily among thistles,
My darling among all others.
Even the lovely blue Water Iris is pale before you, my love." (Kingsley)

Like the finest apple tree in the orchard
Is my lover amongst other men.
I sit in his delightful shade and taste his delicious fruit.
He escorts me to the top of Rhossili Hill,
where the ravens perform their acrobatic dance.
He strengthens me with wild blackberry cakes,
As we sit outside our cave.
He refreshes me with juicy apples,
like the ones we fed to Thunder Spring,
For I am weak with love for my Prince.
Your left arm is under my head,
And your right arm embraces me.
Ah, I hear my lover coming!
He is leaping over Cefn Bryn
and climbing Pennard Castles walls.
Come and find me, my love.
My lover is as swift as the Golden Eagle,
And as graceful as the Red Kite.
Look, there he is behind the wall,
looking through the ancient window,
but with a love that is burning and new.
Come here, my love, for you have found me

In our special room.
Once you have stopped kissing me,
and my trembling has not yet ceased,
you say to me." (Gay)

"Rise up, my darling!
Come away with me, around the Gower.
Look, the winter of our separation is past!
And every spring we shall awake together!
The rains are over.
The flowers are springing up,
and the smell of the wild gorse is upon your breath.
The season of singing birds is upon us,
And the cooing of turtle doves fills the air with our love song!
Rise up, my darling!
Come away with me, my fair one!"
The girl with the sunshine in her hair.
My dove is hiding behind the rocks,
She wears only my rabbit fur robe.
Behind the outcrop on the cliff, I see her lovely form.
Let me see your face.
Let me hear your voice.
For your voice is like music to my ears,
and your hair is so lovely
Like a long, soft horse's tail,
I want to run my hands through it.
And smell your soft fragrance,
More lovely than the wild gorse flower. (Kingsley)

My lover is mine, and I am his.
Our covenant has been made before God
and the people.
He browses among the lilies,
at the banks of the Killy Willy stream,

where the water irises grow.
Before the dawn breezes blow,
and the night shadows flee,
return to me, my love,
and land upon me, like the hovering kestrel,
or as young stallion on the rugged
hills of Cefn Bryn." (Gay)

© Kingsley Ross Hill

Before we slept in love's embrace, we opened one of our cards. It was from Heather, and it was a gift of 300 pounds. We were so blessed!

"Good night, my love." "Good night, my love." I'll blow out the candles now, and they will burn again tomorrow.

"Come rest your head upon me and take your sleep. You thrill me, my Gay, oh love of my life."

"Good night, my Prince. Let us sleep now, until the angel of the morning arrives, and we awaken."

"Good morning, my love. To wake with you in my arms, I am complete. I have waited so long to have the missing part of my soul return."

"Oh, Kingsley, I love you so much! I am complete now too. And I have waited all my life for you!"

We lay in each other's arms until the songbird finished singing his song. Then there was a knock on the door, and Helen and Melody brought us our breakfast in bed. Eggs Benedict, with wild smoked salmon, and Helen's homemade sauce. And Melody brought in champagne and orange juice.

After I had read a story to Melody, she and Helen left for Cardiff. Gay and I slowly started our day.

"Oh, come back to bed my love; I miss you even for a minute."

And we kissed and laughed, and kissed and loved, and slept again until the nightingale sang his evening song. Then I made my love some tea and fed her strawberries and Devonshire cream. I ate more marzipan off the wedding cake.

"Are you going to eat me too, my love?"

"Oh, yes. I want your taste and scent. Breathe for me, my love, and make my heart beat before it stops."

"I love you, Kingsley."

"I love you, Gay."

Three days later, it was time for us to leave on our honeymoon trip around the Gower.

"I've never stayed in bed for three days." Gay said laughing.

"Neither have I, my Queen, but I have stayed in a cave for three days straight. And it rained night and day in November Grey!"

"Will you take me to Bacon Hole, Kings? I want to sleep in the cave with you and lie in front of the fire."

"Yes, I will take you there. We will start our journey at Bacon Hole, and finish at the Worms Head. The rock at the end of the world."

Chapter Twenty-Six
Around the World in Seven Days

Because Gay and I had spent three days in bed, we now had seven days to complete our journey around the Gower, before Gay had to return to work in Cardiff. Seven days was still plenty of time to enjoy our journey around our beloved Gower. And after packing, and an early lunch, we set off for Bacon Hole. We took the East Cliff path until we reached the cliff-top above Bacon Hole, then climbed down the steep path through the gorse, which took us to the entrance of the cave. I smiled as I pointed out my old 'look out seat.'

"This is where I used to start each new day," I said excitedly. And I climbed up on my stone. "Come on up," I said, putting out my hand and pulling her up beside me, and we looked out over the Emerald sea.

Oh, how the gentle winds of memory stirred and blew through my soul, as once again, I sat as the 'Caveman of Bacon Hole.' Only this time, I had a Cavewoman with me. I didn't have to dream or imagine one.

"Come on," I said, sliding down from my stone and helping her down. "Come and be still at the entrance."

"Oh, Kings, the silence speaks so loud. I can feel the past here. Just like when you brought me here for the first time, all those years ago."

"Yes, it is a place of voices. Where the past still calls out to those listening in the present."

"I'd be afraid to go inside on my own, Kings. But if you are with me, I know that I am safe."

"Come on," I said, taking her hand, and as we walked over the hard, stony clay, the still air was heavy with the cries and shadows of a thousand stories. And I was about to live one out with Gay.

"One story," I remembered very well. "It was the story of the cave family that lived in Bacon Hole."

"Do you remember, Kings, when we dreamed of having our own cave family and living here? And we lived in Caveman days? We were the only family living on Pennard Cliffs."

"Yes, I remember. And today, it is only us, my Cavewoman and our family here in the cave."

"Oh, Kings, this is so romantic. Are you going to make me stay here the night with you?"

"Yes, my woman, I am. I will love and protect you in this lonely place."

"I know you will," she said, her eyes excited and looking into my soul, and her face blushed with anticipation.

We dropped our backpacks and knelt at my old fireplace in the heart of the cave. The old stones were still in a circle, telling stories to the listening souls in the silent, shouting air.

"First, we need to collect some wood and build up the fire, enough to keep the fire going through the night."

We laid down our foam mats and sleeping bags on the hard ground, claiming our dwelling place within the ancient walls of Bacon Hole. I pulled out my old rabbit pelt robe from my backpack and rolled it over our sleeping bags. Gay's eyes thrilled when she saw it!

She asked: "Is this your rabbit fur robe?"

"Yes," I said excitedly. "And I shall wrap you in it, and keep you warm through the night."

She then kissed me and whispered in my ear, "I can't wait." And again, she blushed like the pink sky of the rising sun and my heart raced with excitement.

After we had finished reshaping the stones around the fire-place, we went out into the beautiful autumn evening to collect wood. We held hands as we climbed down the steep path at the side of our cave, which led to Hunts Bay. There, we collected a bunch of driftwood that the tides had brought in over the summer months.

"I think it's going to be an Indian Summer," Gay said, as we rested against a rock and felt the warm sun on our faces. It was almost October, and I hoped the sun would keep shining, just for another week while Gay and I made our journey around the Gower. Where we sat against the rocks, I could see the gully where I had found my message in a bottle. God had spoken to me through the scripture verses inside. Now I looked at the gentle swelling tide rolling back and forth, over the pebbles in the gully.

How personal God is! He shouts loudly in the thundering surf, and whispers gently in the quiet rock pools. He is always willing to meet us, right where we are at – in the storms or the stills of this life.

I took Gay's hand and asked her to pray with me. I asked God to bless us with good weather while we traveled, and we both thanked Him for our wedding, and the beautiful reception that David and Jackie had put on for us. And our wedding night at the caravan had been so perfect.

We sat and talked until the sun was low in the sky, and the night clouds began to march their way towards us, but only to make us feel warmer and closer as we said hello to the night sky.

It was time to take our wood back to the cave. We made several trips back and forth to the beach until we had all the drift-wood in the cave.

"There will be enough wood for a good size fire," I said, looking at our wood pile. "Enough to last us all night."

Gay had packed us a supper, and we sat outside upon my lookout stone to eat. The sky was full of oranges and reds, which reflected on the silver-grey sea. The colours were stunning! Purples and yellows were brushed onto the lower part of the sky, with pink windows that looked like tide pools splashing in the clouds. God had painted us a special picture to celebrate our love. Just like He had done on the last day when we had to say goodbye, all those sunsets past.

"Gay, do you know what is even more beautiful than the sunset?"

"What, my Prince?"

"It's watching the sunset together, and knowing we don't have to say goodbye."

At my words, she began to weep, and told me that for years after we had watched our last sunset together, she didn't want to watch sunsets anymore, because they reminded her of the love she had lost.

"But I found you again, Kingsley, and for the rest of our lives we can watch the sunsets together. We don't have to say goodbye. I love you, and I'm so happy!"

"I'm so happy too, my love! And this sunset is a reminder of God's wedding gift to us: a life that we can share together, with all its wonderful colours," I said gently.

We watched as the night tucked away the day in a blanket, and slowly our day went to sleep.

"Well, my love, it's time to build our fire." I used some dead gorse bush that I had collected on the path to light the fire. It burned instantly and Gay handed me some of the smaller pieces of driftwood. We soon had a nice fire burning and we retired under my rabbit pelt robe for the night. The cool, damp air in the heart of our cave soon warmed up. And we held each other tight, glowing in the warmth of our love. As Gay lay her head upon my chest with our hands clasped together, we drifted off to a deep, sweet sleep.

Sometime in the still night, a log moved on the fire, and I awoke. With Gay still sleeping soundly, I could feel the gentle rise and fall of her breathing. With our hands still clasped together, I knew she was warm and safe.

How different it was when I had slept in Bacon Hole alone, with fear and loneliness as my companions. Tonight, my soul was filled with warmth and love. To know and love another so completely! And to be known and loved back! This is surely the longing and the delight of our soul? Oh, my love, I love you so very much! Surely my soul will stop breathing without you.

We woke together, to the song of the dawn. Rock pigeons cooed in the back of the cave, and a rock pipit darted back and forth, catching a hatch of flies for its breakfast. And I made my cave women stay warm underneath my fur robe, which had now become our blanket. And I announced that today was 'Bacon and Eggs Day.'

"How would you like your eggs, my love? Sunny or scrambled?"

"Oh, sunny please, Kings."

("To Loneliness and Fear: We don't do 'over easy' here! So, I suggest you get out of here!")

"Who are you talking to?" my Cavewoman asked.

"Oh, just two old acquaintances that I never held dear."

"Your bacon and eggs are ready. Shall we have breakfast upon my lookout stone?"

"Yes, I want to know everything about what it was like when you lived in here. Even about Loneliness and Fear."

"Yes, they were here, and they taught me a lot."

Gay and I had breakfast upon my stone and we took the forecast for the day. The sun was shy, as he hid behind puffy white clouds that drifted low over the emerald sea. The West wind was awake, but his cousin in the North, still slept. Brother South would arise about noon, as his friend the sea shook hands again with the grey rocks at the top of the beach. The gulls would squawk and dive, and shadows and colours would race across the fields, while the sun brought his sacred spices of warmth from his secret chamber in the East.

"Well, my Cavewoman, it's a two-day journey around the Gower. Where shall we make our destination today? How about Port Eynon beach?"

And she said: "Yes, let's camp at Port Eynon beach tonight.

Then we started our day with a prayer for God's protection and more of His blessings upon us.

"We invite you to come with us today, Oh Lord. To walk with us and talk with us, and to bless us with your friendship and fellowship as we seek to enjoy your creation all around us."

We soon had our sleeping bags and supplies all packed into our backpacks and then climbed to the top of the cliffs. We walked westwards along the east cliff to Pennard village, and then took the west cliff path to Pobbles Beach.

Once we had climbed down the path to the sands, Gay and I raced across the beach to our cove. Gay ran ahead of me as I was carrying the heavier backpack with our pots and pans. I couldn't let her win! I dropped my backpack and chased after her. Catching up with her, I pulled her down to the sand and lay on top of her, staring into her violet eyes. She looked deep into mine, and said, "Okay, I surrender. Is this some Caveman possession thing?"

"Yes, indeed it is," I replied. And as she stopped laughing, I pushed my lips against hers, kissing her as tenderly as I'd ever kissed. My whole being reached for her. And when we stopped kissing, we looked into each other's eyes for a lifetime. Our love was so strong and pure.

We rolled, wrestled, and kissed, until we were surprised by a visitor.

"Autumn Dancer!" I exclaimed, having felt his wet nose come between us.

Gay shrieked with laughter, and said, "No way is this happening!"

"I've got news for you, my Cavewoman. This is happening. He's come to say, 'Congratulations' after the wedding."

And after we picked up our backpacks, the stallion walked the rest of the way to Great Thunder's cave with us.

"He's beautiful, Kingsley! He's not as wild as Great Thunder was. And I think Autumn Dancer is the perfect name for him," she said. When we reached our family cave, Gay reached into her backpack and gave him an apple.

"Gay, this is amazing! He came to our wedding, and now this! When I'm away in Canada, and walking downtown in busy Vancouver, I come here in my heart and think of our Gower and the horses. Just knowing that this life is here comforts me in my crazy grey days. We are so blessed to have grown up here and have this heritage in our lives. And to share it with you, my love, and Melody, is the most wonderful thing in my life!"

"When I moved away to England, and even living in Cardiff, where I like living, I have always come home here in my heart, Kings. Gower will always be my home! I hope that one day we can come back and live here. It would be so wonderful if Melody could grow up here like we did."

"One day we will, Gay!"

"I've been thinking that when I go back to Canada, I will have my belongings sent on to Swansea. Fraser said that I can store them there, until you and I can move them to where we will be living. I'd like to work out of Swansea, even if it does mean a commute to Cardiff. David and Jackie have said there is a demand for counsellors in Swansea, and David asked me to consider coming on-board with him at his church, to do some youth pastoring. They could offer me a part-time position right away."

"Oh, Kings, that's great! I know that working with youth is your passion. You have so much you can teach them."

"Thank you. I believe that's what God wants me to do."

"When the Lord provides a home for us on the Gower, I don't mind commuting to Cardiff, Kings. As I shared before, a few of my friends already commute from Swansea, so we can manage the distance."

We continued to talk and make plans for our future as we left our cave and headed towards Oxwich Bay in the distance.

Autumn Dancer followed us as far as the Killy Willy stream, where he stopped for a drink. Gay and I recalled the time when Thunder Spring was pregnant in the cave, and I would bring water from the stream for her to drink. It seems like it was only yesterday that I watched Thunder Spring give birth to Little Thunder in the cave. So many wonderful memories filled our hearts and minds as we adventured across the golden sands.

Suddenly, Autumn Dancer lifted his head.

"What is it, old boy?" I asked. And he was off! Galloping across the sands towards Oxwich.

"He is leading the way," Gay said smiling. As we continued across the sands, Gay and I shared with each other that our journey around the Gower was like having a honeymoon already.

"Out of all the places in the world where I would like to be with you, Kingsley, on our honeymoon, it's here! The place where we fell in love, and the home of our dreams!'

"I can only echo everything you have said, my love. I feel the same way. You are my most precious dream come true!"

It was late afternoon by the time we reached Oxwich Bay. And our legs were tired after trudging with our backpacks across the sand, along with our running and playing. The tide was low enough for us to walk out to Oxwich Point, and we climbed up onto the headland to rest and have our lunch. Gay made us some sandwiches, as we were too tried to cook, and as we ate our lunch, we looked back across the sands to the Great Tor. And in the middle of the bay, the 'Bell Rock' stood as a proud island in the sea of sand. And the Killy Willy shook hands with the sea at Three Cliffs. And there in the distance, was the dark dot of Autumn Dancer, galloping his way back to Pobbles. The afternoon could not have been more beautiful!

It was time to make our way along the headland path to Port Eynon.

"In about another mile or so, we could pitch our tent up in the sand dunes. What do you think Gay?" Gay liked the idea.

When we reached the Port Enyon dunes, we were spent for the day. And Gay lay down and rested on my fur robe while I set up the tent.

The dunes can offer seclusion and a natural protection, away from the wild open spaces of the sands, and a natural shelter from the sea winds. It was the wild ponies that first introduced me to the lonely solitude of the dunes. Once when I was living in Leathers' Hole, I was caught in a sand storm between Oxwich and the Great Tor. The sand was stinging and blinding in my face, one of the ponies led me into the dunes, where I found shelter amongst the long grasses. It felt like a room as a family of horses was also taking shelter there. After the winds had eased, their stallion led his herd and I back out onto the sands.

Today, Gay and I chose a place deep within the dunes, behind a tall hill and surrounded by the high grasses that stirred in the gentle breeze. By the time I had the tent up, Gay had fallen asleep and I covered her with my sleeping bag. I sat against my backrest of sand and watched the evening sky. There were several stars becoming visible now, as the night sky said hello, and then goodbye to the passing day. This is the time between night and day, it only lasts but minutes, but you can watch night and day play, and tell each other stories of their way.

This is a story they told me that day:

♪❊

THEY MADE A DAY

Once upon a time, there was a man who lived in the dawn and the day. He walked about, and said "this must be the way." But he felt alone, and thought: "I wish I had someone to walk with me in the dawn and the day."

Upon his walk, he met a woman named Gay. And he said to her, "would you please come for a walk with me along the way, and I'll show you my life in the dawn and the day?" The woman agreed, and said: "Yes, I'd like to come for a walk and see your dawn and day, but I walk in the twilight, and night hours of the day. If I walk with you, will you walk with me? And, I will show you my way. And, a walk was arranged with the night and the day.

First the man took the women's hand and showed her the dawn and the bright of the day. And the women said, "you have woken me, and made my spirit come alive and be free! Now come with me!" The women now took the man's hand, and showed him her twilight shimmering sea, and as they walked, a different energy the man began to see, and no longer did he want to leave, because she was so different than he. She took him out, to sit underneath the stars and showed him things that could be, and they went to sit under a tree.

You have shown me so much with your poems and flowers, and you have changed me. I just want to bask in your sunshine for hours, and run with you through the spring showers. You have taught me so much too, the man said, and you have changed me, for in your eyes I can see a missing part of me, your soul touches mine, and I am free.

As time went on, the man did not want to live in the dawn and daytime alone, not now, with everything he had been shown. And he longed for the twilight to come again, his way. Sometimes, he waited all day, until the sun closed the curtains all the way.

And the women no longer wanted to walk in the twilight and night time alone. And under the crescent moon she sat and thought, I will wait for the dawn, he will come soon, because he lives in my heart that no longer has a spare room. And he did! He held her, and kissed her, holding her tight, carrying her all through the night. When the dawn came, they sat in love's glorious light, deciding to marry uniting the day, with the night. Oh, my darling, I shall make you a love-spoon, because my sunshine could not live without your moon.

By Kingsley Ross Hill and Gay Nightingale Tripp
Mumbles, South Wales, June 2017

～

After my meditation of day and night, I went for a walk along the beach, while Gay continued to sleep. As I left the dunes for the beach, I marked my path out of the dunes with small stones or sticks that I found along the way. Otherwise, it would be difficult to find my way back to our camp. There was a moon now rising, and its silver light reflected upon the sea. As I watched the waves gently breaking upon the shore, their florescent colours of greens and blues drew pictures on the sand. The night was still and shouting! I danced my way barefoot along the beach and praised the God of the moon and sun, who shines His love on everyone.

"What a perfect honeymoon, God!" I shouted aloud, and continued to dance along the beach. I must have walked about a quarter of a mile along Port Enyon Beach and I thought I better make my way back, before it got too dark for me to find my love, sleeping in our room amongst the dunes.

I walked back splashing in the waves, making florescent pictures with my feet. As I lifted my head, I beheld the lone figure 'of my love' walking towards me. Or was she dancing too? She twisted and turned, spinning her dress in the breeze. She was dancing!

"Hello dancing Princess," I shouted.

"Hello, my dancing Prince," she echoed back. The sound of her happy voice traveled quickly across the open space of the sands.

Suddenly we ran towards each other, as fast as legs would carry and she jumped into my arms. And I swung her around me, her long hair dancing on the wind.

"You have your pyjamas on under your dress, my love?"

"Yes, these are my beach pyjamas, Kings. I bought them especially for our honeymoon on the beach. Hum, what perfume are you wearing? It smells familiar."

"It's the one you brought me from Canada, my Prince: 'Endless Sea'."

"So, you are wearing my Endless Sea, are you? Well I'm afraid I must ask for a payment for that, my love!"

"Will this do?" she said, taking off her pyjama bottoms and stepping out of her dress. She slowly removed her top, with her eyes fixed on mine.

There were no words spoken. Only the sound of us. Her naked form was a silhouette with the silver moonlight behind her. And her long hair flowed down in front of her, half concealing her pale white breasts, that waited impatiently for me to embrace them. Gay's passionate expression shouted out to me.

"Kingsley, my love! Come and take me! Please me! Thrill me!" was our song and chorus, echoing loudly along the barren sands of Port Eynon beach. While the spirits of drowned sailors envied and mermaids watched from the enchanting waves, our naked bodies crashed and rolled in the singing surf. Gay moaned loudly, and all around us became silent. Together we sang, as loud as the crashing, foaming surf, exploding within our joyous rapture of love! The envious sailors were now silent, and the jealous mermaids dived beneath the waves again to dream that one day they would find such a love!

Gay and I lay trembling in each other's arms, as the glow of our love held us like a warm blanket beneath the stars.

Slowly and gently, the breath of the evening cooled our skin and we dressed each other.

"You dress me so gently, my love," she whispered. "I love how gentle you are with me. You're a wild Caveman, as wild and free as the raging sea! And as gentle as the call of the collared dove in the dawn."

As we walked back to our room in the dunes, it was almost too dark to find our way. A cloud was covering the moon, and I was glad that I'd marked our trail with the stones.

"Here's the one shaped like an arrow," Gay said. "It's this way! Over here, Kings, over here!" And we found our room behind the tall dune. We climbed into our tent and zipped our sleeping bags together. We didn't need a mattress, the sand was so soft, and it shaped to our bodies like a glove. And we were soon asleep.

As morning came, I woke to the chorus of the birds and smell of the sea. And I was reminded of my cave living days. Where had time gone? Surely it waits for no one!

Gay was still fast asleep, so I decided to go for a dawn walk on the beach. The tide had gone all the way out as we had been sleeping. And I smiled as I saw our footprints and the story of our love still written on the sand. And I sang with the morning song, to the God who had made man and woman, in the image of Himself!

"Thank you, oh my God, for the woman you have given me. For she delights me so perfectly!" And I sang and danced along the sands.

After having our breakfast in the dunes, we set off again on our journey. We climbed the cliffs at Port Eynon Head, and started on the 'magnificent five miles,' as this beautiful part of the Gower is called. And as we walked, I remembered so much of my journey around the Gower that I had walked alone all those years ago when Gay and I had been so young and had to part. And now, we were married and together – what a wonderful journey life is!

Life is different for all of us, in what it has to teach us. The lessons of loneliness, heartache and pain that seem so cruel! And yet, they are so necessary in forming and shaping who we are to become. I have walked this journey with a broken heart; and fear and loneliness have been my companions. But now I walk it with a joyful heart and my soul has been enlarged! Enlarged because of all life's experiences. Happy or sad. God sends to us, in His wisdom, all that we need to learn to become the person He has created us to be.

For the next few hours, Gay and I shared with each other the lessons we had had to learn through the events and experiences of our lives – that had made us who we are today. It became evident that God had prepared us for one another.

We talked about the time when we had thought about eloping and running away together, rather than allowing life to happen just the way it was meant to be.

And I shared with her something that Maggie had shared with me, when I was heartbroken because Gay had to move away.

"Kingsley," she said, "if you run away together, it won't work out! Wait, and do what is right! You will have a lot more respect for each other, if you are meant to be together in the future." It was so much easier said than done when I was a teenager in love, but Maggie was right! Looking back today, we are living out the wisdom of her words.

On top of Port Eynon Head, we found some wild pink clover, that grow upon the cliffs, that brighten the days with their pink coloured blossoms. We dug one of the plants up to take to Maggie's grave in the village, and we dug a little hole in the soft earth beneath her headstone and planted it there. The cut flowers would bloom and fade, like Maggie's own life, but just like Maggie's life and her heritage in our lives, the wild flowers would bloom and grow in storms and sun.

"They are a suitable flower for Maggie, don't you think?"

"Yes, Kings, they tell the story of her abundant life! One that overflowed and blessed others like us." Gay and I prayed together, thanking and praising God for Maggie's life.

We had our lunch in the village and picked up some more food supplies. Then, we headed back up the cliff-top. The view from

Port Eynon Head is beautiful and we stopped to look back across the beach to Horton.

"We are surely having an Indian Summer," Gay announced, as the warm sun climbed in the sky. And we both vowed to swim in the sea when we reached our 'most sacred place' of Mewslade Bay.

"We will have to go swimming about half tide," I reminded Gay. "Because when the tide comes in at Mewlsade, the sands disappear completely, and they are lost to the bather for at least two hours around high tide.

(One of my favourite things to do on a winter's day, dear reader, when I want the cobwebs blown out of my soul, is to go down to Mewslade Bay and watch the Atlantic rollers as they are blown in by the strong south-westerly winds. The sea foams and sprays from the thundering waves, and seem to cleanse my soul. The cares of my days disappear in the sea winds and they are blown far away to a distant land.)

Gay and I continued to walk westward until late in the afternoon. It was so wonderful to have my "best friend" at my side, as we waltzed together through Gowerland.

♪✳

GOWERLAND

A POEM

There is a secret place, round which the wild
waves of the ocean
unceasingly roll – sometimes rearing their
snowy crests, huge as
mountains, against the iron rocks
that stand like guardians defying their fury.
Marvelous indeed is the scene when the white clouds
of silvery foam are flung wildly into
the seagull-singing air. Strange

haunting sounds are heard as cavern
after cavern re-echoes in the
dragon's lair, with the wild and deafening chant.
When the storm
fiends flap their pinions in the sailor-screaming gale...
even the fire-breathing dragon won't go outside.

When the south and west winds cease
their cries, and hide again in their caves...
here we find a sweet and lovely nook,
where fairies love to dance,
and mermaids show themselves in the blue pool
and converse with open-minded human kind.
This little spot, dear reader.
is my Gower, the Land of the setting Sun.

© Kingsley Ross Hill

We now reached Deborah's Hole, where we would spend the night. After we put our camping gear in the cave, we walked out to the 'Knave', a curious triangular rock, to enjoy the view, and we waited for the sunset.

I shared with Gay, at Deborah's Hole, when I had been marooned in the fog here. I had listened to the haunting sound of the foghorns and watched the flashing demon-like eyes of the lightships that stared at me through the pocket windows of the fog, from far out at sea.

She held me tight, and said "I don't mind if we get marooned in the fog, as long as I'm with you, my love."

As I held her in my arms, the sun waved goodbye behind the horizon, and left us with its golden smile. As dusk fell, the lightships started flashing their searching eyes at us from far away along the Bristol Channel, giving us an eerie feeling that they could see us! And I found it interesting to learn who these eyes belonged to by the frequency of their blinking flashes.

"Farthest away, to the east is Nash Point on the Glamorganshire coast, (its light occurs every thirty seconds). Closer, in mid-channel is the Scarweather Lightship (one flash every five seconds). Along the Devon coast, are Contisbury Foreland (six flashes every fifteen seconds), then the Bull beyond Ilfracombe (three flashes every ten seconds) and Hartland Point, (six flashes every sixteen seconds). On very clear evenings, the bulk of Lundy Island stands out to the south-west with the two lighthouses of Lundy North and Lundy South. Round to the west and much nearer is the Helwick lightship (one flash every ten seconds), and over the shoulder of Rhossili Downs comes the flash of St. Govan's lightship of the Pembrookeshire coast." (And Dear Reader, that is the complete light circuit of the Channel.)

"Gosh, Kingsley, how do you know all this?"

"I spent many hours, during my caveman days, looking out to sea. Counting flashes and looking at navigational charts was something I enjoyed doing on the cliffs." As Gay lay in my arms, I continued to point out the lights on the horizon.

"Because it's a clear night," I said, "if you look over there, you can see the bulk of Lundy Island standing out to the south-west."

"I can see it," Gay said excitedly.

"Look carefully," I said, "and you can see the two lighthouses of Lundy North and Lundy South. They are a good thirty-five miles away."

"I see them, I see them! This is so exciting, Kingsley!" It gave me joy to share my discoveries with Gay.

We watched the flashing lights at sea until Gay fell asleep in my arms. I no longer regarded the lights as demon-staring eyes; they were lights of 'celebration' – of our marriage! Each flashing light flashed its blessing upon our lives and the sacred journey that we had begun.

"I love you, my sweetheart," I whispered, kissing her gently, as I carried her to our waiting sleeping bag within Deborah's Hole. The curtains of the day were drawn, and the night covers on, and I fell asleep in the arms of love.

Morning arrived with a gentle puff of wind that stirred Gay's long and perfumed hair upon my face. For several minutes I lay watching her, as she slept and dreamed. Slowly I woke her with tender kisses, until a soft smile appeared.

"Good morning, Kings," she whispered, with a smile that never ceased to melt me inside. Ever since that first day, when she turned around and saw me at the Penmaen store. The years had gone by, and I felt that the glow of her love was ever sweeter as I beheld her glowing countenance. As with the rising sun, she thrilled my soul.

It was porridge for breakfast this morning, and our water boiled slowly over a small fire. Gay had brought nuts and raisins, which I stirred into our thickening breakfast. I would have settled for hot water, but she pulled out a small container of milk, still fresh, and a little honey.

"Thank you, Gay, for bringing these little things. They make such a difference, don't they, love?"

"Yes, that's why I brought them. It's the little things that help make life that much more wonderful!"

"Yes," I nodded in agreement, "indeed they do."

There was no fog this morning, as there so often is. Only blue sky in every direction. With our spirits lifted high, we stood again on the knave rock and observed the spectacular rock formations on the golden sands below.

"The tide is low," Gay exclaimed. "It will be perfect for swimming at our sacred beach!"

"It will indeed," I echoed, feeling excited.

After putting away our pots and pans, we started on our way towards the narrow gullies of Foxhole and Butterslade and reached the impressive limestone prow of Thurba Head. (As I have previously mentioned, and again I am inspired to share with you, dear reader, Thurba Head is probably the most precipitous of the Gower Headlands, dropping 200 feet into the sea.)

"It's time to have our swim," I said, taking her hand, and I started to lead her down the path to our most sacred place.

Thurba Head stands like a mighty knight, guarding the eastern side of Mewslade Bay. Mewslade runs down from the hamlet of Pitton, on the main Rhossili road. We followed the path that runs down the slade, alongside the high limestone wall, with crags guarding our path on either side. Suddenly we came to the bay – our most sacred place! And one of the most dramatic in the Gowerland. As we stood on the sand, we looked up at the majesty and might of Thurba Head towering over us. There was nothing else to say in our awe, other than 'I love you', which we both said in the excitement of being in our most sacred place.

Gay then ran up to the rocks and put down her backpack. She stripped all her clothes off and ran towards the waves. I hurried up the beach to undress and join her.

As I stripped off my clothes, I heard her scream that the sea was cold! – but that it was great once you're in!"

There was only one way to get into the sea in late September – jump and brave it! And that's what I did. Whoa! That will wake you up in the morning! But, Gay was quite right! Once you were in, it felt great!

We swam and played in the gentle tide, allowing the current to pull us out a bit, and then we would swim in to shallower water again. The tide was still falling, exposing more of our special beach –we had timed it perfectly. We would be able to explore the beach on the low tide. As we began to get cold, we cuddled to keep warm. The small waves almost ceased for quite some time, as if the sea was contemplating what to do.

"It's reached its low," I said to Gay, now shivering. We swam across the beach again to keep warm. Suddenly, the swells were building again, and the tide turned to come in.

"Quick," I said, "let's go and explore the beach while the tide is still low."

We rode back into the beach, by body surfing on a small breaker. It was like the years were washed away; two best friends had found each other again, we both agreed, and so did the singing sea!

"I love you Gay!" I said, pulling her towards me and kissing her passionately.

"I love you too, Kingsley!" We kissed in the waves until it was time to race up the beach and get warm. I out ran Gay and then caught her in her towel. And she screamed as I lifted her over my shoulders and carried her up to the top of the beach. I lowered her down to the sand and dried her beautiful body.

"Thank you, my love," she said, and dried me.

Once we were dressed, we went to explore our beach. And as the tide was still quite low, we were able to walk from Mewslade to Jacky's Tor, and then on under the towering crag and razor edge of Devil's Truck, and the imposing rock towers of Lewis Castle. Both Gay and I stopped in our tracks to admire these wonderful rock formations. It is not often that one can catch the tide right, when the water is low enough and to see this unique and spectacular part of the Gower cliffs. And I thanked God in my heart, for helping us to time it right to be here at low water.

We continued on until we reached Fall Bay. I pointed out Tears Point. Tears Point, guards Fall Bay to the west, and its slope looks gentle and kind after the succession of limestone pinnacles and sheer rock that lift up so boldly from the sands of Mewslade and Fall Bay.

Before turning the corner around Tears Point, we stopped and had something to eat. Gay had packed some salmon sandwiches which were delicious along with ripe tomatoes which she had bought at Swansea Market. And if that wasn't enough she pulled out some Welsh cakes, and a container of cockles to share. We fed each other in front of a jealous Great Black Backed gull, who watched our every bite until I shared a Welsh cake with him.

The afternoon sun was westering now and it was time to decide where we would spend the night. As we turned the corner at Tears Point, awaiting us, was the 'climax' of the Gower cliffs and rocks - the Worms Head! What a haunting and mysterious site it is, to gaze upon the 'rock at the end of the world!', and hear it calling out to you, in its loud and silent voice, that says 'Come, come and explore my secrets.'

Today, I found the Worm both fascinating and frightening. Its serpent shape, silhouetted in front of the sinking sun.

It was far too late in the day to attempt going out onto the Worm. We decided to climb up onto the cliff path and pitch our tent in a farmer's field. By the time we got the tent up, and had supper, it was dark. And after all our walking and swimming, we soon fell asleep.

We woke up in the middle of the night however, to a howling wind and torrential rain. Our Indian Summer had come to an end in a matter of hours. And above the sound of the wind, we could hear the mysterious booming sound of the blow hole on the Worms' Head.

"It's such a frightening sound," Gay exclaimed, as she held me tightly. And we listened to the pelting rain upon the tent, but we were warm, cozy and safe, and in each other's arms! That's all that mattered, and I went to sleep thinking about the time I had been marooned on the Worm. How different it was tonight, to have the woman I love wrapped around me in a tent, instead of being out on the Worm, exposed and alone. And I drifted off to sleep.

In the morning, the wind and rain looked like it had settled in for the day, so we decided to stay in the tent until the weather improved. We had food, warmth and each other. What more could we want?

After having cereal for breakfast at the entrance of our tent, we returned to bed to cuddle. We listened to the stories of the wind and rain, interrupted only by the sound through the blow hole, who boomed periodically to remind us that the rock at the end of the world was always there.

This pause in our journey, gave us time to talk and think of our plans.

Gay shared with me that she was dreading having to say goodbye to me and return to Cardiff after we had finished around the Gower.

I would be returning to Canada, in just over a week, after we got back. And, I reassured her, that I would come back as soon as I was able and we'd be together again. One thing that we were both aware of already, was the depth of our love, and we held each other all that day, and the following night, only venturing out to go pee, and coming back to make wonderful love once again! I'm sure that our shouts of joy, were louder than the noise of the blow hole on the Worms Head!

At least, that's what the seagull said, as he flew over our tent, telling us to be quiet. "No, Mr. Gull, I'm not stopping now!"

Finally, the wind and rain stopped. We packed up and ventured out into the outside world. The birds sang new songs and the Worms' Head was quiet again, the gentle wind puffed the clouds far out to sea.

Chapter Twenty-Seven
Lives and Lifeboats

We only had three days left now, and Gay would need to be back at the caravan and get ready to return to Cardiff. And I would continue to stay with Fraser and Lynn until it was time for my flight back to Canada. We decided to walk more inland on our return, to be sheltered from the sea winds that remained strong, blowing in from the Bristol Channel. The strong wind soon dried our tent, and we then made our way back to Port-Eynon beach. I had hoped to take Gay to 'Burry Holms,' at the far end of Rhossili beach. But, as often happens upon the Gower, the weather can turn very quickly.

Burry Holms is a small, rocky islet. The word 'Holm' comes from the Scandinavian word 'Holmr,' meaning an island, and it is wise to remember that Burry Holms is an island when you visit it, for, as on Worms Head, unwary visitors who walk over to the islet on the sands sometimes forget that the tide comes in. (As I share in one of my earlier books, 'Cave Days,' Burry Holms has a strange, lost atmosphere all its own, a feeling that you are back in a remote past. The only other place I have ever felt this feeling is at the entrance to Bacon Hole on Pennard Cliffs.)

"Tell me more, my love," Gay said, as we walked. I promised to take her to Burry Holms when I returned from Canada. On Burry Holms are the ruins of a medieval chapel where people came to pilgrimage at the shrine of St. Cenydd, Gower's only Saint. I used to play at the ruins of the chapel with my father, as a boy. He would bring two of his swords, from the collection he had found with his metal detector, and some ancient maps that he had. I loved going on digging excavations with my father – we found so many wonderful things! Shields and swords, old rusted helmets and pieces of armor, from the days of the knights! I found an old dagger once, which my father promptly hid, in fear that the authority's might come and confiscate our find.

Gay has a great interest in history, and especially that of the Gower Peninsula. This was something I looked forward to exploring and enjoying with her more and more. I couldn't have asked for a better match as far as our interests. And Gay pressed me to tell her more of what I knew about the Gower saint, St. Cenydd. And I told her what my father had shown me, when we explored the Gower together.

"We started at the village of Llangennith, where my father and I spent four days in the village, roaming the hills. Llangennith does not quite give you that feeling that you are at the end of the world, like you get from being in Rhossili. The village stands back from the sea – behind the wide expanse of sand dunes that form the Burrows. It is perched on the column between Llanmadoc Hill to the north and Rhossili Downs to the south, and the land to the west slopes down to the sands over the flats of Llangennith Moors. Llangennith is a typical Gower village, compact, with everything around the village green, including the old church and, of course, the pub.

"What I would not give right now for a pint of Guinness and fish and chips!" I said to Gay.

"Me too," she replied. But alas, we were a long way from the nearest pub, so I continued with my story of St. Cenydd.

"Llangennith still remains in this tight little settlement around the village green. This is how it began in the early days of the Norman Conquest, and this is the way it is to this day. The church is dedicated to Gower's own saint, St. Cenydd and, therefore, very properly, it is the largest in the peninsula. The size of the church is not much of a boast, however, as Gower churches are generally very small compared to churches elsewhere. But as my dad always said, 'Us Gower folk are a rare and close-knit bunch.'"

"Llangennith Church was constructed on the site of the sixth century priory, founded by the Saint himself, and which was destroyed by the Danes in A.D.986."

I had to pause in my sharing with Gay at this point, as a precious memory whispered in my heart. I remembered myself standing on the end of Burry Holms islet, with one of my dad's swords in my hand, and shouting out to sea at any listening Viking who dared try to land on my island!

"What are you doing, old son?" my dad asked. "If you want to protect St. Cenydd from the Vikings, you have to hold your sword with two hands, and swing it about like this!" (Okay, reader, I had to swing my sword for a few minutes. And it's back to the story now.)

"The priory was re-founded probably by Henry de Newburgh after the Norman conquest of Gower and its revenues granted to the Abbey of St. Taurinus at Evreux in Normandy. It was thus what was known in English medieval law as an 'alien priory' and its revenue was usually seized by the king whenever he went to war with France, and then he returned it to its French owners when the war ended.

"Did you raise your sword against the French too?" Gay interrupted.

"Indeed, I did!" I said passionately. "I don't like the French or the Vikings!"

"Come to think of it, my Prince, nor do I!"

"That's good, my Princess! So Henry V needed money badly for his French invasion, and in 1414, the year before Agincourt, he seized the revenues of all alien priories, this time for good. Later, out of Llangennith money, he granted a pension of 20 guineas a year to a faithful knight with the improbable name of Sir Hortonk van Klux." (Say that after five pints of Guinness, or backwards after two.)

"There has been some speculation that the lonely farm of Sluxton, between Rhossili Downs and Hardings Down, was originally Kluxton and is thus connected with this curious warrior. In any case, by 1442, pious King Henry VI was building All Souls College as a memorial to those who had fallen in the Hundred Years War. Llangennith came in handy for raising cash to endow his new foundation. He handed over the priory to the Master and Fellows of his new college, who held it until 1838. The glory of the old priory has faded forever, but the old church still stands with its massive tower, complete with the Gower saddle-back roof and its lancet windows. Inside, you are confronted with the usual thorough 'restoration' but there are some points of interest still left untouched.

In a niche on the south side of the nave is the effigy of a knight, with the lower part of his legs cut off to fit the statue into the opening. The old Llangennith folk used to call it the "Dolly Mare" and, as at Oxwich, this gives a clue to the knight's identity. He is one of the de la Mare family that held land around Llangennith, and the style of his armor dates him at sometime before A.D. 1307, when it became customary to mix mail-armor and plate-armor. The old assumption that knights depicted with crossed legs were crusaders, as with the unknown de la Mare, is extremely doubtful.

There are three carved stone coffin lids set in the west-end wall of the nave. Two show simple crosses and are probably from the graves of former priors. I remember standing there with my father and looking at the coffin lids, and asking him if there were knights buried there. He thought not, and that they were most likely priors who lived at the church. Ordinary men, compared to brave fighting knights, I thought! And I remember having this dream of becoming a knight. And I would often feel sad that I wasn't born in the time of the knights.

And my Dad would always say, "You can use my sword, King! And I will teach you how to use it, so then you will be a knight!

And I did learn to fence, and my dad called me 'knight one' or 'first knight'! And my brother, he called, 'knight two.'

"I love hearing about your boyhood, Kings, and you will always be my Knight!" said Gay, and she kissed me.

After my father and I had looked at the two coffin lids with the crosses on the top, he showed me the third one. The third one was more intriguing. It bears a complex interlaced pattern and is decidedly pre-Norman. Tradition maintains that it marked the grave of the holy St. Cenydd himself, perhaps in the earlier monastery, which was destroyed by the Danes.

Now, who was St. Cenydd and what do we know about him? He was the Gower's only saint and thus demands our pious tribute to his memory as we stand before his coffin lid. The story of his medieval life, as told by monks in the fifteenth century, was then retold by the dull but learned capgrave in his Nova Agenda Angliae, printed in Latin and published by Wynkyn de Worde in 1526. It is full of wonderful and strange delights. I think these old Celtic saints were curiously sympathetic, and their lives, as related by the old monastic hagiographers, are almost as much tales of magic as of religion."

I was sure, by now, that Gay would have had enough about my rabbitting on about St. Cenydd, but she hadn't, and she said she found it fascinating. My father, being a local historian, and having taken me with him to spend many long hours at the Swansea public library, had taught me much! And in sharing about St Cenydd with Gay, I was amazed at how much I remembered of my father's explanations.

"Please continue, Kings, I love hearing about it." And I continued.

"Rome looked askance at them; perhaps they never measured up to their own exacting standards of painful martyrdom for the faith. In fact, very few seem to have been interested in martyrdom at all. They all seemed to live contentedly at prayer on some island, fed by the sea birds, or in a romantically placed cell, where they were happy to perform the occasional miracle, to oblige their visitors; and traces of pre-Christian rituals, of ancient Celtic beliefs, still lingered around their dwelling places. The old Celtic saints, with their kindly disposition, did not want to hurt their pagan neighbors' feelings too much!

(If we look at St. Cenydd's life, we can see a classic example of this pattern. He was born, or so the legend goes, of royal stock, the son of Dihocus, a prince of Brittany; but as the translation by Rev J.D. Davies puts it "by a most unnatural sin." And here, the kindly cleric adds a footnote, which has a certain charm for modern readers: "I need scarcely remind those who are acquainted with the Latin tongue that a literal translation of the text is hardly possible." In truth, Dihocus had seduced his own beautiful daughter and made her pregnant. On Christmas Day, King Arthur was holding his court in the Gower and he summoned his vassals to meet him. Among them was Dihocus, who brought his daughter with him. She gave birth to a son among the tents a mile from the palace of King Arthur, but, as a sign of the unnatural sin of his conception, one of Cenydd's legs stuck to his thigh. The prince, who was anxious to hush up the scandal, ordered a Moses-like cradle of wicker to be made; and then the baby was placed in the cradle and cast into the turbulent waters of the little River Lliw, which flows into the bigger River Loughor. This stream swiftly carried the frail bark out to sea, but as it drew near to the dangers of Worms Head, the seabirds flew to the rescue. They lifted the boy from the waves, placed him on a safe rock on the Worm, stood around him in great flocks, and "kept off the wind and hail and snow with the shelter of their wings." On the ninth day, an angel of God descended and placed a brazen breast-shaped bell in the infant's mouth, through which he was miraculously fed with "the sweetest savour of infantile nourishment ... and in Welsh, to this day, it is called Cloch Tetham, which is interpreted as Titty Bell.

"The birds and the wild deer were determined to look after him. When he was unexpectedly found by a kindly farmer and taken home to his wife, the gulls tore all the thatch off the farmer's roof until little Cenydd was taken back to his cozy nest on Worms

Head. There, a doe politely filled the Titty Bell with her milk. And clothes were not a problem. 'The clothes in which he was wrapped adapted themselves to the circumference of the boy, according to his size and increasing measurements; just like the bark growing around a tree, and neither were the little clothes affected with any decay. Then, as the boy grew older, an angel looked in at regular intervals to complete his education.

"At eighteen he was ready for the saintly life. An angel directed him to the spot which is now the village green at Llangennith, where a stream sprung out of the ground to refresh him. Could this be the old village well, which is still crowned with a great slab of hard Old Red Sandstone rock still carrying faint traces of a cross? Opposite this, Cenydd constructed his rude hut, and in the oratory built there, a heavenly host frequently met him and conversed with him." His fame spread throughout Gower and beyond, and his Titty Bell had surprising power. One touch of it forced an evil doer to repent and gave him the power to skip across the waves into exile with St. David in Pembrookshire. The good Saint used the Bell to restore stolen booty and to convert thieves. He became the friend and ally of St. David, and his leg was temporarily cured by a miracle to allow him to take part in an important religious conference. Then leaving the earth to receive rewards in heaven, he departed on the calends of August."

A modest saint was St. Cenydd, a kindly man spreading a quiet happiness around him. He seemed to suit the Gower. And he would have turned a blind eye to the splendid saturnalia that was celebrated in his name every July 5th right up to the turn of the century. This was the renowned Llangennith Mapsant . Most Gower villages had their Mapsants or festivals on their saint's day. Rhossili's, for example, took place in the winter on February 12th, and Lllanmadoc's on November 12th. Everyone agreed, however, that for sheer carefree exuberance, Lllangennith Mapsant took the prize. But then, Lllangennith men were always famous for the way they enjoyed themselves. This was the place to come for cock-fighting, prize fights, dances and 'bidding' weddings. A fine independent lot were the 'Llangenny oxen,' So much so, that when the government introduced daylight savings during World War One, and clocks had to be put back one hour, Llangennith held a public meeting in which it was decided not to accept the new law right away, but to give it one month's trial.

At the Mapsant, the booths lined the village green; the fiddlers played outside the "Welcome to Town" public house; there was endless dancing at the Kings Head; and everyone consumed enormous quantities of ale and 'whitespote' or 'milked meat,' which was a mixture of flour and milk and other ingredients that were then boiled together in commemoration, so they say, of the milk left by the kindly hand in St. Cenydd's Titty Bell. All Mapsants celebrated by having something special to eat. Llanmadoc had its pies, made of chopped mutton and currants; and Rhossili had a kind of plum pudding known as 'Bonny Clobby.'

"Did you ever go to a Mapsant festival, Kingsley?"

"I can only remember going to one, Gay. And that was when I was about 10. The real Maspants had finished years ago, but they had a modern-day version of one in Rhossili, which my father took me to. And I remember vividly a wooden cock dressed up in ribbons, and he was supposed to be a representation of the birds that fed St. Cenydd. It was hoisted up to the top of the church tower."

"Wow, I wish I could have seen the Mapsant with you, Kingsley!"

"It was pretty amazing when you think about the history and traditions around the Mapsants. My dad is a great historian, and he taught me so much about the Gower Peninsula with its rich history and legends!"

Gay and I reached Port-Eynon beach, and we decided to go into the village and have our lunch on the green. It was there where I had once found Thunder Spring and Little Thunder on my journey around the Gower to find my horse family! Today, with every step towards Port-Eynon village, I became more excited, as I remembered my sacred adventures of the past, and to have my love with me made everything extra-special!

As we continued our journey, we became more aware of the 'life journey' we were now walking as husband and wife, and our love and appreciation for one another seemed to grow by the hour.

My Mum's words spoke loudly to me again, as they had done when I'd first met Gay in the days of my youth. "When you are in love, you see the world differently, and the little things that once seemed ordinary, become extraordinary when you share them with the one you love."

Mum, you are so right! I am falling in love with Gay more and more each day. To want her and need her, and to feel her as part of my very soul, is such a wonderful thing! Love does make the world go round! And I am so in love, Mum, and so very happy. I never thought my life could be this good!

Gay and I approached the village, and we left our camping gear on the green to set up later in the day. There were pockets of blue sky above us now, and the morning fog was beginning to lift. Familiar places became mysterious in the fog and morning mists, as they hung over the hills and houses, as if putting them under a magic spell. And as we arrived at the village this morning, the thatched roofs of the houses appeared here and there, like floating islands in the rising mists. The howl of the sea winds blew in, as if wanting to visit the village so drowned sailors' souls could come and haunt the warm and the living that dwelt this side of the grave. Gay held onto me tightly.

"I'll protect you," I reassured her.

"I know you will, Kings."

When we arrived at the old church, the prominent memorial statue for the lifeboat men of Port-Eynon stood above the fog, like a man resurrected out of the cruel sea that covered the tombstones with its grey and white blanket, as if to symbolize the fallen.

"The 'lifeboat man' looks like he is standing upon the sea," Gay commented. And indeed he was! Let me tell you, dear reader, the story of the brave Port-Eynon lifeboat men.

So this morning, I told Gay their story! Only then would the cool fog lift from the shivering tombs and the spirits go back to the restless heaving sea.

⁓

"The establishment of the Port-Eynon lifeboat occurred in 1894, and the vessel was movingly named 'a Daughter's Offering,' The wild coast that runs westwards from Port-Eynon has always been a shipping graveyard, especially in the days of sail, and in 1833 the terrible wreck of the steamer Agnes Jack off Port-Eynon Head shocked everyone. The rockets failed to reach the twenty-one survivors clinging to the rigging, and when the mast collapsed they were all flung into the boiling surf. They drowned in a matter of minutes before the eyes of the helpless watchers on shore. And it was this incident that led to the building of the lifeboat station and the beginning of the distinguished career of the Port-Eynon lifeboat."

Gay seemed memorized by the history of the lifeboat men, which added to my pleasure immensely as I continued the story.

"In 1906, a new 35-foot self-righting lifeboat, 'The Janet,' was sent to the station. This was the boat that my Grandfather told me about as a boy. He said that he would go and watch the vessel as it was brought out to practice launching every summer. It was moved down the beach by a team of four stalwart horses supplied by the local farmers, and my Grandfather, with *his* Grandfather, watched in awe as Billy Gibbs, the coxswain, and his men, all armored in oilskins, were dragged into deep water with the great horse's breast high in the waves. Then out came the oars and the heavy boat was rowed towards the point.

"That's how tough you had to be in those days," Grandpa said, "before you became a member of a lifeboat crew!"

"Alas, there came a sad day, in January 1916, when the Glasgow steamer Dunvegan went ashore on Oxwich Point in a howling gale. The Port-Eynon lifeboat rowed to the rescue, but found that the rocket operations could not reach the ship-wrecked men. The lifeboat turned for home as darkness descended. The great wind drove it eastward, and in the tremendous seas off Pwlldu Head, the boat capsized twice. Most of the men managed to struggle back into the boat, but three were never seen again – the coxswain Billy Gibbs, the second coxswain William Eynon, and lifeboat man George Henry."

Are you sure I'm not going on too much about the Lifeboat Men, my love? Its rather a long history isnt it! And when I get into local history, I can talk for a long time. No, my love, I really do find it so interesting. Do you know any ghost stories or scary legends, I really like ghost stories and legends!

⌒

"There is also a legend that an old man told me..."

"There is a legend, boy!"

"Yes, Sir!

"I'll tell you, boy!"

"Yes, Sir, please do!"

"During particularly bad storms off Port-Eynon beach, the spirit of coxswain Billy Gibbs inhabits the statue in the Port Eynon churchyard, walking through the village and looking for his drowned crew."

As Gay and I watched the statue standing in the mist, there was no doubt in our imaginations, that we could almost feel that the Spirit of Billy Gibbs was getting ready for his walk around the village. And Gay held me tight as we walked through the village in the eerie fog.

After walking around the village and reminiscing, we decided we were hungry, and we headed back to our gear on the green and had breakfast. Within an hour, the fog had lifted, and Port-Eynon put on his friendly sunshine face. Gay and I smiled at each other and at the world. Before we left the village, we went to visit Maggie's grave. Meanwhile, the spirit of Billy Gibbs had once again left the statue and gone back to the waves of Port-Eynon beach. Gay and I left the village and continued on our journey.

As the tide was low, it allowed us to walk back towards Oxwich Point along the sands. We looked for treasurers along the tidelines, which always seemed to lead us to some new adventure. When we reached the Point, we climbed up from the beach and found the path through the woods that would lead us to old Oxwich Church. It seemed that Gay and I were still in the mood for scary stories and she asked if there was any legend about the Oxwich Church.

"And indeed, there is! But it's a frightening story and would likely keep us up tonight!"

"I would still like to hear it, Kings. And besides, there are far more wonderful things that we can do rather than sleep!"

I needed no more persuasion than that, as I looked deeply into her eyes of promise.

(Before I start telling you this story, dear reader, it is important for me to share with you that the following account is of something I actually saw as a boy. And it is an experience that has both haunted and perplexed me over the years.)

The story starts one cold January afternoon when my two friends, Steven and David Tucker, and I went night fishing on Oxwich Beach. Steven and David's father, Doug, was doing some work in Port Eynon, and would give us a ride home the next morning if we met him down in the Port Eynon village. It had been a good night fishing; we each caught a good-sized bass, and then Steven caught another one.

The three of us walked excitedly along the path that would take us to Oxwich Point, where we would climb the headland to Port-Eynon and meet Doug. It was a dark, grey morning as we approached the old church. Suddenly my friend Steven glanced behind us, then looked back at his brother David and I, as white as a ghost!

"Look behind us," he said, obviously scared. So David and I glanced back and saw what appeared to be a white horse walking upright on his hind legs! And the horse proceeded to walk leisurely along the path behind us! The strange creature followed behind us until it reached the stone stile of a gate that led into the church. Then we watched in fear and amazement as the animal climbed over the stile without the slightest difficulty, still standing on its hind legs! The feeling I got was that the creature might not have even been aware of us boys walking in front of him. Like it was in a different dimension! Once over the stile, the uncanny thing disappeared!

For the next several minutes, the three of us walked in a heavy silence, not knowing what to say, and taking turns to look behind us to see if the horse-man had re-appeared. When we reached the safety of Oxwich Point, we all shouted out: "Oh my gosh! What the heck was that?" We discussed many theories. Steven thought it was Satan, the Devil. David and I decided it was half-horse and half-man – a horse in appearance and a man in intellect – a 'horse-man.'

Our day didn't get any less haunted when Doug described having seen the same creature when he had been fishing on Oxwich Beach as a boy. He and his father had seen the horse coming out of the sea and walking on its hind legs like a man across the beach.

"What did you and your father do?" I asked.

"Run like heck, boy! Run like heck!" That's what he told me, and that's what we did.

We didn't set up our tent near Oxwich Point that night. We walked a mile or so until we reached the sand dunes and the stream of Crawly Woods so we could set up the tent there and spend the night in the friendly dunes!

As Gay and I lay in our tent, we talked about how we used to swim in the sea, run up the beach to the dunes, and lie in our warm blankets of sand, falling asleep in each other's arms.

Gay turned to me and said, "It's so wonderful to say goodnight and still be together. When I was away at university, I used to say goodnight to you each night, and pray to God that you heard me."

"I did too!" I said, looking into her eyes that flowed with tears of love. "I heard you every night. Each morning I would wake up from my dreams and reach for you. Sometimes I could feel the warmth of your body and smell the perfume of your hair. You were always there with me, my Princess."

"Oh, Kingsley, my love! For years I would reach for you! Sometimes I would wake up from my dreams of you, and I could not find you and hold you. I pictured you and Great Thunder galloping across the beach, and I was always looking for you around the Gower and wondering where you were. But now, my love, you are here with me! And I love you so much! And I'm so happy! And this is the best honeymoon that I could ever have asked for."

"I love you too, my Gay! You are my first thought when I wake, and my last thought when I lie down to sleep."

And we made love in our place in the dunes.

♪✻

LOVE IN THE DUNES

Here in the dunes, to the roar of the wild sea,
where the tall singing grasses tell the story of you and me,
I celebrate you, my love.

Your soft lips, tender with promise, taste and tease me
like the autumn sun that hides behind Thursday's clouds,
and then bursts forth with the flavors of blazing June.
And my hope of summer is very soon.
Welcome my love, to my sand dune room.

Your touch is gentle, like the calling of the sea breeze that whispers,
and then sings fragrant songs with the gossiping pines.
They shout out of all my fantasies with you, my love, in the dunes.
My hopes and dreams are fulfilled.
Dreams I didn't know I had, come to greet me,
Born within your love.
They hold me tight within your arms,
where I bask in your smile and your charms.

Lives and Lifeboats

Your eyes, like the deep green rockpools,
pull my dancing soul into yours,
where we swim in our sea of love,
where birds sing and soar above in skies of orange
and indigo dreams,
that tell our secrets behind the crying sunset
that will never set on our perfect love.
You squeeze and caress me within your sacred place,
and my passion wakes like the first dawning of creation, as our
love sings like the collared doves calling.
You pull my soul into yours, where I find myself waiting.
And my manhood explodes like the blow hole
on the Worms Head,
Shooting high above Rhossili Beach,
Where the ravens perform their acrobatic dance
on the winds of North Hill.
Your cries of passion echo across the lonely hills that
are barren no more.
For they have heard our love song!
Your love excites me more than Cefn Bryn,
and swimming in the Pennard Pill.
And we love until our bodies are spent as the twilight still,
And we lie glowing like the sunset on Llanmadoc Hill.
Good night, my love, I love you!
I love you too, my love!
Blow out the candle and we will burn again tomorrow.
Nighty night, nighty night.

© *Kingsley Ross Hill*

We woke to the crashing surf that splashed high up to our fortress
of dunes. The gulls and a kestrel said good morning to my love and
I. We had our breakfast on the highest dune and looked out upon
the Bristol Channel. A strong breeze blew Gay's perfumed hair

across my face and thrilled my senses; I danced before the rising sun. Gay smiled and laughed in excitement. She jumped to her feet and we danced together, saluting to the warm sun that now kissed us, as it rose higher in the jealous sky. White horses rode in on the waves from far out at sea; and we undressed and went swimming in the waves.

"Where is our destination today, my love?" Gay asked, as I dried her, and she dried me.

"I would like us to reach Three Cliffs and the valley, and sleep under Pennard Castle! Only a short walk today, my Princess. And we can talk more about our plans."

"Yes, my Prince! Now take my hand as we walk across our golden sands."

Roughly half way around the curve of the beach, we came to the stream that originates from the Oxwich Marshes: The Nicholaston Pill, which flows out over the sands.

"Let's go inland," I said, "and explore some of the marshland."

So we turned inland, and crossed over some low sand-dunes that led us to a "rather strange landscape," as Gay called it.

"It's like finding a lost garden," she said.

The plants and dune flowers called out to us from the invading sands, and the limestone shapes above us were clothed in ivy and waving leaves as they look down at us."

"What a lovely secret place we have found, my love," Gay exclaimed.

"Yes," I replied. "I've only ever been here once before, when Great Thunder brought me here on his back!"

We stood now directly under Nicholaston Woods. And in front of us was a shallow sheet of water that mirrored everything around us like a parallel world. Farther back, it turned into a reed swamp and small salt marshes that were a vivid green. Here and there patches of Yellow Iris dotted the marsh like little tropical islands. I'd only ever seen the yellow marsh iris in the spring, not in autumn.

The water was too deep for us to venture any further into the marsh. But beyond the willow scrub and the low alder trees, I could see a familiar meadow that pulled at my heart. In my soul, I felt the gentle winds of memory stir. Soon they spoke louder and then began to shout!

"What are you staring at?" Gay asked. "Do you see an animal or a bird?"

"No," I replied. "It's the meadow of the stallions!"

"The meadow of the stallions?" Gay echoed.

"Yes! When I was learning to ride Great Thunder, he would take me to all these secret places. I remember him bringing me to that meadow. There were other stallions there, and I remember counting about eight of them! It was the sacred gathering place of the stallions!"

"A real men's club!" Gay said. "Oh, I wish I could have seen them, Kings!"

"There must be a way around the marsh to get to it," I said. "I know Great Thunder brought me there from the other side of the marsh, because we didn't cross the swamp."

After walking a fair distance in front of the swamp, we came to a narrow path that ran beside a steep bluff. We followed the path further inland until we came to a thicket of gorse bushes. The ground was dry, and the autumn leaves crunched beneath our shoes. The trees spoke loudly in yellows, greens and oranges.

"Can you hear them calling to us, my love? "

"Yes, I love their song! "I took Gay by the hand, and started dancing with her.

"Wait," she said. "Let's take our shoes and socks off, and feel the leaves." So we danced barefoot in the leaves.

"What shall we call our dance?" she said, kissing me gently.

"Why, 'Autumns Last Dance,' of course!" And I held her close, and fell deep into her beautiful eyes, and kissed her with a summer's kiss.

ᏚᎬ

After we finished our dance, we noticed a path through the thicket – seldom used, but a path! There were broken twigs in the gorse, and here and there were hoof marks that had been made when the ground had been softer. We knelt to inspect them.

"These are big hoof prints!" I exclaimed. "Those of a large stallion!"

We cautiously continued. We didn't want to come upon a stallion and startle him. Then we would have a chase on our hands, for sure! We could see that the path through the gorse was about to open into a large meadow, so we slowed to a stop.

"Wait here," I said, and I took a few more steps until I could peer around our gorse cover. As I looked around the corner, the years melted away instantly, and I felt my heart beating faster. There under a large oak, I counted six mature stallions! Two of which had their heads up and were looking right at me. I was half expecting them to give chase, for we were intruding on their territory. To my relief, the two stallions lowered their heads again, and went back to grazing with the others.

And I went back to Gay and whispered: "Come and see this!"

"My gosh, Kingsley, I've never seen anything like this! All the stallions are together. They are usually so solitary. Surely this is a sacred place!"

"It is," I said, "it's the sacred place of the stallions!"

"I wish Melody could see this, Kingsley. She'd be talking about it for weeks."

"We will bring her here in the spring," I replied, "when I come back from Canada."

We watched the stallions for about half an hour, and they were very tolerant of us being there, I thought. They obviously sensed that we were only there to observe them.

"Yes, I think you're right. Not everyone gets a friendly invitation to the stallion's men's club," said Gay, laughing.

It was time to make our way back along the sands to Three Cliffs Bay, and head up the valley to the castle to set up camp.

Time seemed to be going by so quickly now, and after tonight we would only have one night left before we met up with Gay's mum and Melody.

"I'm so glad that no one can steal you away to England again, Gay! I could not lose you twice in a lifetime!"

"You will never lose me again, Kingsley, because I belong to you!"

At her words, my heart filled with joy and the reality of our marriage covenant sank into my soul even deeper. We set up our tent on the Three Cliffs Woods' side of the river, with the northern face of Pennard Castle staring at us from the hill.

Once we were set up for the night, we sat on the banks of the Killy Willy and dipped our feet into the slow winding waters. Pennard Castle stood as he always did, guarding the valley and shouting out his silent stories to the listening creatures below.

"The past always lives here with the present, doesn't it, my Prince?"

"Yes, Princess, it does! And my soul can hear Pennard Castle calling from the past. Can you hear him calling, my love?"

"Yes, I hear him."

And we ate our supper on the river bank, and waited for the sunset to make our valley orange and gold, and Pennard Castle read us a story that had never been told.

౿

By the light of the moon, Gay and I walked up the sandy path to the castle, and then lay in the soft sand of the castle room. As darkness fell, we undressed each other and lay under the stars.

"I love you, Kingsley," Gay exclaimed to the listening past. "How romantic is our love!"

"Surely the moon and stars are jealous," I answered.

"They are indeed!" Pennard Castle agreed.

And before he became too jealous, Gay and I held hands and ran laughing down his golden slope as fast as our legs would carry us.

Kingsley Ross Hill

"What about our clothes?" Gay asked, as we jumped into the slow flowing turn of the river.

"We'll pick up our clothes in the morning," I said, pulling her towards me and kissing her passionately, as the slow current cooled our burning bodies.

I led her by the hand and dried her body at the entrance of our tent. After Gay had dried me, we went inside and snuggled in our sleeping bag.

"Good night, Pennard Castle!" I called up to the moonlit hill. And all was still in the valley. Pennard Castle sang us a love song as we made love to his music.

We woke tangled and warm in our sleeping bag, as we listened to the patter of gentle rain upon our tent. And we snuggled and cuddled some more until we fell asleep again. Somewhere between the rain drops and a morning's first kiss, we drifted off to sleep, and we didn't stir until the wood pigeon called us to wake up, in the late afternoon.

"Good afternoon, my Cavewoman!"

"Good afternoon, my Caveman! Shall we stay in the tent after breakfast?"

"Yes, my love!"

It was evening before we ventured out of our tent. The wind and rain allowed us to have our supper outside, and then the wind started blowing again.

"It's back to our tent, my lovely lady."

"Yes, lovely man, it's back to our tent," where we giggled and laughed, tickled and played, loved and slept, and then kissed together in the rain. What a perfect honeymoon!

Then it was time to pack up our tent and go to meet Helen and Melody at the caravan. And as we walked through the dunes and across the Burrows, there seemed to be a heaviness over Gay.

"What is it, sweetie?"

"Oh, I'm okay, Kings! It's just the thought of us having to be apart again. But I know it won't be like before. We are married now and I'm so happy. And we will soon be back together again in the Spring!

"And I'll write to you while I'm away, sweetie, and we can Facetime on the phone," I reassured her. Soon she was her bubbly self again, and we waltzed across the burrows like two teenagers in love.

When we reached the caravan site, Melody saw us from the window and came running out to meet us. She raced into our arms and asked, "Did you bring me a horse?"

Gay and I both laughed, and I said: "No, we didn't bring one back, but we found the 'meadow of the stallions!'

"The meadow of the stallions?"

"Yes!" Gay replied. "Kingsley and I found the special field where the stallions go!"

"You mean, you and Daddy found the field! I have a Daddy now, Mum!"

"Yes, you do!" I said, lifting her up and putting her on my shoulders. "And you're getting to be a big girl," I said, lowering her down to the ground again.

"Yes, we are a family now," Gay added.

Helen now arrived on the scene, and she asked about our trip around the Gower.

"Oh, it was wonderful, Mum!" Gay and I said together.

"One at a time, please, children," Helen said, smiling.

And Melody giggled, and whispered in my ear: "Grandma thinks you and Mum are children!"

"We are," I said, and Melody laughed out loud.

"Now ask him, ask him, Grandma!" Melody shouted out in excitement.

"Not just yet, Melody, they have only just got back from their trip!"

"Ask me what?" I said, feeling Melody's excitement.

"Melody was wondering if you would come back to Cardiff with us, Kingsley...

"… so you can walk me to school tomorrow." Melody interrupted.

Gay now entered the conversation, and said, "Can I talk to Dad alone, please, Mum and Melody?"

Helen took Melody into the caravan, and Gay said, "What do you think? I know it means you traveling all the way back to Swansea tomorrow, but Melody is so excited that you're her Dad, and she's never had a Dad to walk her to school. She wants to show you off to her friends."

"Of course I will."

"I'm her Daddy now!"

"Yes, you are," Gay said, and kissed me.

"I heard that!" said a voice from behind us.

"Come here, young lady," I said, lifting Melody up onto my shoulders. "Of course I'll walk you to school tomorrow."

"Yippee! Yippee! That's what I told Grandma," she said, beaming.

My mind then flashed back to the school yard at Pacific Christian School in Victoria, Canada. Where I had always walked my daughter, Samantha to her classroom, ever since she had started kindergarten, until she was ten years old. We were standing in the playground, and she let go of my hand, and said, "Dad, you don't have to walk me to the classroom anymore. I'm a big girl now!"

Well, I just stood there stunned! I wasn't ready for this! My little girl had grown up!

"Are you alright, Mr. Hill?" another parent asked, waking me from my daze!

"No, I'm not alright," I said. "Samantha doesn't want me to walk her to the classroom anymore! She's grown up now!"

And on that Thursday morning in Spring, I wanted to turn back time so that I could hold my Sam's hand forever. But over the next few weeks and months, God reminded me that Samantha's heart and mine would always be together. And when our children grow up, it's a good thing! Life just goes by so quickly, doesn't it?

But today, another little girl was asking me to walk her to school, and I was so happy to be 'a young dad again.' A little wiser, and with some grey hair, but always young at heart. I did a dance in the caravan site, and Gay joined me. And Melody laughed and danced with us. And Helen came out of the caravan, and I'm sure she thought we were all nuts!

But all she said was: "Had I known there was a party, I would have taken off my high heels and put on some flat shoes."

Melody giggled, and then Helen said, "We have to stop the disco now, because tea is ready."

"Didn't you know. Mum? The music never stops!"

Helen looked around to make sure there were no neighbours watching, and then she spun her dress around in her high heels. (And that, Dear Reader, was our first 'family tribal dance.')

And then we all went in for tea. After tea, we soon had Helen's car packed and we were on our way to Cardiff. Melody was so excited that I was coming with them to Cardiff, and she mentioned me taking her to school in the morning four times. It made me feel so special!

Gay poked me in the shoulder from the back seat and said, "See Honey, all us girls adore you!" And Helen smiled.

Once we got unpacked, it was time for an early night, as we were all tired. And I told Melody a bedtime story about my pet magpie Jerry.

After a nice cooked breakfast, I walked Melody to school. She took my hand like a Princess, and as we arrived at the school yard, she introduced me to several of her friends, saying, "This is my Dad, he's the best! He had a pet magpie called Jerry."

I think I grew another four inches as I strolled around the school like a male peacock, feathers puffed up with pride.

As the bell rang, Melody marched me into her classroom to meet her teacher. Mrs. Lewis was thrilled to meet me, and she shared how happy she was that Melody now had a Dad in her life. After Melody showed me her desk, insisting that I sat at it, I headed back to Helen's house to spend the morning with Gay.

As I walked, I felt God speaking to me as I remembered the expressions of pride and joy on Melody's face as she introduced me to her friends, and then her teacher. It was like God was allowing me to feel Melody's heart, and how she had felt when she had seen the other Dads walking her friends to school, and she not having a Dad in her life! Today was a victory for her! A day when her inner sadness had turned to joy! She now had a complete family, like most of her friends. And oh, what a responsibility I had! And such a great privilege to be Melody's Dad! And I prayed and asked God to give me His wisdom and understanding, so that I could be a good Dad and husband.

Gay met me at the door, and I shared with her my experience taking Melody to school. We spent the morning together, and in the afternoon she drove me to the bus station, where she waited with me for the bus. Waiting for the bus gave us more time to talk, and to just hold each other.

"I miss you already, Kingsley! But I know you are coming back to us, my love. And I'll wait for your call to let us know you're back in Swansea, safe. And next week I'll drive out to Swansea and pick you up, and take you to London for your flight. I want to be there to see you off!"

"Thank you, my love!"

The bus arrived, and with the bus driver beeping his horn several times, it was time for me to stop kissing Gay and get on the bus.

Fraser picked me up at Swansea bus station, and for the next several days, he and Lynn and I shared a great time together. The days flew by, and it was soon the day of my departure. My heart was feeling torn already!

Gay arrived to pick me up, as planned, and with my suitcase and saddle, we were soon on our way to Heathrow. It was a three-hour drive from Swansea, and Gay and I enjoyed a special journey together, making plans and talking about what it was going to be like to share our lives together. We shared our hopes and dreams, as always, and our fears were few. After we prayed together in the airport chapel, God gave us His perfect peace!

Gay gave me a scripture verse, one she had especially picked out for my flight. We read it together from her Bible.

[Romans 8 vs 31, What, then, shall we say in response to these things? If God is for us, who can be against us?]

And Gay and I, both answered together, and said, no one!

It was the perfect verse for both of us as we put our trust in God to work everything out for us and bring us back to each other in the spring.

As the call came for me to board the plane, I felt good knowing that Gay was doing well and wasn't feeling sad. It's so wonderful to know that in our weakness is God's perfect strength, and He had given us both His peace that passes all understanding!

[John 14 vs 27, peace I leave with you; my peace I give you.
I do not give to you as the word gives. Do not let your hearts be troubled and do not be afraid.]

"Bye, my love! Call me when you arrive in Vancouver."

"Bye, Princess, and give little Princess a hug and kiss for me." We kissed until the final boarding call was announced.

"Why are you bringing a saddle to Canada?" the Canadian security officer asked.

"To ride a horse, of course! I wouldn't be without it." I smiled.

"Have a good flight, Sir.

"Thank you, Sir, I will!"

*The End of the Second Book of the
Gower Peninsula Adventure Series*

Lightning Source UK Ltd.
Milton Keynes UK
UKHW021029271220
375899UK00014B/1649

Lightning Source UK Ltd.
Milton Keynes UK
UKHW021029271220
375899UK00014B/1649